VOLVO
GOTHENBURG
SWEDEN

Christer Olsson

&

Henrik Moberger

ISBN 3–907150–58–9
(English edition)

©
Christer Olsson, Henrik Moberger and Norden Publishing House Ltd.
St. Gallen, Switzerland
1995

Project leader, principal author (main text, tables, bibliography) and layout:
Christer Olsson

Co–author (information panels):
Henrik Moberger

Cover illustration:
Lasse Jödahl

English translation:
Tom Byrne, Techtrans Ireland, Cork (body text)
Gordon Paget, KB Swengel Göteborg, Sweden (information panels)

Photographs and other illustrations
supplied by Volvo Central Archives and other sources.
Most of the new photographs were taken by
Roland Brinkberg, Peter Haventon, Christer Olsson and Tommy Wiberg.

Photosetting and repro:
Lennart Larsson Reklam AB, Göteborg, Sweden
Technical coordinator: Sören Backman
Scanning: Kåre Larsson

Printing:
Västergötlands Tryckeri AB, Skara, Sweden

Binding:
Sambok, Farsta, Sweden

PREFACE

As the story of a company which touches the lives of tens of thousands of employees, and of millions of motorists in Sweden and around the globe, the history of Volvo is important. It explains why a Volvo is a different car from others – and why Volvo is a different company to work for than its counterparts in Japan, Germany, the USA, France or Russia.

The author has been a student of Volvo products for many years. However, since a history dealing only with the products would be far too selective, as would a company history which excluded its products, this volume by my co–author, Henrik Moberger, and myself is a synthesis of both. We hope that its readers will find it entertaining as well as instructive.

Hundreds of people contributed to the project during its seven years of preparation. Henrik and I thank each and every one sincerely. In the hope that I will offend none, I would like to mention just a few individuals who deserve our special gratitude. In this respect, motoring historian Sven W. Bengtson occupies a special place. Many fruitful discussions with him gave me a broader understanding of the complex history of Volvo as an automaker. Three of the management staff at the Volvo Central Archives, Olle Högberg, Ingrid Alexandersson and Ulla Bergwall, made the book possible by their enthusiasm and generosity in giving us access to the treasures under their care, while Gunnar Söderblom's knowledge of motoring literature contributed greatly to its final presentation.

Three Volvo people are worthy of special mention: Leif Strand (now vice–president of Volvo Penta) who, in my days as a raw recruit to the company, gave me the assignment of researching the history of Volvo trucks (a love affair which has never died), Sten Langenius (currently vice–president of AB Volvo and executive chairman of Volvo Construction Equipment) and Torsten Dahlberg (now head of Product Planning at Volvo Truck Corporation), who gave me the chance to initiate VTC's truck restoration programme, a project which contributed in no small measure to the establishment of the Volvo Museum in Göteborg as an exhibition portraying the history of Volvo as a whole. Any reader who has not yet visited the museum has a treat in store!

Not every author has the good fortune to collaborate with a publisher who combines the qualities of professionalism and personal enthusiasm. Sven–Erik Gunnervall is the exception to the rule. My co–author and I would like to express our sincere gratitude to him for many years of stimulating cooperation, culminating in the publication of this work.

To print a large volume of this nature can be a difficult undertaking beset by many problems. However, thanks to the dedication of Lennart Johansson in Skara, it proved an enjoyable rather than a painful task.

Finally, a proviso or two. The book does not set out to describe every single detail of Volvo's history, but is intended as a subjective rhapsody in which the chronology is occasionally interrupted to describe the entire history of a model several years ahead. Furthermore, information which is either contentious or no longer available has been omitted from the tables at the rear.

Lerum, November 1995

Christer Olsson

FOREWORD

Now THE LARGEST industrial group in the Nordic countries, Volvo started life as a carmaker in 1927. Today, it is the manufacturer of a wide range of products for the transportation industry, from cars, trucks and buses to construction equipment, marine and industrial engines, and aircraft engines.

In addition to its operations in Sweden, Volvo produces cars, trucks, buses and construction equipment in the EU, has a complete truckbuilding operation in the USA, and manufactures trucks and buses in Brazil. The company also has production plants in countries including Canada, Australia, Malaysia and Thailand.

The Volvo Group operates a worldwide marketing and service organisation (over 85% of its products are sold in markets outside Sweden). As one of the most powerful brand names in the world, Volvo stands for quality, safety and care – both for people and the environment.

In 1924, Economist Assar Gabrielsson and engineer Gustaf Larson pooled their talents to pursue a common dream – to build a Swedish car for Swedish roads. A series of

ten prototypes was built in 1926 and the first Volvo car – the ÖV4 – left the works at Lundby, near Göteborg, on 14 April 1927.

Gabrielsson and Larson coined the phrase 'to build cars the Volvo way'. Unlike its contemporaries, Volvo designed and manufactured its own car components, while parts purchased from external suppliers were made to the company's own specifications. Its competitors, by contrast, merely assembled their vehicles from bought–in parts.

The Volvo way laid the foundations for Volvo quality – a core value which the company has consistently upheld and remains one of its guiding principles even in this high–tech age.

This book traces the history of Volvo from the ÖV4 to the present–day range of cars, trucks, buses and other products, and includes many of the exciting developments on the company's road to success. The first vehicles are naturally included, as are descriptions of prototypes and many other little–known products. Of central importance is the account of how Gabrielsson and Larson formulated the philosophy

which was to become Volvo's guiding star – concern for people and our common environment.

One of the most interesting chapters deals with the PV444, the model which, more than any other, was to symbolise Volvo's success and was destined to become Sweden's 'people's car' in the years after World War II. Other fascinating products include prototype models such as the Philip, a huge American–inspired car with a V8 engine, and a number of experimental models, such as the VESC (which preceded the 240 series), Volvo's first electric car, the New York experimental taxi and the LCP, a car built from new materials and designed to run on new fuels.

Another chapter deals with the exploits of Tom Trana and Gunnar Andersson in their PV on the world's rally circuits and the more recent success of the Volvo 850 in the British Touring Car Championship.

The development of Volvo Aero Corporation and Volvo Penta forms a natural part of the story. Pentaverken built its first engines less than twenty years after the appearance of the first Volvo car, and went on to

develop its revolutionary Aquamatic and Duoprop drives. The history of Volvo Aero Corporation deals with products such as the radial piston engines of the early 1940s and the RM2B, the first jet engine to be equipped with an afterburner.

We are convinced that a knowledge of the company's history – with all its successes and failures – is essential if you, the reader, are to understand our value judgements and how we see the future development of Volvo. We believe that this volume is a significant contribution to a history which is not only fascinating, but has contributed to the development of mankind and society as we know it today.

Göteborg, November 1995

Sören Gyll
President, AB Volvo

Assar Gabrielsson was born in Korsberga, in Skaraborg province, on 13 August 1891 the first of three children. His father was an administrator at the Korsberga brickworks but later became tenant-farmer of the Spännefalla farm estate next to the Dairy in Tibro. There he started up an egg business, which later grew to include imports from Russia.

The family moved to Stockholm, and Assar completed his higher 'student-examen' certificate studies at the Norra Latin sixth-form college in 1909.

Assar Gabrielsson was one of the famous 'first-year' pupils at the Stockholm School of Economics. His teachers, who were legends in their day, included Walter Ernest Harlock and Eli Heckscher. Assar graduated from the School in October 1911 in five subjects, and he gained a 'passed with great credit' award in economics following a written test on the subject of 'How spirits distillation and distribution is organised in Sweden'. He gained top marks in both English and Russian. He also learned shorthand, and this enabled him to work as a stenographer in the Chancellery of the Lower House of the Swedish Parliament from 1911 to 1916. He also helped out in his father's egg business.

In 1916, Assar Gabrielsson embarked upon a rapid career at the Svenska Kullagerfabriken, SKF, in Göteborg. From 1921 to 1922 he was managing director of the SKF subsidiary in France, and he was later appointed head of sales of the entire SKF Group. In this capacity he negotiated with the Soviet leaders, who during the Russian revolution had confiscated the SKF plant in Russia.

Whilst working at SKF, it occurred to Assar Gabrielsson that Swedish ball bearings were cheaper than those available on the international market. The idea of producing a Swedish car – which would be able to compete in terms of price and quality with the American cars that were dominating the market – grew ever increasingly in the mind of Assar Gabrielsson.

During the period 1917-1920, Gabrielsson had co-operated with Gustaf Larson, who was an engineer, at SKF and had come to admire his immense knowledge and skill. He also knew of Larson's experience of working in the British car industry. The fact that Gustaf Larson also nurtured the idea of starting up car production in Sweden enabled the two partners to work much easier together after their chance meeting in Stockholm in the summer of 1924.

While Gustaf Larson engaged young engineers to make the drawings for the new car, Assar Gabrielsson analysed the economics of the venture and the prospects of obtaining financial backing. In the summer of 1925 SKF declined to provide support for the project, so Gabrielsson decided to invest his own savings of 150,000 kronor. It was not until August 1926 that SKF decided to make the registration

ASSAR GABRIELSSON

documents of its dormant patent company Volvo available to the prospective car company. At the same time, SKF signed a share capital of 200,000 kronor.

Meanwhile, the ten prototype cars – nine of them with open tourer bodies and a single one with a four-door saloon style – were produced in Stockholm. The bodies were made by the well-known coachbuilder Freyschuss, and final assembly was carried out in Galco's premises on Hälsingegatan. The Pentaverken in Skövde provided the engines, Bofors the chassis frames, and Svenska Stålpressings AB in Olofström the body shells.

A competitor ball bearing manufacturer, Nordkulan, had been formed but it went out of business a few years later. The remains of this company had been acquired by SKF and this meant that they had an impressive factory on the island of Hisingen in Göteborg.

After completing an adventurous journey with a convoy of three prototype cars on atrocious roads from Stockholm to Göteborg in October 1926, the newly-formed Volvo company moved into these premises on Hisingen.

An office was set up on the top floor of the 'L' building next to the 'BC' factory building. Production in the BC building was started up with a conveyor belt running through several floors of the building. On 14 April 1927 the first series-produced car was driven out of the factory building, and thus Volvo was born.

Assar Gabrielsson remained the company's managing director for almost 30 years until his retirement in 1956. He then continued as Chairman of the Board for the period 1956-1962.

Gabrielsson was known for his untiring strength and a never-ceasing belief in the possibilities for achieving a Swedish automobile industry. He combined brilliant business skills and economic expertise with a bold concentration on products and production resources.

Assar Gabrielsson and Gustaf Larson created a unique spirit and willingness to co-operate within Volvo. Despite the depression years in the 1930s, and the problems brought about by the Second World War, the Volvo management and workforce battled on unyieldingly. During the War, Gabrielsson committed himself to the cause of the other Scandinavian countries, but also to ensuring Volvo would be able to survive. After the War, the PV444 car model was introduced and this proved to be the real breakthrough for Volvo. In the mid-fifties Gabrielsson decided, even if rather reluctantly, to export Volvo cars to the USA. As chairman of the Volvo Board he was party to the decision to build the Torslanda plant, but did not live to see the opening. Assar Gabrielsson died 28 May 1962 leaving behind him one of the greatest 'life-time achievements' in Swedish history.

Gustaf Larson was born 8 July 1887, the third of eight children. His father, Lars Larson, was a 'freehold-farmer', and his mother was Hulda, whose maiden name was Magnidotter and who was born in Göteborg. Gustaf Larson was born on Falltorp farm in Vintrosa a few miles west of Örebro. As a child he was interested in sports and was one of the founder members of the 'Örebro Sportklubb', playing left wing on the football team.

Gustaf Larson completed his higher 'studentexamen' certificate studies at the Technical Elementary school in Örebro in 1911, and later graduated as an engineer from the Royal Institute of Technology (RIT) in Stockholm in 1917.

His skill is apparent from a letter written to Larson by RIT professor Edvard Hubendick, in which he asked Larson to 'donate the pressure diagrams and valve diagrams from your undergraduate thesis, as well as your calculations, to the RTI where they can be used as a model for future generations'.

From 1911 to 1913 Gustaf Larson worked for the engine manufacturers White & Poppe in Coventry, England, where he became involved with the W&P contract to supply engines to a new car company in Oxford, to be called Morris Motors.

After graduating from the RTI, Gustaf Larson moved to Göteborg and to SKF where he worked on various engine and carburettor projects. It was here he first met Assar Gabrielsson, who had joined SKF one year earlier in 1916. In 1920 he moved to Stockholm and to Galco (G.A. Lindquist & Co.). There he began once again to think of cars – whilst working on carburettors and lubricators and designing the Agrippa binder.

On Midsummer's Eve 1924, Gustaf Larson met his former colleague from SKF, Assar Gabrielsson, and they had the following brief conversation:

"*How pleased I am to meet you Gustaf. You have experience of car production, and I would like to discuss it with you.*"

"*Gladly, Assar. But I must rush off to catch the train. Perhaps we can meet again after the summer?*"

After the now famous crayfish dinner at the Sturehof restaurant, work was soon under way on the drawings for the car. The children's nursery in Gustaf Larson's apartment became the drawing office and design studio. While Larson was working at Galco, young engineers – one of the first being Jan G. Smith – got to work on the drawings.

In the Autumn of 1925, Larson employed Henry Westerberg to bring the work on the drawings to completion. He is generally regarded as being the first Volvo employee.

In 1926, the first Volvo prototype cars were built in Galco's premises in Stockholm, and on 14 April 1927 the first series-produced car was driven out of the factory in Göteborg.

Larson's famous comment on the pandemonium caused by the final drive being incorrectly assembled thus causing the car to set off backwards was: "*Fingal (the workshop manager) has really bridled up the horse back to front this time!*"

From his years at Morris, Larson had adopted the idea of designing most of the car's constituent parts 'in-house'. These would then be manufactured by external sub-contractors working to Volvo's precise specifications. 'Building cars the Volvo way' became a widely-known concept.

Gustaf Larson's immense technical knowledge and skill made him a well-known and respected figure far beyond Volvo's and Sweden's borders. He spared no pains nor costs when it came to designing. His motto was: "I*t's cheaper to do something right first time than it is to do something wrong and then correct it.*"

In the same way as a water-diviner, Larson could detect a possible weakness in drawings made by colleagues with almost uncanny precision. This helped to breed very good engineers within the company and was a major factor in creating Volvo's well-known standard of quality.

Gustaf Larson headed Volvo's technical development with great authority right up until his retirement in 1952. After that he continued as a member of the Volvo Board until 1958, and was a consultant to Volvo until he died on 4 July 1968.

Urban's cafe and Sturehof

In the mid-summer of 1924, Assar Gabrielsson was in Stockholm. We do not know why he was there, but he was probably visiting the home of his parents. He was then living in Göteborg, where he was sales manager for SKF. Gustaf Larson lived in Stockholm, where he was technical manager for Galco AB. On this particular day he was on his way to Trosa to celebrate mid-summer with his family, wife Elin and son Eric who had just turned three (there were later additions to the family with the birth of another son and two daughters).

At the corner of Drottninggatan and Adolf Fredriks Kyrkogata there was at that time a cafe which Larson later called Urban's cafe (someone else called it 'Hurtigs').

On his way to the central station, Larson went into a cafe to buy a box of chocolates to take with him to Trosa.

At the same time, Assar Gabrielsson walked into the same cafe to buy something. Both men had worked at SKF between 1916 and 1920 and knew each other well. Unaware of each other's ideas and ambitions, both men had for many years given serious thought to the possibility of starting up car production in Sweden.

Gabrielsson told Larson how pleased he was to meet his former colleague, who 'knew all about cars and engineering matters', and told him he wanted to discuss car production with him.

Larson did not have much time to spare, however, as he had to catch a train, and the two men agreed to meet again after the holidays, but did not set any exact date. Therefore, the next time they met was also out of the blue. It was on 25 July 1924.

Assar Gabrielsson loved eating crayfish fished in Swedish lakes, and on that day he decided to go out alone to the Sturehof restaurant in Stockholm to eat crayfish.

The Larson family were also lovers of crayfish. Gustaf Larson, in fact, had an elder brother who ran a 'crayfish speciality' shop in Vetlanda.

On 25 July 1924 Gustaf Larson also felt the urge to go out alone to eat crayfish, so he decided to go to the Sturehof restaurant.

Already inside the restaurant, sitting behind a proverbial mountain of crayfish, was Assar Gabrielsson. Gabrielsson invited Larson to sit at his table and they both dined sumptuously on the delicious crayfish. Neither man spoke. It was not until they had finished their meal that they started to discuss the project which many years later was to develop into a global enterprise called 'Volvo'.

In all Swedish diaries, the name-day for 25 July is 'Jakob', and a reliable source claime that it is this red-letter day which gave its name to the very first Volvo car.

IN RETROSPECT, PERHAPS the most surprising fact about Volvo's early years is not that Assar Gabrielsson and Gustaf Larsson succeeded in their enterprise, but that they embarked on it at all! The challenge was daunting; the prospects of creating a new, Swedish car industry appeared remote in the light of earlier, unsuccessful attempts, tough competition from abroad and the gloomy predictions of prophets of doom at home.

However, these very cynics had made the fundamental error of equating 'remote' with 'impossible' (although it must be said that the enterprise of the two founders was complemented by a fair degree of luck).

Although the repercussions of the First World War were still being felt in the mid–1920s, the postwar economic depression was beginning to subside, and both the national morale and the economy were beginning to recover. Optimism was growing and free enterprise was flourishing.

At the time, Scania–Vabis was in the process of phasing out car production to concentrate on truck and bus manufacture, two areas in which it was meeting stiff competition from Tidaholm, the other domestic manufacturer.

However, undue importance should not be attached to the opposition which faced Gabrielsson and Larsson. There was a definite willingness on the part of the many mechanical workshops and factories then in existence to participate in the industrialisation and mechanisation of the Swedish engineering industry. And willing suppliers of

appears to have been fully convinced of the prospects of success. In hindsight, it is difficult to identify the reasons for this optimism, although his excellent contacts with SKF and Swedish commercial life in general, including the banks, must certainly have been compelling.

Volvo was not alone in its efforts to establish a Swedish car factory; Thulinverken of Landskrona (which had been founded originally to build aeroplanes and aircraft engines, but had also produced cars) had made considerable progress in the area, and had even built a small number of prototypes of an advanced design with overhead–valve engines and all–round braking. In all likelihood, however, it was Assar Gabrielsson's excellent contacts with the banks which put paid to its competitor's plans, otherwise the history of the Swedish car might have been vastly different.

components to the infant car industry were certainly not difficult to find – despite the fact that Gabrielsson was an extremely tough negotiator who extracted the best possible deal from his suppliers by imposing strict conditions of delivery and demanding extremely low prices.

Despite all, Assar Gabrielsson, in particular,

Rådmansgatan 59 in Stockholm – a shrine to all Volvo enthusiasts – where the first car was designed and the plans for what was to become a great international company were laid.

Drawing office in children's nursery

Volvo's first drawing office was in fact the children's nursery in the Larson family's apartment on the third floor of 59 Rådmansgatan in Stockholm.

In the autumn of 1924, Gustaf Larson started work on the drawings for the first Volvo prototype cars. The draughting work was carried out by young engineers recruited from the Royal Institute of Technology in Stockholm. They went to the Larson home in the evenings, and Gustaf Larson checked each detail in his usual meticulous way. But he needed someone to correlate the work and bring it to completion, so in the autumn of 1925 he employed the young Henry Westerberg for the princely salary of 300 kronor a month to complete the work on the drawings.

A year later, production of the ten prototype cars was in full swing. Gustaf Larson wrote a letter on 6 December 1926 to his sister Vivan and her husband Henning in Göteborg – with whom he had lived almost 15 years earlier while working with the Morris company in Coventry. In the letter, Larson complained of tiredness brought on by continuously working with two jobs – Galco during the day and car production in the evening. He was particularly worried that they were finding it difficult to complete the drawings. The letter concludes: "*It will be a great relief when all the drawings are finished, and all I will need to do then is supervise the work.*" The letter was signed "Guss".

In his letter he also asked his sister to take a look at the Nordiska Kullager's factory premises on the island of Hisingen to assess its suitability as a car manufacturing plant. He also offered his brother-in-law a good job once production got under way. He had designed a spring bracket, and he asked Henning if the design of this bracket from Morris was in a special type of cast iron and if it was machined at one particular end. He requested an immediate reply.

1925 WAS A BUSY year for the hopeful employees of the new – as yet unnamed – company. Although a handful of those who had been recruited were paid a salary, most were working more or less out of idealism, to gain experience of design work and, perhaps, in the hope of finding employment in the new industry.

Many indigenous car manufacturers were established around the world at this time and most of their products differed from the new Swedish car in one essential respect – they were built from existing components (indeed, in many cases, the radiator badge was almost the only item designed by the 'maker'!). Since Gustaf Larson certainly realised that the new car (which was still without a name) would be successful only if it matched the standard of the best foreign makes in the medium–price class, it was designed 'from scratch' with no preconceived ideas.

At this time, Europe was a polarised society, in which the advent of industrialisation had created a yawning social gap between the upper and lower classes. As yet, the middle classes did not play any significant role in political life.

As a result of these social distinctions, the differences between the various cars on the market were enormous. Luxury marques, such as Rolls–Royce, Voisin, Maybach and Hispano–Suiza, were sold alongside 'cycle cars' – small, functional models, mostly with engines with a cubic capacity of only about 1 litre. Although medium–sized models were also sold, these were 'squeezed' between the other two categories.

As a result, it was natural that Gustaf Larsson should have opted to develop a medium–class car capable of attracting buyers from the rapidly growing middle class. And, since it was clear that this could neither be a complicated design, nor a model offering sporty performance or luxurious bodywork, the choice was a conservative car which, although old–fashioned, would also be reliable. Planning of the next model was initiated at the same time. Although this was also to be of a simple, basic design, it was to be considerably more sophisticated than its predecessor. Offering more space, a more lavish level of equipment, a covered body, a more powerful engine and a more modern gearbox, this would enable the company to charge the higher price which was essential to the long–term viability of the venture.

Today, it seems incredible that a car could be designed in a matter of a single year. However, the fact remains that the model was not only built in time, but also proved to be reliable in service.

The first Volvo car was an open four–seater of the touring type. The styling was the work of Helmer MasOlle, a contemporary artist from Dalecarlia province in central Sweden, who opted for straight, elegant lines, although those of the last

Helmer MasOlle.

Helmer MasOlle

The landscape and portrait artist Helmer MasOlle (born 1884, died 1969) was commissioned to draw the first Volvo cars. He was generally regarded as Anders Zorn's successor, and was very interested in cars. He actually owned a 1914 French Voisin car, and several features of this car were incorporated into the first Volvo car model.

The first editor of the magazine 'Ratten', export manager Rolf Hansson, wrote a pen portrait in 1933 of MasOlle and his artistic achievements. Of his work on Volvo's first cars, Hansson wrote among other things:

"MasOlle had drawn and modelled the body for our first open car, and we enjoyed the same relationship when working on our current six-cylinder saloon car, for which he modelled the body, engine bonnet and radiator, and he has also advised us on choice of upholstery etc. You do not need to look at our latest car for any length of time to realize just how well MasOlle has succeeded in combining interior body space with a first-class exterior. And anyone who has sat behind the windscreen and observed the pure elegant lines of the engine bonnet, or admired the other exterior features, can testify that MasOlle has succeeded in fulfilling his assignment in a way that does credit to his artistic taste".

The Volvo management were later given reason to officially announce that MasOlle did not draw the first closed car, the PV4, so-called 'Orrekojan', as many people considered it to be so ugly that MasOlle's name should not be associated with that car.

Designed by Helmer MasOlle, the lines of the new Swedish car were simple and classical.

three open cars and the series–built models were slightly modified compared with the first series of six test cars. Features of the early prototypes included steel wheels, smaller doors, different wings and a rear end which was not used on the production cars.

Henry Westerberg.

Henry Westerberg, Volvo's first employee, drew the ÖV4 in Larson's children's nursery

When Gustaf Larson and Assar Gabrielsson decided to start producing cars in Sweden in 1925, Larson lived in Stockholm. Larson started work on designing the ÖV4 in his home. He was assisted by a young consultant engineer called Jan G Smith, who made most of the drawings.

One year later, in the autumn of 1925, Larson employed the 23 year-old Henry Westerberg to help him complete the drawings for the ten prototype cars which were to be built at Galco, where Gustaf Larson was then employed.

Henry Westerberg thus became the first person to be employed on the project which was to continue another two years before it was given the name 'Volvo'. Westerberg was set to work in the Larson family's children's nursery in their apartment on 59 Rådmans-gatan in Stockholm. It is said that the eldest son, who was then five years old, told Henry Westerberg that *"mummy doesn't like uncle Westerberg because uncle Westerberg smokes in our toilet"*. The working conditions could have been better, obviously.

"I was the first person to be employed by Volvo – or more correctly the project which was to become Volvo", said Henry Westerberg in an interview a few years before he died. *"But I was also the first to be given the sack. The reason was that when the ten prototype cars were completed and ready for testing in the spring of 1926, my work was concluded and I was given notice to leave. But shortly after the holidays Gustaf Larson phoned me and I was employed once again"*.

Another memory which amused Henry Westerberg greatly was the first ever accident involving a Volvo:

"It was when the first three prototype cars were to be driven to Göteborg", he says. *"Unfortunately, two of the cars had the alternator turned the wrong way so the electric power supply ran out. While driving through the night in the forests of Småland we tried to follow the tail lamp of the car in front, but those of us in the rear only succeeded in driving into the ditch. No-one was injured but Larson was very angry when he eventually returned to find us sitting on the footstep calmly smoking"*.

Henry Westerberg worked in many different car design departments, and he was always well liked by his colleagues, and was asked time and time again to stay on even after reaching retirement age. It was not until at the age of 79 after spending 55 years with Volvo that Henry Westerberg decided to finally retire in 1980 and enjoy the rest of his days with his wife Magdalena. He died in 1991.

The imposing facade of the former Galco premises, where Volvo's first car was built for a time while Gustaf Larson was still an employee.

Where the prototype cars were born

In the early 1920s there was a company called Galco which had its premises at 42 Hälsingegatan in the north of Stockholm, and since 1920 Gustaf Larson had been employed there as technical manager. He started by designing 'conus' cups, a type of automatic fully-mechanical lubricators for belt-driven machines of that day. You can be sure that later lubricators supplied for all Volvo machines were conus cups. In his first year with Galco Larson also designed the so-called 'Agrippa binder', which was to sell in countries all over the world for about 50 years, providing the main source of income for Galco.

When this invention was to be given a name, Gustaf Larson suggested that it should start with the letter A. He looked up the first volume of the Nordisk Familjebok's Uggla edition, turned to the letter A and found Agrippa. And that's how it got its name.

The open bodies were manufactured by the world known coach-builder Adolf Freyschuss. Final assembly of the prototype cars was performed in Galco's premises on Hälsingegatan. There was to be no more car production as far as Galco was concerned, but the company continued to be an important supplier to Volvo well into the 1970s. From the outset, Galco was Volvo's main supplier of small pressed parts. As opposed to Volvo's normal policy relating to suppliers, Galco owned all the tools themselves, and this gave competitive benefits. This was a result of a friendship between the company's owner G A Winqvist and Gustaf Larson. Up until well into the 1960s, parts for Volvo products accounted for about half of Galco's sales, and the Agrippa binders for the other half.

849

THE FIRST PROTOTYPE of the new Volvo car was completed in May 1926, less than two years since Gabrielsson and Larsson had agreed to undertake the project, and the first series–built cars were delivered less than a year later.

It would be wrong to glamorise the work carried out in 1925–26 by pretending that no mistakes were made. On the contrary, there was much to put right. The first prototypes were driven long and hard by various company employees and the teething problems which emerged from time to time were corrected before series production was commenced.

The engine was, perhaps, the weakest link. The first hand–built units were under–sized and the dimensions of the bearings, among other components, were increased, greatly improving the reliability of the 2,000 or so type DA four–cylinder units manufactured subsequently.

Volvo's first factory at Hisingen, near Göteborg, is now in a built–up area surrounded by housing and shops. The setting was more rural in the 1920s.

The 'BC' building

The legendary BC building initially housed most of Volvo's operations. But after just a few years larger factory premises were required and new assembly halls were put into operation.

Gabrielsson and Larson moved into the BC building in 1939, and the Volvo Head Office was housed there up until 1967 when the new VAK Head Office was completed close to the new Torslanda plant.

The BC building has its own special place in the history of Volvo as it has been in use almost unchanged since 1926 up until the present day. Thousands of Volvo employees have worked there (including the principal author of this book…)

Although the low doors on six of the open prototypes were undoubtedly attractive, they made entry and exit difficult for the occupants. As a result, they were replaced by larger doors which, however, spoiled MasOlle's elegant body lines to some extent.

Hand–built in Stockholm, the first ten cars were finished in different colours, as seen from the photographs which have survived. In other respects, they were more or less technically identical, although representative of three generations – an initial series of six closely resembling MasOlle's design, a later series of three open models similar to the series–built cars and a single covered model.

Although no production site had yet been selected, Göteborg was probably one possible location. The entire development project, including the purchase of components and the assembly of the ten prototypes, cost a total of SKr200,000. Since the model was sold for SKr4,800 in 1927, this was equivalent to the price of just 42 cars. Given the same relationship today, the Volvo 850 would have cost almost SKr8 billion to develop up to its launch in 1991. In actual fact, the cost of developing the 850 model and the necessary production facilities was SKr16 billion (or 16 thousand million)!

The forerunners of millions of Volvos to come, ten prototypes (nine open–top and one covered) were built in 1926.

Car exports by climbing mountains

In 1939, the Swedish magazine 'Business Economics' carried an article with the above heading. It was about a journey with a Volvo car from Buenos Aires, over the Andes to Santiago de Chile, where a successful deal was concluded.

This article highlighted the difficulties encountered during Volvo's export drive, and also the will and unyieldingness which characterized the structure of the export organisation. For many years the Export Manager was Rolf Hansson.

As early as in Larson's and Gabrielsson's detailed and famous 'Memorandum concerning the possibilities of manufacturing automobiles in Sweden' dated 1926, we can read of the importance of exporting the company's products. Seasonal variations in Sweden meant that the main consideration was to export to the southern hemisphere, as sales in Sweden were far too low during the winter. The memorandum also stated that sales to car-producing countries was practically impossible owing to the high import duty charges imposed by these countries.

The prospects were considered to be good. And the aim was set high from the outset. However, no cars were exported during the first year, and only 24 cars were sent for export in 1928, and 27 in 1929.

Finland became the first export country, and a subsidiary was set up there in 1928. In 1930, companies were set up in Norway and agents were accepted in Denmark. A modest attempt at selling cars in warmer climates came in 1931 in Cuba. In the autumn of 1931, the way was suddenly opened up to both exports and increased domestic sales, as the Swedish krona fell substantially in relation to the dollar in particular. Successful export sales to Holland in 1932 were quickly followed by agencies being set up in Palestine, Syria, Egypt and Morocco. These were later followed by agencies in Spain, Portugal and Rumania. The attempt in Cuba was also successful, and this led to the setting up of agencies in Brazil, Argentina, Uruguay and in Chile – after the journey over the Andes.

Following an order for the purchase of 40 buses in 1935, Argentina became an important export country. And so it has continued. Some countries have become less important as far as exports of Volvo products are concerned, while other countries have been added. 1955 was an important milestone. That was the year when the first cars were shipped over to the USA – the home of the car, where it was considered to be just as impossible to sell imported cars as selling refrigerators to Eskimos.

Today, we can count on Eskimos having refrigerators, in exactly the same way as Americans own thousands of Volvo products. Export sales to the USA became so successful that the country has long been Volvo's most important export country and the biggest individual market.

At present, about 90 per cent of Volvo's total production is sent for export outside Sweden.

VOLVO'S FIRST CAR, the ÖV4, (the designation was an acronym for 'Öppen Vagn', meaning 'Open car', while the figure '4' stood for four cylinders) was a functional model which was superior to its immediate competitors in terms of quality. However, it was also old–fashioned and lacking in speed. In the advertising brochure for the model, the top speed was optimistically quoted as 90 km/h and it was also stated that the car could negotiate Ramberget (a hill near the factory in Hisingen) in top gear, although it is not known if either of these claims was true.

In mechanical terms, the car was of simple design. Developing 28 hp, the 1,944 cm³ engine was a four–cylinder, side–valve unit manufactured by Pentaverken in Skövde. (Assar Gabrielsson's original intention was to have the engines built by marine engine manufacturers Albin in Kristinehamn; however, the company declined the order.)

The gearbox was a three–speed unit without synchromesh. The brakes were mechanical and acted only on the rear wheels on the first models (front–wheel brakes later became available as an option at extra cost).

Apart from the standard four–seater version, the ÖV4 was also built (mainly for the Royal Swedish Telegraph Service) as a small, open, two–seater delivery truck with a small load compartment, under the designation ÖV4TV. In addition, a few ÖV4s were sold as chassis, with a two–seater truck cab and a small goods platform for service as light delivery trucks.

Despite its limited power, the ÖV4 was entered in a number of competitions (usually winter events) equipped, in some instances with a specially tuned engine with aluminium pistons. However, Gustaf Larsson put a stop to these activities as soon as he became aware of them.

It quickly became clear that the open–top car was a mistake; Swedish buyers wanted a covered model for use in all weathers. As a result, it was decided to build one of the ten prototypes (No. 9) as an enclosed type with a metal body on a timber frame, as was customary at the time. Styled by MasOlle, this car also boasted elegant lines with oval side windows to the rear of the back doors.

Before long, it became apparent that the light chassis designed for the open–top model was not sufficiently strong to carry a heavy, rigid, covered body. As a temporary measure, it was decided to use a Weymann–type body, the timber frame of which was covered with imitation leather rather than metal cladding. This made the body more flexible and less prone to cracking as the chassis moved. Known as the PV4, this was the first Volvo car to be assigned the PV prefix, which was used for many years afterwards (the letters 'PV' stood for 'PersonVagn', the Swedish for 'Passenger car', while

the figure '4' stood, as before, for 'four–cylinder'). Although it became more popular than its predecessor, sales continued to disappoint and the infant company was operating at a heavy loss. In fact, by the end of 1927 and the beginning of the following year, its prospects appeared anything but bright.

With its unattractive lines and abrupt transition between the foreshortened bonnet and the rest of the body, the styling of the PV4 was not a success. As a result, it was modified substantially in autumn 1928, when the 'Volvo Special' appeared with a longer bonnet, a bigger, rectangular rear window (which was oval in the PV4) and bumpers as standard equipment.

Over the years, Volvo has become known as one of the leading makers of estate cars. In this context, it is worth noting that the company was building this very type of model to order (as a commercial travellers' car) as far back as the late 1920s. In this version, the vehicle was equipped with a full–sized, side–opening door at the rear.

Volvo's first open–top car was a cabriolet. With its 28–hp engine, its speed was modest.

Although robust and functional, the first enclosed saloon was of staid appearance.

The Mars symbol, the diagonal stripe, and 'VOLVO'

Many vehicle manufacturers have a symbol which they use for advertising and design purposes. But Volvo is probably alone in having no less than three symbols, all of which have been used ever since the first car was produced.

From the very first time it was shown, the ÖV4 car was called 'The Swedish Car'. This meant that a symbol was needed to associate with this heritage. The symbol chosen was the one for iron, and Swedish iron processing, as the car was made of 'Swedish steel'. The 'iron symbol', or Mars symbol as it was initially called because it is also the symbol of Mars the Roman god of war, was placed in the middle of the radiator on the first ever Volvo car (and on trucks some years later).

The Mars symbol had to be firmly affixed to the radiator, and the easiest way was to place a metal stripe diagonally across the radiator. Gradually, this diagonal stripe became an even more powerful symbol for Volvo and its products – in actual fact, it is the most powerful symbol in the automotive industry.

The third and final Volvo symbol is the trade mark 'VOLVO', designed in the characteristic 'Egyptian' style with equi-thick bars and hair-lines.

These three symbols were placed on the first Volvo car and they are still used in 1995 on all Volvo products. This unbroken line of tradition is without parallel throughout the entire automotive industry.

14 April 1927 – Volvo is born

When was Volvo born?

Was it on 11 May 1915? The day when, at 3.30 in the afternoon, the patent agency AB Delmar & Co acting as a representative for Aktiebolaget Volvo submitted an application to have the trade mark 'Volvo' registered as a name for several different products – 'bearings especially ball bearings and roller bearings, machines, transmissions, automobiles, bicycles, railway material, all types of transport equipment, as well as parts of and accessories for the afore-mentioned products…'

Or was it on 25 July 1924, on 'Jakob day' (as it is called in Swedish diaries), when Gustaf Larson and Assar Gabrielsson met by chance over a plate of crayfish at the Sturehof restaurant in Stockholm, and after enjoying their meal agreed to start up production of 'The Swedish Car'?

Or was Volvo born on the June day in 1926 when the first prototype cars drove out from Galco's premises in Stockholm?

No, Volvo considers 14 April 1927 as being the date when the company was born. After experiencing 'labour pains' all through the night – the final drive had been installed back to front, for example, thus making the car to drive backwards only – Sales Manager Hilmer Johansson was able to drive the first series-produced Volvo car through the factory gates at 10 o'clock in the morning.

ASSAR GABRIELSSON WAS convinced that the car would one day become the property of the common man. However, he misjudged the time scale, believing that sales of quality, medium–class cars would increase rapidly at that time. In fact, the anticipated explosion in sales did not take place until much later, after the Second World War.

Gustaf Larson, the second founding father, had a more realistic outlook. Although he did not believe that the average Swede could afford to pay an extra high price for high quality, he did take the view that buyers who used the vehicles for commercial purposes (hauliers, bus companies and taxi owners) were more concerned with quality and running economy than price.

Design work on Volvo's first Series 1 truck had now been in full swing since the end of 1926. Although the model was based on the same engine and gearbox as the car, the rest of the components were considerably heavier. The track width was the same as in the car; however, a sturdier frame and rear axle were used to accommodate the 1.5 tonne payload (and the type of overloading which was common at the time).

Unlike the car, sales of the truck were successful. By the time it was launched in 1928, a number of customers had already placed orders for the new vehicle and the series was sold out a mere six months later. By then, the handful of energetic designers had carried out comprehensive modifications and improvements.

Exactly like its predecessor, the Series 2 truck was equipped with the underpowered 28–hp engine driving a three–speed gearbox. However, the narrow track width of 1,300 mm had been increased to 1,460 mm, while the slower of the two final drive ratios previously available as options was now standard. The differences between the new model and the first series and, especially, between it and the cars, were now obvious.

Although the Series 1 and 2 models became popular mainly as trucks, a few examples were also sold as buses or attractive delivery vehicles. In general, these commercial vehicles were short–lived, most of them being taken out of service by the mid–1930s and used as agricultural tractors. As a result, many have survived to the present day and are being restored to their original condition as examples of Volvo's earliest commercial vehicles.

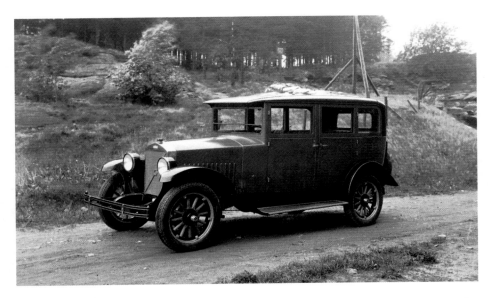

The Volvo Special – a modified and more tasteful saloon – was introduced in 1928.

The first Volvo buses were built on the four–cylinder truck chassis. The interior was simple, functional and extremely attractive, with generous use of real wood trim and tasteful fabrics.

The first truck bore an oval badge similar to that on the car, but without the 'Göteborg Sweden' legend.

THE FLEDGLING COMPANY began to fly on its own in 1929, although its financial returns were still poor. In fact, it had made a loss every month since its foundation, mainly because of the small number of cars built during that time. However, the growth in truck sales was making a positive contribution to Volvo's finances.

Most of the criticism levelled at the company during the first few years focused on the fact that the Volvo car, despite its high price, lacked power. This problem was now finally rectified. At the end of May, the company unveiled its DB engine, which was designed in Göteborg and produced in Skövde. The new six–cylinder unit was based largely on the experience gained from the first four–cylinder type; however, the cubic capacity had been increased from 1,944 to 3,010 cm3 by

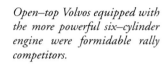

Open–top Volvos equipped with the more powerful six–cylinder engine were formidable rally competitors.

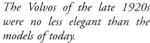
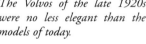

The Volvos of the late 1920s were no less elegant than the models of today.

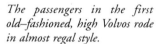

The passengers in the first old–fashioned, high Volvos rode in almost regal style.

increasing the bore, while the output was almost doubled from 28 to 55 hp.

Technically, the new six–cylinder PV651 car bore only a limited resemblance to the first Volvo car. The new model was a saloon which, like the open ÖV4 before it, had been styled by the artist MasOlle. Although clearly inspired by American thinking, and although they were conventional rather than daring, the strong lines immediately won the approval of the solid, prosperous middle class which represented Volvo's main group of customers.

Because of the PV651's slightly longer wheelbase (295 cm), both the driver and passengers rode in almost regal style. The legroom was generous and the high roof ensured that the occupants could keep their hats on while travelling (which, in fact, may well have been advisable, given that heaters did not become generally available until the mid–1930s – and even then were installed only as an extra!).

With its 55–hp engine, the model possessed adequate power, if not exactly in the sports car class. By now, the Volvo was already a strong and robust car, with a weight to match. The chassis was well–dimensioned and was obviously influenced by the company's two years of experience of vehicle manufacture.

A variant known as the PV650, in the form of a chassis which was used to build small trucks for delivery applications, was produced concurrently with the PV651.

The DB engine had undergone practical testing even before the new six–cylinder model was introduced. During the winter of 1928–29, a couple of ÖV4s had been fitted with the unit and entered in a number of competitions (these cars were clearly distinguishable by the longer bonnets used to accommodate the two extra cylinders). At this time, both of the test cars (as well as a PV650

chassis) were fitted with light, simple, open bodies, which contributed to their sporty appearance.

While the more powerful engine and the four–speed gearbox were welcome improvements to the car, they were even more useful features of the new Series 3 trucks, which were introduced more or less at the same time. In most respects, the new models were identical to the previous series; however, the much higher engine rating enabled drivers to maintain respectable average speeds even when heavily loaded.

The front of the Series 3 trucks was identical to the PV650/651; in other words, it featured the same more rounded radiator and extended bonnet. There was, however, one important difference; whereas the PV650/651 radiator carried the characteristic diagonal Volvo 'stripe' and Mars symbol, the new truck did not.

In its longer version, the Series 3 truck was also suitable for service as a country bus. Several bus andrail companies, mainly in western and southern Sweden, now bought Volvo buses, providing a major social service at a time when those who used them could only dream of owning their own cars.

The significance to Volvo of the product innovations introduced in 1929 can hardly be exaggerated. For the first time, the Volvo car was aspacious, robust and safe vehicle which met the requirements of the Swedish middle class, while

The six–cylinder cars were much more readily accepted by customers than the first, rudimentary model.

Volvo was building estate models by the end of the 1920s.

truck owners could now avail of a mass–produced Swedish truck of a size ideal for most long–distance transport applications.

However, Volvo was not the only company engaged in product development.

Engine manufacturer Pentaverken in Skövde had commenced production of a new version of its successful U–2 outboard engine under the designation U–21. Compared with the original 1921–22 unit, this featured lighter mountings, an aluminium flywheel, a pull–cord starter and an olive green painted finish.

Developed originally in 1921–22, the U–2/U–21 and the U–22 variant were to remain in production in almost unmodified form until 1962, an unbroken period of four complete decades. (Although Volvo Penta produced a 'U–22' model until 1979, this was not a relation of the original 1930 U–2, but was actually a descendant of the renowned Archimedes BS opposed–piston engine designed originally in 1912!).

A major advance on its predecessor, the first six–cylinder truck became equally popular in the bus version.

Facing page: Pentaverken, which was to be acquired by Volvo about a year later, unveiled its legendary U–21 outboard engine in 1929. The unit was to be produced in almost unmodified form until 1962.

Volvo almost became American

Volvo's executive management – which then consisted of Assar Gabrielsson and Gustaf Larson – had many problems to wrestle with in 1929. For one thing, the company was very close to being sold off to the Nash Corporation in the USA.

As Volvo was still running at a loss well into 1929, its owner – SKF – began to give up hope of ever making a profit. The president of SKF in America contacted Nash, the giant car manufacturer, and the initial discussions were so favourable that Charles Nash himself decided to sail to Sweden to seal the deal. The evening before his arrival, Assar Gabrielsson contacted SKF President Björn Prytz and beseeched him to persuade his board not to sell off Volvo. Gabrielsson offered to invest everything he had made so far from the company – 220,000 kronor – to eke out SKF's loan to Volvo. He was adamant that Volvo would start to show a profit very soon.

After a long discussion lasting well into the small hours, Björn Prytz decided to hold a telephone conference with the board of SKF before receiving their American guests at the dock the following morning. The decision went Gabrielsson's way, with Volvo escaping from the clutches of a foreign take-over by the narrowest of margins.

But there was a condition attached to this: SKF insisted on receiving 25 kronor for every Volvo car sold. This proved to be a difficult problem for Gabrielsson to solve, and his successor Gunnar Engellau 'inherited' the dilemma in 1956. It was not until 1959 that this extremely delicate matter was finally resolved, following a decision by the Swedish Supreme Court. In September 1929, Volvo showed its first-ever profit: 1,579 kronor. Assar Gabrielsson marked the occasion by cabling the American contact who had assisted in forging the contact with Nash. He wrote: 'At last we are beginning to see the light of day. Last month we made a profit – even if it was a small one'.

October saw the figures back in their accustomed red, but from the month of November, Volvo obliged the board of SKF by remaining permanently and soundly in the black.

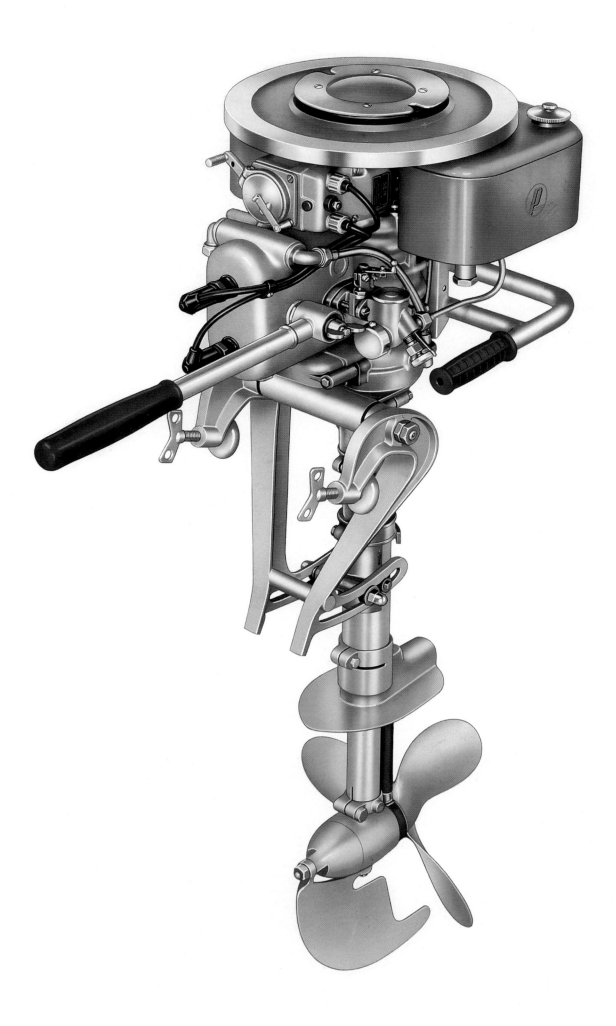

By the beginning of 1930, the management of Volvo was at last able to breathe a little easier. Thanks to successful truck sales, the company had finally become viable.

Although produced in small numbers, the cars had found their niche in the market as one of the most reliable – albeit boring – and high–quality makes. Nevertheless, since most Swedish motorists were still buying low–priced, good quality American cars, Volvo decided to concentrate its attention on taxi owners.

Special taxi versions which were mechanically identical to the PV650/651 were introduced in 1930. Initially, these were designated the TRS and TRL (Swedish acronyms for 'urban taxi' and 'rural taxi' respectively). The main difference between the private car and taxi versions was the longer wheelbase of the latter, which afforded the rear–seat passengers extremely generous legroom. Two folding seats were also installed between the front and rear seats to increase the passenger capacity.

Outwardly, the TRS and TRL were identical. Inside, the urban version was provided with a glass partition between the front and rear, most likely to protect the driver from cold as the passengers entered and alighted (at this time, most passengers were well–behaved and sober, and the screen was not intended as protection against unruly fares).

The PV651 and TRS/TRL were fitted with mechanical brakes of obsolescent design on all four wheels, at a time when their American competitors had long been equipped with efficient hydraulic brakes all round. In 1930, the PV651 was succeeded by the PV652, with this feature as the main improvement. The body of the new model, mainly the redesigned rear end, was also modified. These changes were made somewhat later to the improved TR673 and TR674 taxis (town and country models in which '6' stood for six–cylinder,

When Volvo equipped its cars with efficient, all–round hydraulic brakes in the 1930s, it added a warning triangle on the boot lid to advise motorists with less powerful mechanical brakes to keep their distance.

The Volvo engine plant in Skövde is the inheritor of a long tradition. The photograph shows the original factory building in the late 19th century.

'7' for seven–passenger and '3' or '4' for the version). At this time, the earlier taxis were redesignated TR671 (TRS) and TR672 (TLS).

The Series 3 trucks had become extremely popular and were not modified. However, Volvo now introduced a new Series 4, which was almost identical mechanically but carried a higher payload.

Meanwhile, Pentaverken in Skövde had achieved enormous success with its U–2/U–21 outboard engine, which was a simple, two–stroke unit for utility purposes.

Penta's new S–2 (later known as the S–21) was launched in 1930. However, this was not intended as a successor or competitor to the hugely successful U–21, but was introduced as a 'top–of–the–range' model.

The four–stroke S–2 was a bigger outboard engine with a cubic capacity of no less than 496 cm3. The unit featured two horizontal cylinders, side valves and light alloy pistons, with the crankshaft supported in roller bearings. The four–stroke design made the unit quiet, economical and environmentally sound (the same rationale behind the 1990s 'innovation' of using four–stroke outboards).

The S–2 was a robust engine. However, since it was also heavy and relatively expensive to manufacture and sell, production of this epoch–making unit ceased in 1937, before even 200 examples had been made.

The two–cylinder L–2 was added to the Penta L series in 1930, the four–cylinder L–4 having been introduced the year before (the bigger, six–cylinder L–6 was to follow in 1931). The side–valve L series engines retailed at a reasonable price, and soon acquired a high reputation for their quality and excellent running characteristics.

The success of the L series and the popularity of the U–21 were the reasons which prompted Volvo

Volvo Pentaverken

In 1930, Volvo acquired a share majority in Pentaverken (formerly Skövde Gjuteri & Mekaniska Werkstad, with a history dating back to 1868).

Five years later the Pentaverken was fully incorporated into the Volvo Group (and the name was changed to Volvo Pentaverken). However, a special company responsible for sales of Penta marine engines was retained with the aim of further developing that part of the business.

'Penta engines are sold in countries all over the world. They are expensive, but good. It may be well worth remembering that the lifeboats on the big Atlantic steamships, the Europa, Bremen, and Rex, were powered by Penta engines'. (Extract from the Sales Manual dated 1936).

to take over Pentaverken in 1930, the first of many such acquisitions. However, the growth in car engine production was crucial to Pentaverken and the company was unlikely to have survived on its own.

When Volvo took over Pentaverken, the range included both inboard and outboard engines. A few S–2 four–stroke outboards can be seen at front right, with a number of ordinary two–stroke U–21 outboard units behind. Inboard engines of various types are shown on the left.

'Ratten'

The Volvo magazine 'Ratten' (The Steering Wheel) was first published as early as 1930. The first editor was Rolf Hansson, who was the company's export manager. The magazine was distributed to various interested parties outside Volvo as well as to all Volvo employees. In time it became an out and out customer magazine. By 1980, the circulation had grown to one million copies published four times a year.

Ratten is now not only one of the biggest magazines in Sweden, it is also the oldest customer magazine in the country. For a few years, however, distribution of the magazine was discontinued for political or economic reasons.

A special edition of the magazine was printed after the Second World War. Except for an 'explanation and apology to Swedish readers' on the front cover, the entire magazine was written in English. This was because the company's sales force outside Sweden had not received any information at all about the development of the company during the six years war raged.

In the fourth number of 1964, an appeal was made to the magazine's 230,000 readers. They were asked to fill in a questionnaire stating their interest in receiving the magazine. This was because there was a risk of the magazine going out of circulation as a result of substantially increased distribution costs. There was obviously not enough interest – or the budget was too small – because after 35 continuous years, the magazine did not appear in 1965.

In 1966, however, there were some major new products in the pipeline and money was made available. The magazine reappeared first with an entire issue devoted to the Volvo Amazon car, and this was followed by an issue devoted entirely to the new Volvo 144 car model.

Ratten did not appear for a couple of years in the 1970s, but the Volvo Swedish sales organisation decided in 1979 to concentrate seriously on the magazine. Instead of being distributed only to owners of the newest Volvo car models, as it had been up until that time, it was decided that all owners of Volvo cars in Sweden – more than a million readers – would receive a copy.

When Volvo became the Renault agent in Sweden in the early 1980s, some Renault-owners also received the Ratten magazine.

After some years there was a desire to keep the contents relating to the two manufacturers separate, and this led to the formation of the customer magazine 'Renault Revue' in 1988.

Over the years, many Volvo market companies have also started up their own customer magazine based on the one in Sweden – some of them rather simple in form, others extremely elegant.

The cover of the first issue of Ratten was anything but exciting. It featured a solemn picture of Hjalmar Wallin, the Volvo dealer in Göteborg.

LITTLE VOLVO WAS at last attaining success. Its trucks were selling like hot cakes, its taxis dominated Swedish taxi ranks and a growing number of its cars were finding favour with buyers willing to pay for high quality. The capital necessary to give the company stability was finally available.

By now, Volvo was anxious to expand its customer base to include the more exclusive end of the market. Only a few years earlier, open–top cars had been for 'ordinary' people, while saloon models commanded a considerably higher price. Things had now changed and 'upper class' customers were demanding elegant cabriolet models with hoods to provide total protection against wind and weather all year round. As a result, Volvo commenced development work on a series of expensive cars of this type and several prototypes were built, leading to the production of 26 examples (on the 650 chassis) during 1931 and 1932. Unfortunately, not one of these has survived to the present day.

The Swedish roads of the period were of extremely poor quality and local authorities in many areas permitted only low axle weights. This led to the development of a three–axle Series 4 truck known as the LV64LF (the prefix 'LV' denoted 'LastVagn', or 'Truck', while the suffix 'LF' signified 'Long Frame' – a designation which was used for three–axle models until the 1950s). Based on a Danish patent, the suspension arrangement used on the two rearmost axles has, in principle, survived to this day on three–axle Volvos with a single driving axle and twin wheels on the rearmost axle also. In the event, the LV64LF was used almost exclusively as a bus, although some chassis were finished as platform trucks.

By this time, it was clear to the new Swedish automaker that the bigger the vehicle, the easier it was to sell it at a higher price. Until then, the company had been party to a gentleman's agreement whereby Scania–Vabis built large commercial vehicles and Volvo confined itself to smaller models. This tacit agreement came to an end in 1931, when Volvo introduced its biggest trucks to date in the shape of the LV66–67 and LV68–70 series, which were also the first to be built originally as trucks and bore no relation to the cars. A powerful overhead–valve engine, the 4.1–litre DC developing 75 hp, was also introduced in the new series. Although intended for use only in heavy trucks and buses, about ten of these units nevertheless found their way into cars. A rugged gearbox of a new design was used to transmit the engine power to a single–reduction (LV68–70) or a double–reduction (LV66–67) final drive.

The LV68–70 became a popular medium–sized series, a segment in which their was a real gap to be filled since American trucks of this class were of less robust construction and the company's two

Based on the ageing LV Series 3/4 of 1929–30, the LV64LF was Volvo's first three–axle commercial vehicle. With the exception of a few trucks, most of the vehicles were built as buses.

Simple is beautiful, as shown by this retouched photograph of the LV64LF chassis.

Swedish competitors were building genuinely large models virtually by hand. Volvo was established as a producer of medium–sized trucks.

The powerful LV66–67 series was designed to meet the challenge from Scania–Vabis and Tidaholm in earnest. While the ruggedness of the chassis helped it to gain acceptance among customers, the somewhat low engine power (relative to the gross weight of the vehicle) prevented it from becoming a success in the most important application of the day – road maintenance, often combined with snow–ploughing in winter. Thus, it was to be another six years before Volvo would be able to compete seriously in the Swedish heavyweight division.

Volvo's first head office was located in what was known as the 'L Building'. Pictured in front of the offices is a fleet of LV67 trucks.

The most impressive of this generation of trucks were undoubtedly the LV66LF and LV67LF bogie models with gross weights up to 9 tonnes. This super–heavy chassis was introduced in 1933, the year in which Volvo also launched its Hesselman engine, a DC petrol engine converted to burn less expensive heavy fuel oil.

The LV66/67 became best known to the public for its service in humanitarian operations during the war in Abyssinia (now Ethiopia), when several of the trucks were fitted out by the Red Cross for the distribution of emergency supplies (just as numbers of Volvo N and FL models have been used by the UN in more recent times to distribute food and medicines to areas of war–torn Bosnia).

The LV67LF was an extremely powerful three– axle truck. The model is pictured above in a finished version and (above right) as a bare chassis in the workshop.

The winged emblem (right) is an attractive example of 1930s design.

The 'L' building – the first Head Office

The first head office consisted of a corner of the top floor of the L-building, which was really a parts warehouse. The two founding fathers moved into this building in the autumn of 1926 together with a few other engineers who worked intensively on completing the first car and preparing the 1929 car and truck product news.

The L-building has now been pulled down but the foundation remains, and on this the truck laboratory which carries the name 'L' is built.

The winged trade mark

Now when Volvo was producing really large trucks, there was a need to highlight this by having a more elegant type of symbol on the radiator. This led to the creation of a new emblem in the form of a familiar triangle, which adorned the large trucks (but not the earlier PV65 cars and the older truck models, Series 3 and Series 4).

However, it soon became apparent that it was not a good idea to have several different company symbols, and a return was made to the classical trade mark 'VOLVO', together with the Mars symbol and the diagonal stripe.

INTRODUCED IN 1932, the highly successful LV70B was part of the LV68–70 series. Volvo had already delivered a large number of truck chassis for bodyworking as buses and the demand was now so great that the introduction of a purpose–built chassis was warranted. The model consisted of an extended, right–hand drive LV70 chassis provided with mountings for a bus body, extra instruments and chromium–plated lights. The decision to produce dedicated bus chassis was taken when company management realised that bus companies were prepared to pay more for the product than 'tight–fisted' hauliers!

A special 'Volvo standard bus', consisting of an LV70B chassis and a body by Arvika Vagnfabrik, Aktiebolaget Svenska Järnvägsverkstäderna of Linköping or Svenska KarosseriVerkstäderna of Katrineholm, was also introduced in 1932. Due to differences in legislation in different parts of Sweden, the same bus was available in two alternative widths. Of these, the narrower version was fitted with only a single row of lateral seats and a long bench seat running the length of the bus.

In the early 1930s, Volvo's small and medium–sized trucks were painfully old–fashioned, with wooden, spoked wheels and brakes on only one axle. To rectify these deficiencies, two up–to–date new series, the LV71–72 and the LV73–74, were introduced in 1932. In appearance, these were similar to their predecessors and were based on the same components. However, the larger series was considerably more robust, with heavier frames, stronger suspensions and bolted–on wheels (five nuts on the LV71–22 and six on the LV73–74). Both series were powered by the same type EB engine, which was introduced at the same time in the PV650/652 and TR673/674 cars. The engine was a bored–out version of the DB, with a cubic capacity of 3.27 litres and a higher rating of 65 hp. Increasing numbers of chassis were now being fitted with bodies built by specialist firms, many of them by the Åtvidaberg company.

Volvo LV70B standard bus.

Every new engine is the product of exhaustive laboratory testing. The picture at bottom right is of the first single–cylinder, test version of the HA engine. The picture below shows the finished version of the unit installed in a car. Right: The inventor, Jonas Hesselman.

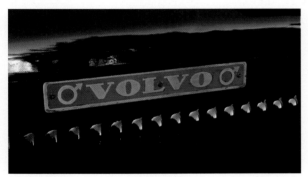

Above: The interior of the Volvo standard bus. The other three photographs are of the LV73 truck.

YET ANOTHER MODEL in the LV73 series appeared at the beginning of 1933. Intended mainly as a forward- control bus (without a bonnet), the model, the LV75, was also built to a limited extent as a truck. Mechanically, it was the same as the LV74 except that the front axle from the heavier LV68 series was used to compensate for the higher front axle loading. The main advantages of the new model were its superior weight distribution, which reduced the axle weight and had a less damaging effect on the roads, and the fact that the a platform or body of the same length could be accommodated within a shorter overall length, affording better manoeuvrability. The standard version had a wheelbase of 4.1 metres; however, customers had the option of specifying another wheelbase, such as 4.6 metres or even longer. As an early example of Volvo's internationalisation, the LV75 was launched, not in Sweden, but at the Amsterdam Motor Show.

In retrospect, the young company's design engineers must have worked day and night, given that their number was so small and that the product range was not only very wide, but was expanding rapidly.

Developments in the car sector were proceeding at an extremely fast pace. A new, updated generation of cars with more rounded styling was introduced in 1933. These consisted mainly of cosmetically refined versions of the existing models. The PV653 boasted softer lines than its predecessor, the PV652, featuring a gently sloped front and windscreen, and a rounder body. The standard model was supplemented by a 'luxury' model (PV654), which was available in a range of attractive body finishes and boasted a more luxurious interior, twin horns and two spare wheels. Buyers who wanted a bare chassis had the option of the PV650.

The LV75, Volvo's first forward–control (F–type) chassis became popular both as a truck and a bus.

Below: Volvo's first concept car, the Venus Bilo, was the forerunner of the streamlined PV36 introduced two years later.

Several exciting and – in the opinion of many – beautiful special models were built on the PV650 chassis. The most unusual of these was ordered by Volvo from the Nordberg coachbuilding firm in Stockholm. Nicknamed the 'Venus Bilo', this was strongly influenced by the 'functional' style which was then emerging in the fields of architecture and interior design. This unique vehicle was, in effect, Volvo's first concept car – a model used to test customers' reactions to modern innovations –and may be regarded as the forerunner of the PV36, which was introduced barely two years later. Thanks to its wide body without running boards, the Venus Bilo had a wide, spacious interior. Although the car itself is no more, the version used as a model is now on show in the Stockholm Technical Museum.

A number of attractive cabriolets was also built on the PV650 chassis, the most famous of which were bodyworked by Norrmalms Karosserifabrik of Stockholm. The one survivor of these two open–top models not only had a unique body, but concealed a powerful 75–hp DC truck engine under the extended bonnet – a feature which was not entirely unnecessary given the weight of the car.

Yet another 'special' on a PV655 chassis was

designed by Oscar Montelius, who converted the model by fitting hydrostatic transmission units (known as 'IMU' pumps) to each wheel to replace the mechanical transmission.

The earlier taxi models were also revamped and given slightly softer lines when the stock of parts was exhausted. The TR673 urban taxi was succeeded by the TR676 (on the same wheelbase but with a taller body so that 'posh' passengers could keep their top hats on!), while the TR674 was superseded by the TR677 (on a longer wheelbase). The TR678 (built on the same short wheelbase as the TR676) and TR679 (with the longer wheelbase) were available to buyers who wanted custom–built coachwork.

The PV653/654, which was also built in a cabriolet version (above) at the Norrmalm works in Stockholm, was perhaps the most attractive of the cars built between 1929 and 1937.

A GAP HAD EXISTED between the PV655/TR678–679 chassis variants and the LV71 truck series in the otherwise fairly comprehensive truck range. In 1934, this was filled by the LV76 series, which strongly resembled the cars in appearance. Far from being a coincidence, this was due to the fact that the front section, including part of the door, had been taken from the PV650/TR67. These series may justifiably be regarded as the first to be equipped with 'Volvo cabs' since they were normally delivered complete with steel cabs from Svenska Stålpressningsaktiebolaget in Olofström. The LV76 was a small truck which, the different versions of which were fitted with a rigid platform, all with single rear wheels of different sizes depending on the variant. The model was modified in step with the corresponding cars; when the EB engine was superseded by a more powerful unit, the LV76 series trucks were similarly modified.

The LV70B and LV75 had been well received by bus operators despite the fact that they were based on truck chassis. Volvo had taken due note of the trend and had developed purpose–built buses – a step which was almost certainly not welcomed by Scania–Vabis, whose busbuilding operations were much more extensive than its truck production.

Unveiled in 1934, Volvo's first bus, the B1, found an immediate market niche, proving ideal as a large rural or suburban bus (although it still posed no threat to Scania–Vabis's big, prestigious city models).

The B1 was a forward–control model in keeping with the trend of the day. In technical terms, it was quite similar to the LV66 truck and was powered either by a DC petrol engine or a Hesselman HA unit, both 4.09–litre units developing 75 hp. The gearbox was the same four–speed unit used in the LV6, while the final drive was the same as in the LV68, with single reduction. The B4 model, which was equipped with the same powerful double reduction drive as the LV66, was developed for service in especially tough conditions or in very hilly terrain. The axles and wheels were also taken from the LV66, although the suspension was redesigned to improve the standard of comfort and lower the floor height.

Volvo was now an export company. Although the forward–control bus had been accepted and become common in Sweden, conventional bonneted models were still the norm in most other countries. To supply these markets, the B2 and B3, which were exact counterparts of the B1 and B4, but which featured a decorative front with a short bonnet and wings, were introduced in parallel. Unrelated to the rest of the product range, these models were built only in small numbers. However, the B1, in particular, sold well in several export markets, especially in South America, where it laid the foundation for the company's success in

supplying the rapidly expanding network of bus services.

Volvo included both traditional bonneted (right) and forward –control models when it introduced its first generation of purpose–built buses in 1934. The latter are shown in the top pictures on the facing page in Swedish (left) and Brazilian– bodied (right) versions.

The LV76 finally provided Volvo with an powerful, up– to–date, light truck capable of competing with American Ford and Chevrolet models which, although cheaper, were also of lighter construction.

1935 WAS ONE of the most dramatic and exciting years yet in Volvo's history. Profitability was now at a highly satisfactory level, thanks to the truck and bus sectors, while the dealer network was firmly established – at least in Sweden. The product range was comprehensive, and since all of the vehicles were solidly built without extravagant features, their quality was acknowledged.

The company realised that it was now time to move ahead in the car sector also, to which end Assar Gabrielsson and Gustaf Larsson engaged a number of Swedish–American engineers from the USA to design a modern Volvo capable of competing with the leading American marques.

The introduction of the PV36 in spring 1935 was a source of pride to Volvo's employees, who had designed and built a car considered to be in the same class as the newest American models, with the aerodynamic styling which was popular at the time. Described in the first advertisements as the 'streamlined car', the PV36 later became known as the 'Carioca' (although the origin of this name, with its suggestion of hot–blooded Latin American dance rhythms, is unknown).

The Chrysler Airflow is generally regarded as having provided the inspiration for the Carioca, although Dodge and Hupmobile also had similar models, and it is hardly a coincidence that the project's chief designer had been recruited from the latter company.

However, the high expectations of the employees were dashed. Instead of the anticipated success, the 501 cars built (500 complete vehicles and a chassis finished with a Nordberg cabriolet body) proved extremely difficult to sell. It was several years before the cars of this first (and last)

The Volvo TR701 was a spacious and stately taxi version of the 'new' cars which formed the last link in the chain of models dating from 1929.

Even in the 1930s, the rugged construction of Volvo cars provided the occupants with an unusually high degree of protection. Despite the severe damage to the front of this PV36 Carioca, the passenger compartment is intact.

series were disposed of, an experience which was not conducive to the development of a successor.

In technical terms, the PV36 did boast a number of innovations. The front axle was now split, improving the standard of comfort although increasing the weight. The EC engine – a bored–out EB unit with a cubic capacity of 3.67 litres and an output of 80–84 hp – compensated to a degree for the higher weight. This engine was to become a legend. Adapted by Penta, it was the first Volvo car engine to be used in large numbers in marine and industrial applications.

Buyers of cars are usually both knowledgable and fair–minded. The failure of the PV36 was deserved; compared with its Volvo predecessors as well as its competitors, it was far from being an advanced car, either in terms of features or engineering. The model was solidly built, so much so that its frame was more like that of a small truck. This was a major departure from its American counterparts which, by virtue of their frameless monocoque construction, were considerable lighter. The nearest equivalent, the Chrysler Airflow, was equipped with an in–line, eight–cylinder engine of considerable power which, combined with the low weight of the car, gave it a decisive advantage over the heavier and less powerful PV36. The American cars on which the PV36 had been modelled (the Hupmobile Aerodynamic, DeSoto Airflow and Chrysler Airflow) also performed poorly in the market and were succeeded by conventional models.

Since the Olofström plant was still unable to produce pressings of all sizes, the middle section of the PV36 roof was of woven fabric (the body was still built on a timber frame by Åtvidberg). While the roadholding was reasonable on good roads, the handling on winter roads appears to have been quite the opposite.

Despite its shortcomings, the Carioca became something of a cult model, occupying a special place in the hearts of motoring historians alongside

the Volvo ÖV4 (1927–29), PV444 (1947–58), P1900 (1956–57) and Amazon (1956–70).

Volvo has historically shown a reluctance to place 'all its eggs in one basket'. Thus, the introduction of the PV36 was paralleled by that of the PV658 (standard version) and PV659 (deluxe version), models derived from the earlier PV653/654. Although these also displayed a little of the streamlined shape, the designers were content to conceal the radiator behind a sloped and slightly pointed grille (the first time this had been done). Apart from this, the changes were minor, except that the engine was the same EC unit used in the PV36.

Apart from the finished cars, these models were available in chassis form as the PV656 (on a normal wheelbase) and PV657 (on an extended 355 cm wheelbase). The PV657 was used mainly as an ambulance, with the exception of one chassis which was built as a four–door convertible for the reigning King of Sweden, Gustaf V. This particular model, which was built for service during the royal hunt, is now part of the Svedino collection in Ugglarp, Sweden.

Taxi owners were not neglected. New taxi models were introduced in parallel with the PV656–659 cars, in the shape of the TR701 (a tall urban taxi on the shorter 310 cm wheelbase), the TR702 (a 325–cm wheelbase chassis), the TR703 (a long urban taxi on a 325–cm wheelbase, with an

Although it attracted a great deal of attention, the PV36 Carioca found few buyers.

Volvo employees were actively involved in sports from the very beginning, fully supported by the company's founding fathers. Both enthusiastic golfers, Assar Gabrielsson and Gustaf Larson even encouraged their managerial staff to take golf lessons in company time! The photograph shows a Volvo soccer team of the 1930s (note the familiar design on the jerseys).

Volvo quoted on the Stock exchange

By 10 August 1926, Assar Gabrielsson's positive forecasts had satisfied the SKF Board that the company was doing well, and it was thus decided to make the registration documents for the dormant patented company Volvo available. The board also decided to subscribe for a share capital of SKr200,000 in AB Volvo.

Two days later, an employment agreement was signed between Assar Gabrielsson and the shareholder, SKF. Gabrielsson was employed as Managing Director of AB Volvo as from January 1927. SKF then reimbursed Gabrielsson for the money he had invested out of his own pocket to produce the ten prototype cars – a total of about SKr220,000, which at the time was a staggering amount of money.

SKF also granted AB Volvo a loan of one million kronor, and even more money later, to cover the losses. AB Volvo reported a loss for the first three years of operation. It was not until October 1929 that the unbroken sequence of profit-making began.

By 1935, the company had shown a profit for five years in succession. The owner, SKF, had made several share emissions, and the share capital amounted to SKr13 million. SKF then considered it was time to quote the company on the Stockholm Stock Exchange, and their shareholders were offered the opportunity to subscribe for Volvo shares. There was already a very wide spread of SKF shares, and this helped the Volvo share to quickly become the 'people's share', which it has remained to be ever since.

Volvo IF

The Volvo Sports and Social Club (Volvo IF) was formed in 1935. It grew quickly in pace with the company, and more and more sections were added. When the club celebrated its 60th anniversary in 1995, Volvo IF was proud to be one of the biggest sports clubs in the whole of Sweden.

internal glass partition and a low roof) and the TR704 (a rural taxi with the same body as the TR703, but without a partition). Apart from the more powerful EC engine and the radiator grille (the same as on the PV658/659), the 'new' taxis were identical to the earlier TR676/679 models.

The LV76–78 light trucks introduced a year earlier were now fitted with the same radiator grille as the cars and also with the EC engine (although only with a 75–hp rating).

Several new truck series appeared in summer 1935, when the LV81, LV83 and LV93 replaced the LV71, LV73 and LV68 respectively. The new models were of a streamlined shape, now with a rounded grille concealing the radiator.

The bonnets on the new trucks were shorter than before since the engine was now installed above, rather than behind the front axle, a modification made possible by redesigning the oil sump. The new configuration afforded much improved weight distribution between the axles and permitted better utilisation of the front axle loading. As a result, the demand for forward–control (non–bonneted) models declined for a several years subsequently.

The new styling was probably determined in consultation with the Åtvidaberg cab company, which simultaneously launched a cab series displaying much more rounded lines in harmony with the rest of the new Volvo range. However, these were not exclusive to Volvo but were used by other makers, such as Chevrolet and Ford, and, on occasion, by Scania–Vabis. As before, the cabs consisted of a sheet steel structure on a timber frame, with the roof covered in imitation leather.

The LV8 was equipped with the EC engine, while the L9 series was still powered by 75–hp DC and HA units (although Volvo had probably intended to have the more powerful FC and Hesselman FCH engines ready in time for the launch of the new models). This resulted in a paradoxical situation whereby the cheaper side–valve models and the more expensive OHV models were both equipped with 75–hp engines for a year.

The basic LV81–84 versions were soon supplemented by two special chassis, the LV85 (for small buses) and the LV86T (for small tipper trucks).

Trucks were commonly used to deliver the milk from farm to breakfast table in the Sweden of the 1930s and 1940s. The picture shows an LV84 milk delivery truck in Göteborg.

FAR FROM BEING ignored, the bus companies were the object of considerable attention and were soon in a position to welcome the introduction of a series of new models. Volvo still offered the option of forward–control models, like the 'Boxer', or normal–control types with a bonnet.

The first really popular Volvo bus series was the B10/11, which eventually came to comprise the B10 (forward–control, short wheelbase), B11 (normal– control, short wheelbase), B12 (forward–control, long wheelbase) and B14 (normal–control, long wheelbase).

Technically, the B10/11 series were the equivalent of the L9 trucks, with a modified frame and a lower, more comfortable suspension. The buses were medium–sized models accommodating 29 to 33 passengers depending on the wheelbase. Although Swedish bus operators were still buying large numbers of bonneted models, the B1 was, in effect, the last series–built Swedish bus of this type. From 1940 on, the bonneted model became the exception rather than the rule on the nation's roads.

The PV650/TR700 cars series were now obsolescent and the PV36 had proved a disaster. However, the disappointment led to the emergence of Volvo's very first mass–produced cars, the standard PV51 and the deluxe PV52 (which was launched a year later). For this first time, Volvo had opted to produce a small car which, although basic, offered adequate room and (thanks to its low weight) an acceptable standard of comfort. Advertised as the 'five–one', this was the first Volvo car to have an all–steel body without a fabric–covered roof. Compared with the PV36, the dimensions of the model were small and the expensive, independent front suspension in that model had been replaced by a conventional beam–type front axle. The windscreen was undivided and the recessed headlamps on the PV36 were replaced by two individual units mounted on the body.

Since the mechanical equipment was the same as in the PV36, the in–line, six–cylinder EC engine gave the new, considerably lighter PV51 relatively good performance. The gearbox was a three–speed unit.

The PV51/52 was a 'fastback' with a fairly straight, sloped rear end and a boot lid with a recess to accommodate the spare wheel. The boot lid of the PV52 Special (which was introduced in 1937) protruded outward to increase the luggage space, the spare wheel being stored underneath a shelf in the compartment.

Since the market trend at this time was towards softer and more pointed shapes, rather than straight horizontal and vertical lines, Volvo introduced a modified version of the PV51/52 two years later under the designations PV53 (the standard model with the spare wheel in the boot lid), PV54 (the

Above: The forward–control B10 and the normal–control B11 were Volvo's first major sellers in the public transport field.

Below: Bus design was also influenced by the current 'streamlining' trend. Despite its appearance, this is a normal–control Volvo bus.

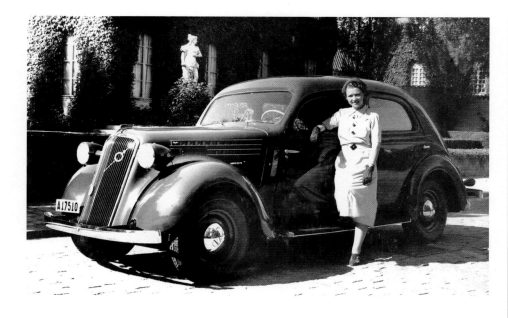

same as the PV53, but with the protruding boot lid and the spare wheel in the luggage compartment), PV55 and PV56 (deluxe versions of the PV53 and PV54 respectively). The only difference between these and the PV51/52 was the more pointed front, which was clearly of American inspiration. Since the PV53 and the other versions were introduced shortly before the start of World War Two, large numbers of the series were purchased by the Swedish Defence Forces, mostly in a military grey or camouflage finish. Some of these were fitted with radio communications equipment or used as staff cars.

The conventional saloons were also accompanied by chassis versions of the PV51/53 and PV53–57, which were bodyworked for a wide range of special applications, ranging from delivery vans for shops and stores to small, open trucks or even elegant open–top cars coachbuilt by the Nordberg company in Stockholm.

Top: The PV51/52 represented Volvo's breakthrough as a car manufacturer; earlier models had sold only in small numbers.

Above: The elegant cabriolet version was built by Nordbergs Karosserifabrik in Stockholm.

Sales Manual dated 1936

Brown, leather-lined binders enclose a very special publication dated 1936 – a Sales Manual. Each copy of the manual is numbered and an acknowledgement of receipt was signed by the person receiving it. However, there was a condition that it was to remain in Volvo's possession.

The manual contains about a hundred pages, and was intended for use as an aid for salesmen in Volvo dealerships throughout Sweden. The name of the author is not given, but it has always been generally regarded as being written by Assar Gabrielsson himself, apart from a technical section written by Gustaf Larson.

The introduction to the manual carries the following declaration:

"Selling is an art. Anyone who does not have the natural ability to be an artist in a particular field can never become one, no matter how much education and training he receives. Likewise, anyone who does not have the natural ability or the will to sell can never be turned into a salesman through training."

The manual contains many other words of wisdom on the difficult art of selling. Paragraph §120 describes how to deal with customers when selling the PV51 car – which was being introduced at that time:

"Rule No 1: Let him drive the car!
Rule No 2: Let him drive the car!
Rule No 3: Let him drive the car!"

This was undoubtedly sound advice, and it is just as valid today as it was in 1936, as is also the question of service, which is dealt with under item no 37:

"As far as selling is concerned, nothing compares with personal service which the individual salesman can offer his own particular customer. If you have sold a car, do not rely on the company's repair and service workshops being able to deal with all types of problems. Follow up the car yourself to check how it is running and to what degree the customer may have reason to complain. Personal contact between the person who has sold the car and the customer who has bought it means more to customer satisfaction than anything else."

Gabrielsson put the customer firmly in focus as early as 1936.

The first time the word 'safety' is used officially in a Volvo context is in the first paragraph of Gustaf Larson's technical section in the Sales Manual. Safety being Volvo's second fundamental key-word after the original – and 'everlasting' – quality:

"An automobile conveys and is driven by people. The fundamental principle of all design work is, and must be, safety. Each individual supporting part and component in the car must be dimensioned in such a way that it will withstand all forms of stresses and strains which it can be expected to be subjected to, apart from collisions and similar types of impact. This applies chiefly to all supporting and driving parts... we should in future also allow caution to be our guiding-star."

THE L8 AND L9 SERIES had been well received. Similar in appearance but of much more substantial dimensions, the L18/19 and L28/29 series appeared early in 1937. In practice, these were the successors to the ageing LV66 series. The L18 (with single reduction) was the direct successor to the LV68, while the L19 (with double reduction) replaced the LV66. The single–reduction L28 and the double–reduction L29 were direct competitors to the big, powerful and well–regarded Scania–Vabis models. The two smaller trucks were powered by the relatively new 90–hp FC engine or the Hesselman FCH unit of the same rating, whereas the L29 and L28 (which never entered production because of weaknesses in the final drive) were equipped with the new 6.7–litre, 120–hp FA or with the Hesselman FAH. Trucks with the bigger engine were distinguishable from their less powerful counterparts by a longer bonnet. This was the first time that Volvo had produced trucks which were large as well as powerful, and the models duly became successful. The L29 became popular in many versions, from long–haul vehicles with trailers to rugged tipper trucks and road maintenance vehicles, which were often used for tough snow–ploughing duties.

Bus customers too had the option of buying ever bigger and more powerful Volvo buses with the introduction of the forward–control B20 and normal–control B22 as the passenger transport equivalents of the L29 series trucks. Outwardly, these models were very similar to the B10 and B11; however, the heavy wheels with their eight nuts provided the clue to the heavier frame and the higher capacity. The B23 (forward control) and B24 (normal control) versions on a longer wheelbase were introduced later.

The large B40 city bus made its appearance later in 1937. As the first genuinely large and powerful bus in the Volvo range, this posed a threat to the dominance of Scania–Vabis models on the urban traffic scene. Equipped with frames, axles and wheels which were even more rugged than those of the B20/22, the B40 models were powered by the big 120–hp FA/FAH engine.

Penta was now an integral part of Volvo, a position which was exploited to rationalise its development, production and marketing programmes.

Until this time, most marine engines were purpose–built, a factor which minimised the resources available for their development. However, the sale of the Penta EC–6 in substantial numbers for the first time in autumn 1937 marked the end of one era and the start of another, in which efficient and relatively inexpensive car engines, designed and tested using major resources, were first installed in boats. The Penta EC–6 was based on the EC car engine, the output of which was limited by lowering the top speed.

The EC engine (shown here in the 1937 EC–6 marine version) was now the mainstay of the Volvo engine range.

Successful heavy commercial vehicles introduced in 1937 included the B41 bus (left) and LV29 truck (above and below). Some of the components used in the models were common.

In 1938, THE PRODUCT range was further expanded with the addition of the large B50 bus which, although based on the B40, was built to meet the specific requirements of Stockholms Spårvägar (Stockholm Tramways), an obdurate customer which had previously been disinclined to buy Volvo buses at all. Even bigger than the B40, the new model was equipped with a Lysholm–Smith gearbox and modified steering. Although only a small number was built, the B50 played a vital role in establishing Volvo as a recognised manufacturer of large city buses.

The 'Americanisation' of the company's cars proceeded apace. Volvo kept a close eye on trends in the USA and was quick to copy ideas. The taxi market was carefully cultivated by the company and a completely modernised taxi series, the PV800/810, was introduced in 1938. Internally, the models featured no revolutionary innovations; however, the streamlined design and the all–welded steel body represented a radical departure from the reliable and proven, though ageing TR700 series.

Built for a decade as the PV800, PV810 and PV820, the new series became extremely popular (a small number even found their way to customers outside Sweden, for example in Holland and Belgium). Like all taxis of the day, the models were painted blue until 1947, when black became the predominant colour. Apart from taxi service, some of the vehicles in this series were used as company cars, usually with a maroon finish. During the war, a small number (in a military grey or camouflage finish as before) was also used by the Swedish Defence Forces.

Just as the PV650/TR700 series shared their appearance with the LV76–LV79 trucks, two new, modified series of medium–sized trucks of the same 'pointed' appearance as the PV800/810 were launched in 1938. The L10 was a small truck for light delivery duties while the L11, which was suitable for medium–heavy cargoes or for use as a small tipper truck, was more or less a replacement for the LV79.

Since Volvo engines were now recognised for their reliability, they began to find application, not only in cars and boats, but in fire–tenders and even military tanks.

Publicity photographers used other attractive models to emphasise the elegant styling of the 1938 cars.

Although basically the same as the PV51/52, the PV53/54/55/56 featured a sharper, more rounded grille.

The LV101, which replaced the LV76–78 series, combined the appearance and components of the new 801/802 taxis with a heavier frame, springs and wheels.

Produced in parallel with the small cars, the spacious PV801/802 taxis offered a superb standard of comfort.

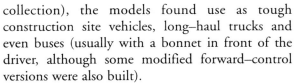

collection), the models found use as tough construction site vehicles, long–haul trucks and even buses (usually with a bonnet in front of the driver, although some modified forward–control versions were also built).

At the outbreak of World War II, Volvo was an established vehicle manufacturer with a wide range of products and sound finances. The company had even developed a substantial export trade, mainly to non–European countries without their own indigenous automotive industries. Although strongest in South America, Volvo had also exported some products to Japan, China and Israel, as well as to European nations, such as Ireland, Holland and Belgium.

THE FAMOUS 'Roundnose' series, initially the L12 and L13, which superseded the L8/L9 and L18/L19 respectively, made its debut in 1939. The transatlantic influence was also clear to be seen in these models. In mechanical terms, there was little new since the models were powered either by the 84–86 hp EC (LV120–123) or the FC/FCH/FDH engine, and the gearbox was an unsynchronised, four–speed unit as before. While all of the LV12s had a single–reduction final drive, the LV13 was available either with single reduction (LV130–133) or double reduction (LV135–138). Similarly, all of the L12s were single rear–axle types while the L13 was available either in a single or twin configuration.

Both series were extremely versatile and were used in transport applications of all kinds. In addition to light delivery duties (such as milk

With the exception of the renowned 'Roundnose' truck (above), Volvo's activities in 1939 were focused exclusively on the production of producer–gas units for cars, trucks and buses. Burning wood or coal, the units were produced to keep new and secondhand vehicles on the road during the war years.

Since Volvo's prosperous business was based exclusively on vehicle production, the situation at the start of the war appeared bleak. In the event, however, the war years were to prove extremely profitable for the company, which supplied large numbers of vehicles to the Swedish Defence Forces, as well as large quantities of spare parts for the increasingly decrepit fleet of civilian vehicles operating under tough conditions on dreadful roads, often badly maintained and running on fuels and lubricating oils of less than the highest quality.

Initially, the company facilities for manufacturing military vehicles in high volumes were limited. Two specific solutions were applied to this problem: the manufacture of producer gas units and the production of military vehicles of other makes under licence.

Although national supplies of petrol quickly became depleted, Volvo had developed a couple of producer gas units – designed mainly to burn coke and coal – in almost record time. These became available for manufacture in mid–September 1939 and stretched the company's production resources almost to breaking point. The production of a small number of trucks, as well as a few buses, taxis and cars (mainly for government use), was carried on simultaneously.

Volvo's producer gas units were of reasonable quality and quickly became popular. The heavier coal gas burners developed for trucks and buses never achieved quite the same popularity, and were frequently replaced immediately after delivery to the expectant customer, usually by a wood gas producer, which was easier and cheaper to run.

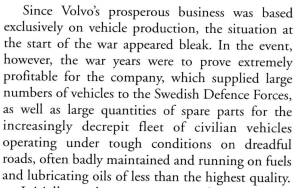

The 'Main Council'

In 1939, the artist Liss Sidén (born 1902, died 1975) made caricature drawings of all Volvo staff employees. It appears, though, that the artist did not dare to make a caricature of the two top managers, Gabrielsson and Larson. Instead, she drew them in a more face-on position and more 'life-like', surrounded by their closest colleagues in what was popularly referred to as the 'Main Council'.

Apart from the two founders, this included several people who had been part of the company since its formative years, and others who had made significant contributions to the formation and development of Volvo.

Legendary figures include Rolf Hanson, Carl-Einar Abrahamsson, Rolf Johansson, Ture Gehre, Anders Johnson, Nils Langborg, C. A. Thiberg, and Gunnar Pettersson – just some of the engineers, economists, etc. who had contributed to Volvo's success.

The formation of a staff union in 1939 led to the establishment of a social club without equal in the history of a Swedish company.

UPPROPET FÖR BILDANDET AV TJÄNSTEMANNAKLUBB

Volvo Staff Union (VTK)

On the 4th of October 1939, Volvo and Penta staff employees gathered in the 'classroom adjoining the canteen'.

By the late 1930s, trade unions had started to flourish in Sweden. SIF, the Swedish Industrial Salaried Employees Union, had also started to 'sound out the ground' among Volvo staff employees. Assar Gabrielsson did not like this one bit. He was averse to trade unions, so he asked Bertil Hälleby to appoint a representative for the salaried employees with whom the company could negotiate on salaries and other important issues.

At the same time, the food in the canteen was a disaster and something had to be done about it.

It was for these two reasons the meeting was convened on the 4th of October. The meeting resulted in 14 staff employees putting their signatures to an appeal to form a 'Volvo Staff Union'.

The new association got off to a flying start and 250 staff employees became members, with the exception of two, who declined for religious reasons. Both Assar Gabrielsson and Gustaf Larson became active members. Although Assar Gabrielsson was regarded as being of a 'mean disposition', he always gave his full support to the Staff Employees Union. The company, for instance, has always paid the salaries of the Union's office staff.

In this way, the SIF union was kept at bay, but it gained a strong foothold some years later, and grew alongside the voluntary Staff Union.

As Volvo grew as a company, so too did the Volvo Staff Union. Activities included excursions and the renting of leisure cottages to members, and during the first decades of its existence in particular, a sports competition called 'Decathlon' which attracted a lot of attention. Parties and large-scale celebrations were organized, especially around 'Lucia-time' in December. A crayfish party was held every year in memory of the famous crayfish dinner enjoyed by the two founders of the company at the Sturehof restaurant in July 1924.

The Union started its own magazine, called 'Ljuddämparen' ('The Silencer'), but which eventually changed its name to 'Luftrenaren' ('The Air cleaner'). The magazine was taken over by the company and later became 'Volvokontakt'. During the 1980s it was replaced by the present house journal 'Volvo Nu'.

The Volvo Staff Union celebrated its 25th anniversary on 2 October 1964 with a banquet for suitably attired members at the 'Börsen' in Göteborg.

This rather unusual 'club' celebrated its 50th anniversary in 1989. Today, not all staff employees are members, but 5,000 members is not a bad figure for an association whose aim is to enhance the enjoyment and well-being of staff employees, and to improve the 'spirit of affinity' between the various Volvo companies.

DARKNESS WAS DESCENDING on Europe in autumn 1939. The interwar years were drawing to a close and were soon to have proved no more than a breathing space. Since 1937, Volvo had been developing special military vehicles on a modest scale, with the aim of building large, unique terrain (or off–road) vehicles.

However, Volvo's activities in the military sphere were of older origin; a number of chassis intended mainly as ambulances had been delivered in 1928, the year that the company built its first trucks. Prior to that, in 1927, Volvo had sold a number of its first cars to the Swedish forces for use as staff cars. Throughout the 1930s, the company had also completed several major vehicle deliveries, mainly medium–sized ambulances, beginning with LV71s and LV73s.

The first true military vehicles were built in the early 1930s. These were LV64 and LV73 trucks equipped with armament and protected by armour plating. One of these m/31 armoured cars has been restored and is now on show in the Axvall Military Museum, about 10 kilometres from Skövde in western Sweden.

An Hungarian by the name of Hollos joined Volvo around 1937 and remained with the company for some time. Assisted, among others, by Sigvard Forsell, he produced the basic design for a rugged, three–axle artillery tractor, with the two rearmost axles driven. Known initially as the TVA (Terrain Vehicle A), the vehicle was equipped with individually mounted pendant axles. A pair of 'auxiliary' wheels was installed between the front and rear axles to further reduce the risk of sinking in particularly soft and muddy ground. To provide sufficient power, the TVA was equipped with a special version of the powerful FA engine with dry–sump lubrication. The vehicle underwent field testing under actual conditions some time at the beginning of 1939 and performed very satisfactorily. However, the Swedish army displayed little interest in it; its financial resources were modest and the risk of war may, perhaps, not have been taken seriously. As a result, efforts were made to export the product. As part of the sales campaign, demonstrations were held in southern Europe and although the results were again excellent, no orders were received.

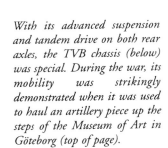

With its advanced suspension and tandem drive on both rear axles, the TVB chassis (below) was special. During the war, its mobility was strikingly demonstrated when it was used to haul an artillery piece up the steps of the Museum of Art in Göteborg (top of page).

As the clouds gathered over Europe, the interest of the Swedish army was reawakened. Realising that Volvo had built and tested an advance terrain vehicle 'free of charge', the defence authorities placed a contract for a considerable number of TVBs (the improved version of the TVA), now powered by a bigger and more powerful dry–sump version of the FBH engine known as the FBI.

Volvo has never been a sub–contractor to other companies – with just two exceptions (the Lynx armoured car and the Lago tank). In 1940, it improved the workload in its plant by contracting to build the Landsverk m/40 'Lynx' armoured car, a unique vehicle which, by virtue of its special design, could be driven backward as well as forward at the same speed. In the Volvo variant, the model was equipped with the FBL engine, a special version of the FB developing 135 hp, and with a powerful 20 mm cannon.

Until the Second World War, the car had been an albatross around Volvo's neck. However, the company had persevered with its production pending the advent of popular motoring. Following the success of the PV51–57, Volvo dealers were anxious for a smaller model to compete with successful makes such as Opel and DKW. This project had been commenced in earnest before the war and by early 1940, a full–scale wooden model of the proposed PV40, a medium–sized, two–door car with a pointed front and a steeply sloping back, had been finished in the design studio. In the new model, the engine was at the rear and the luggage compartment in front.

The GA engine – a two–stroke unit with four cylinders and eight pistons (two per cylinder) – was equipped with a Roots blower.

In actual fact, the PV40 was not a Volvo design, but a discontinued General Motors project which Chief Design Engineer Olle Skjolin had brought with him when he left GM in the USA to return home to Sweden. In the USA, the project had been one of three small car design projects, known as AD1, AD11 and Martia (although the two largest of these were closer to medium–sized models by European standards). The PV40 was most similar to the smallest model.

In the event, the PV40 project was (perhaps happily) abandoned, probably at the instigation of Gustaf Larson who, although receptive to advanced ideas, usually preferred the tried and tested when it came to series production.

A new L11 'Sharpnose' truck series was introduced in 1940. The model was occasionally equipped with a special cab, as in the forward–control model (above) built for the Swedish Post Office.

Right–hand column: These design models of the PV40 show how the PV444 might have looked.

Bottom: Volvo built the m/40 armoured car under licence during World War II.

The B17 was one of the aircraft equipped with the My series engine, the unit which led to the establishment of NOHAB Flygmotorfabriker/Svenska Flygmotor (later Volvo Flygmotor and now Volvo Aero Corporation).

Svenska Flygmotor

Volvo's operations grew very rapidly during the war years, despite the fact that much of the vehicle production programme was at a low level. Production for the Swedish Defence Forces continued at a furious rate, however – the only limitation being the supply of materials.

Volvo's success led to banks, other parts of industry, and the Swedish State having a high degree of confidence in the company. It was, therefore, a natural progression when Volvo was offered the opportunity to take over the share majority of the Trollhättan-based aircraft engine company Svenska Flygmotor (formally NOHAB Flygmotorfabriker).

Svenska Flygmotor was for sale not because it was in any financial difficulty; on the contrary, Svenska Flygmotor was 'making money hand over fist', and the Royal Swedish Air Force had what seemed to be an insatiable demand for aircraft engines. It was certainly difficult to get hold of production material, but flexibility and improvisation had ensured regular production of high quality aircraft engines.

Svenska Flygmotor was dominated by the Wallenberg empire through the Stockholms Enskilda Bank, which also controlled the aircraft manufacturer SAAB. The State authorities wanted to prevent at all costs a monopoly situation in the field of aircraft and aircraft engine manufacture. Therefore, it was decided to offer the well-established high-technology company to Volvo.

AB Volvo took over Svenska Flygmotor in 1941.

The company was not all that old. It had been formed in 1930 as a subsidiary to Nydqvist & Holm Aktiebolag as a result of a study carried out by the Swedish State, which wanted to create on-going domestic production of aircraft engine for military preparedness and to meet the needs of the Swedish Defence Forces.

For ten years or more, the company had manufactured 9-cylinder engines of a British design, based on products manufactured by the 'Bristol' company in England.

The engines were of the 'Star' type and were used exclusively for military applications. Manufacture of the engines was carried out under strict state quality control, and the Swedish products manufactured under licence were, if anything, better than the originals from the United Kingdom.

The addition of Svenska Flygmotor to the Volvo Group meant not only that the company grew, but also that high technology was now readily available 'in-house'. Aircraft engines have always represented leading-edge technology, in which technological advances are made use of long before they reach more common-place objects such as cars.

THE ENTIRE PERIOD of the war (1939–1945) was a golden time for Volvo. Product development proceeded at a more intensive pace along the same lines as before (and after), with one significant exception: development activities were funded completely by the state and the defence authorities. During this period, the Swedish automotive industry laid the foundations of its postwar expansion.

An extremely wide spectrum of vehicles was developed during the war years, a time when all product development was governed by three criteria: function, durability and mobility. The TVB had been developed in record time at the start of the war, Now as the company was preparing to produce the first major series of large terrain vehicles for the Swedish army, it unveiled that model's natural successor, the TVC.

Two very significant advances had been made. Firstly, the model was Volvo's first all–wheel drive vehicle and boasted even better mobility than the TVB (on which the front wheels were not driven). Secondly, since the TVC was a forward–control vehicle, it had no bonnet and its manoeuvrability was better than ever. However, the model was heavier and the front wheels had a tendency to sink when operating under difficult conditions in soft, wet terrain.

The level of activity at Svenska Flygmotor was high. The company was involved in the production of engines for all of the Royal Swedish Air Force fighters, whose role was to defend the nation's neutrality and repel intruders from the belligerent nations.

The need for a new, modern aircraft engine was acute. The 14–cylinder TW C3 'Twin Wasp' engine built by Pratt & Whitney in the USA was well–known and ideally suited for the purpose; however, it proved impossible to negotiate a manufacturing licence and even more difficult to locate a recent version of the unit from which to 'borrow' ideas. Fortunately, a solution was at hand.

Out of the blue (or, perhaps, the clouds), an allied plane powered by a TW C3 made an emergency landing in Sweden, providing a heaven–sent opportunity of copying and producing this modern radial engine.

The unit was dismantled, copied and built to top–class engineering standards – and, before long, the first units were in service with the air force. The model was christened the STW C3 ('S' denoting the Swedish version).

Although the Swedish action was, obviously, a serious contravention of international law, it was overlooked by the Allies. In fact, after the war, American observers were said to have acknowledged that the Swedish copy was actually of higher quality than the original engine!

During the difficult war years, Sweden was defended by its ordinary heroes in the field – and their Volvo trucks. The model pictured is an LV11.

Köping

There had been intensive cooperation between Volvo and Köpings Mekaniska Werkstad (KMW) ever since the first gearboxes were delivered in the late 1920s. Deliveries to Volvo eventually accounted for an increasing proportion of KMW's total deliveries, while deliveries of the more traditional product – tool machines – declined.

It was therefore a natural step when Volvo took over the operations of its transmissions supplier in 1942 whilst war was raging. This enabled gearboxes and rear axles to be designed, developed, and produced intimately with each other, thus resulting in faster development and lower costs.

The 1942 TVC was Volvo's first
all–wheel drive terrain vehicle.
Basically identical to the TVB,
it boasted a driven front axle
and a forward–control cab.

IT WOULD BE tempting – but incorrect – to assume that huge numbers of high–technology special vehicles were manufactured during the war. In fact, most of the vehicles built by Volvo between 1939 and 1945 were standard types, sometimes modified to improve their mobility and durability.

The 'Roundnose' trucks played a vital role in the transport of supplies. A modified version of this model was introduced in 1943. Known as the TLV, this was a specially adapted twin–axle, all–wheel drive, off–road vehicle.

The first version was the TLV13, essentially an L13 with a driven front axle. This was followed, a year later, by the TLV14, a model powered by the 5.65–litre, 105–hp FE engine and developed specifically for military applications. A civilian version (L14) was introduced after the war and the engine was also used in the popular B51 bus.

The Swedish government laid down clear guidelines governing the products which Volvo was allowed to manufacture. Thus, the production of private cars was a luxury which was prohibited. However, agricultural tractors were a different matter; since these were essential to food supplies, the production of limited numbers was permitted, provided the models were gas–driven and did not use scarce petrol.

Volvo developed a tractor model in 1943–44, not because it was especially anxious to enter the field, but simply because the manufacture of other products was prohibited. In the event, what was essentially a stopgap measure was to become an enormously successful operation for the company; over the next thirty years, more than a quarter million Volvo tractors were to roll off the production lines in Göteborg and Eskilstuna.

To rationalise the production of the new tractor, it was decided to collaborate with Bolinder–Munktell (BM), a well–established Eskilstuna company, which was then a supplier to Svenska Flygmotor. As a result, the rear end of the first Volvo tractor (T4) was identical to that of the BM20. However, this was not the first joint project between the two companies. During the war, BM (which, until then, had only built tractors with hot–bulb ignition engines) developed a model powered by a Volvo FC engine converted to burn producer gas.

The first version of the T4, the T41, was naturally designed to run on producer gas during the war years. Although the chassis was of a completely new design, the engine consisted simply of two–thirds of an FAH unit, with four cylinders instead of six. In this configuration, the cubic capacity was 4.48 litres and the unit developed 48 hp on producer gas.

Since the A4 engine used in the T4 was the first of a generation which was to be produced for the

Equipped with a Hesselman producer–gas unit, the first tractor (T41) was related to the Bolinder–Munktell models and became known for its high quality.

next decade, the system of designations used from 1944 to 1956 should be clarified. The designation consisted of three elements, the first being a serial letter indicating the particular engine in the series, the second a figure denoting the number of cylinders and the third a letter describing the type of unit or the fuel. The most important of these was the middle figure. The first four–cylinder engine (for the T4 tractor) was known as the A4, the second (PV444 car) as the B4, the third (T2 tractor) as the C4 and the fourth (T3 tractor) as the D4.

Since the Swedish Defence Forces also needed tractors to haul equipment, a series of T4s designed to burn petrol, paraffin and motyl (a mixture of petrol and motor spirit) was developed under the designation T42. The war ended just a couple of years after these entered production and the T4 was introduced in an 'optimised' version (T43) with the Hesselman A4H engine. However, since the availability of the Hesselman injection pump (the 'Injector') was limited, this was supplied initially only to buyers of the T41, who were now busy dismantling their producer gas units. Thus, production of the T43 was effectively postponed until practically all of the T41 tractors had been converted.

The Landsverk m/42 'Lago' tank was manufactured under contact in 1943. Known as the EH (the Swedish acronym indicated that the model was equipped with a single engine driving an hydraulic transmission), the Volvo version was powered by a unique 22.6–litre V8 petrol engine developing 410 hp (excluding auxiliaries) or 380 hp with the cooling fan is service.

The engine consisted simply of two–thirds of a Daimler–Benz DB605 aircraft engine, a unit which was shortly to be series–built in Trollhättan by Svenska Flygmotor AB for the Royal Swedish Air Force J21 and B18B aircraft. These units were also built by Bolinder–Munktell as a supplier to Svenska Flygmotor in an underground, bombproof workshop between Eskilstuna and Torshälla. Most of the non–Volvo versions were equipped with twin Scania–Vabis six–cylinder petrol engines which, in hindsight, proved a better choice than Volvo's V8 'monster'.

A Volvo T43 tractor with a Hesselman engine.

Bottom left: The 1943 half–track tractor (or HBT) was one of the remarkable vehicles developed by Volvo during the war.

Below: The 1943 TPV terrain vehicle.

THE TLV141VKP WAS the only Volvo–designed armoured car ever built (the Swedish acronym 'VKP' stood for 'Volvo Armoured Car'). In truth, this statement is only partly true; two versions of the body were actually developed, one by Volvo and the other by Scania–Vabis. However, the Volvo version was found less suitable by the military authorities and it was the Scania–Vabis 'SKP' body which was used on the Volvo vehicle! The TLV141 has achieved international fame through its long service with the United Nations. Most of the UN vehicles were fitted with the SKP body; for various reasons, the Volvo body was used only in Sweden and was phased out sooner than the version built in Södertälje.

The most elegant Volvo product of the war period was the m/43 terrain personnel carrier (TPV). This was not a truck but a converted taxi of a more rugged construction, equipped with a heavy–duty, light truck frame and all–wheel drive. To provide an aircraft spotter with a clear view, the body was a four–door 'cabriocoach' type with a fabric roof which could be removed as required. Manufactured in a couple of hundred examples, the TPV m/43 was used as a staff car and as a communications vehicle, in which case it was fitted with radio equipment for operational command and communications purposes. The TPV was a large vehicle with a generous wheelbase and small, car–type wheels, for which reason its terrain mobility was not comparable to that of a small jeep or a purpose–built off–road model. Nonetheless, it was valuable as the precursor of later Volvo terrain vehicles, which were to set new standards of mobility.

Gustaf Larson had turned down the proposed PV40 small car with its unusual two–stroke, rear–mounted engine. Now, in anticipation of peacetime sales, the new Volvo PV444 was being designed along conventional lines, with a longitudinally mounted, in–line engine at the front, driving the rear wheels through a three–speed gearbox with synchromesh on the two highest gears. The body was Volvo's first monocoque type, reducing its weight, while the engine was the first Volvo car engine since the early years to be available only in a four–cylinder version, as well as the first OHV unit to be used by the company in a production model.

In September 1944, almost a year before the end of the war, Volvo invited the public to a major industrial exhibition held at the Royal Tennis Hall in Stockholm.

All of Volvo's existing products and its full range of military vehicles were displayed; however, the undisputed star of the show was the little PV444 (the three '4's were said to denote four cylinders, four seats and 40 hp). And, since the new model retailed at the same price (SKr4,800) as the ÖV4 seventeen years before, interest in it was enormous.

The first PV444 prototype was extensively photographed, in this instance with an attractive young lady who was probably one of the company secretaries.

Although described as a small car, the PV444 was actually medium–sized, with reasonable space for the driver and three passengers. The design showed the American influence, albeit on a smaller scale. Like the famous Model T Ford, it was available in a range of colours – all of them black!

It was to be another three years before the first cars were delivered, due mainly to a shortage of body materials. By that time, it was clear that the originally quoted price of SKr4,800 was a gross miscalculation; the production cost was higher than estimated and those customers who had signed contracts had the fortunate choice of buying the car at an exceptionally cheap price or selling their contracts at a substantial profit. Several years were to elapse before supply exceeded demand and delivery times were shortened.

The version unveiled in 1944 was produced more or less unmodified until 1950, when it was retrospectively renamed the PV444A (no letter suffix had been necessary until then).

In summer 1950, the company produced a deluxe version (the PV444AS) in a dove–grey finish instead of the standard black, with more luxurious upholstery, bumper overriders and chrome trim – all at a slightly higher price.

The 1951 model (PV444B) was unveiled in autumn 1950. Now, six years after it had been first announced and almost three years in production, the car had naturally undergone a considerable number of improvements. The mechanical changes were few since the somewhat more powerful 44–hp engine had already been installed in the last of the PV444As. However, the gearbox had been refined and was now quieter.

The external modifications were comprehensive. The bumpers were now in three sections and overriders were fitted on the standard model. The rear number plate, previously located in the middle of the boot lid, was now mounted on the bumper. On the 'B' model, Assar Gabrielsson had succeeded in having the direction indicators relocated on the roof in the form of a single fixture known officially

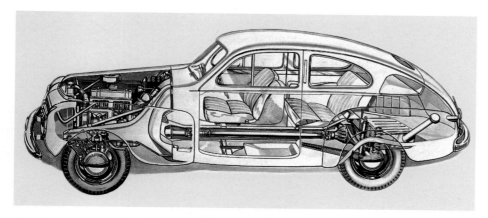

Safety body and laminated windscreen

The first of many Volvo inventions in the field of safety is said to be the introduction of the PV model in 1944. An important safety feature on that car model was the laminated glass windscreen.

Another, and perhaps less certain feature was the 'safety body'. Nonetheless, great play was made of this later. Perhaps the most dramatic example of this was a demonstration in the German town of Bad Soden in March 1961. Volvo GmbH in Frankfurt had invited the press to a safety conference to give information on Volvo's ambitions and attempts at improving road safety.

The journalists and photographers who were present were later given a highly dramatic demonstration of the safety properties of the PV544. Wearing a crash helmet, Orvar Aspholm, a stuntman from Göteborg, drove a standard car at a speed of 80 km/hour on a sloping ramp to get the car to move – and that is exactly what it did. It not only moved, it ended up first on its nose and then on its roof. When the driver climbed out through the hole where the windscreen once was, completely unharmed, the demonstration was concluded.

Under the skin, the new model was equipped with the latest technology. The characteristic rear end design differed slightly from later versions in details such as the location of the number plate.

The Royal Tennis Hall

The Volvo management realised that demand for cars would be high after the war. But not demand for the big cars of the 1930s, but for smaller and more fuel efficient cars. Under a veil of secrecy the PV444 was developed – a 4-seater, 4-cylinder car developing 40 horsepower.

The PV444, and the new PV60, were to be presented after the summer of 1944, and the Royal Tennis Hall in Stockholm was booked for the period 1-10 September for a special showing.

It was decided to exhibit the Volvo Group's entire range of products. AB Volvo exhibited cars, trucks, agricultural tractors, and a whole host of military vehicles – war was still raging – including armoured vehicles, tanks, and cross-country vehicles. AB Pentaverken exhibited its range of marine and industrial engines, including a 'fully-automatic electricity plant'. Köpings Mekaniska Verkstad exhibited gearboxes, reverse and reduction gears for Penta's marine engines, and its own machine tools Ulvsunda Verkstäder presented 'independent manufacture of precision spindles and hole grinding machines'. Svenska Flygmotor exhibited various types of engines, including a cut-away engine in motion.

The exhibition was an outstanding success. Most interest was directed at the PV444. A car was put up for lottery every day, and this helped to attract 148,437 visitors to the exhibition. Pricing the PV444 at 4,800 kronor – the same price as for Volvo's first car, the ÖV4 – resulted in 2,300 people signing contracts. These contracts became something of a commodity during the two and a half years before the first cars could actually be delivered – and by then the 'right price' had leaped to 6,050 kronor.

Once sales of the PV444 got off the ground it signalled the start of a fantastic period of expansion. The PV quickly became a Swedish 'people's' car.
The exhibition at the Royal Tennis Hall was a spur for the whole of Volvo as the entire workforce – even if there were some doubts about this – was invited to take the expenses-paid trip to Stockholm.

The Staff Union joked about it in its journal 'Ljuddämparen' with some typical lines of verse and Göteborg humour.

as the 'Fixlight' – but sarcastically nicknamed the 'cuckoo' – which, unfortunately, admitted rain and prevented the use of a roof rack!

Inside, the upholstery was new while the instruments – previously located in the centre of the dashboard in keeping with the prevailing fashion – were now directly in front of the driver.

The next model, the PV444C (and the CS special version), was introduced in June 1951. In this case, the only changes were to fit 15" instead of 16" wheels and to increase the number of wheel nuts from four to five. The quarter lights in the front doors were also slightly smaller.

Introduced in August 1952, the PV444D was the first of the series to be equipped with a Volvo–designed heater, which was a better fit in the car although still only available as an option, while a heavier–duty electrical system was also installed. As of 1953, the exacting customer could buy a Special finished in maroon instead of the usual dove grey (however, the standard model was still available only in black).

The PV444E, which was launched in April 1953, was more or less identical to its predecessor, with the exception of the new bumper which was introduced during the life of the model and the fact that the heater was now standard equipment. The original dove grey finish of the Special was replaced by a lighter, pearl grey shade.

Significant modifications were made to the PV444H and HS (no F or G version was produced). The windscreen was bigger and mounted between slimmer pillars, the divided rear window was replaced by a wider, single–piece type, the rear lights were located at waistline level and a cross–piece incorporating the number plate light and a red lamp was mounted on the rear bumper above the number plate. The boot was bigger and the spare wheel, previously stowed flat, was now stored upright on the right–hand side. Synthetic paint replaced cellulose in the middle of 1955 and the interior was finished in black rather than grey.

Money was short in postwar Europe and simple, functional cars, such as the Citroën 2CV, Renault 4CV, Volkswagen 1200 and Morris Minor, were in demand. Volvo's entrant was the PV444 Export, which had first been introduced during the production life of the H model and was also marketed as the PV444L before it was discontinued. The Export was available only in black and sea green, while the earlier chrome was replaced by silver–plated trim and no front bumper overriders were fitted. The interior was spartan; the seats were of a simple, tubular–frame type and a heater was extra.

As the first Volvo exported to the USA, the PV444H (and the special HS version) represented a milestone in the company's history when it was launched there in autumn 1955, powered by a

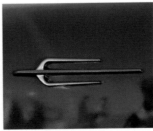

The second version of the model (PV444B) introduced in 1950 featured the unusual – and much derided – 'Fixlight' roof–mounted direction indicator.

B14A engine (an advanced version of the B4B), which had been developed for the P19 sports car and featured a modified camshaft and twin SU carburettors).

The PV444K appeared in December 1955. This was equipped with a more powerful 51–hp engine and a new, mesh–type grille with a chromed surround with slightly protruding corners. The rear lights, now round, were again located at a low level.

The luxury California model (which was also available in Sweden, but with a single–carburettor engine) was introduced for the growing American market.

The last version of this long–lived series (the PV444L) appeared in early 1957. The grille had once more been redesigned and now featured a fine–mesh pattern with a large 'V' in the centre (except in the USA, where this symbol was used by Cadillac, and where it was replaced by a small chromed iron symbol in the top left corner). The same 'V' symbol was also used on the boot lid.

The most significant change was to the engine (B16), which had been bored out to make it bigger and more powerful. The standard version now developed 60 hp (compared with 51 hp), while the sports version (which was still unavailable in Sweden) was rated at 85 hp (70 hp previously). The suspension had been improved and the much–criticised vacuum–powered windscreen wipers (which had a tendency to stop when they were most needed) replaced by efficient electric wipers.

The PV444 had been introduced to attract new customers interested in smaller, more economical cars. Naturally, however, the company was also anxious to retain those existing, loyal customers who preferred large, comfortable and safe Volvo models with six–cylinder engines. As a result, the new PV600 (the introduction of which had originally been scheduled for 1940, but had been delayed by the outbreak of war) was unveiled at the

same time as the PV444 at the company's Stockholm exhibition in September 1944.

The PV60 was a big, comfortable, four–door model which was an obvious copy of the 1939 Pontiac (so obvious, in fact, that many of the finished body parts were purchased in the USA!). While the styling was completely new to Volvo, there were clear echoes of the PV53–56 series.

In mechanical terms, the PV60, with its three–speed, column–shift gearbox (a fourth gear was available, if required, in the form of overdrive) was a conservative car. The model was equipped with the last of the side–valve engines, a modified EC with the same cubic capacity and a slightly higher output (90 hp) than the original version, bearing the designation ED.

The first PV60s were delivered at the end of 1946. Buyers who preferred an elegant convertible, an attractive estate model or a light delivery van could specify the PV61 chassis for the purpose.

The new postwar bus, the B51, which was basically a modified and improved version of the B20 chassis, was also unveiled at the Stockholm exhibition. At this time, a third digit was added to the designation to indicate the wheelbase or other variation. Thus, the B511 was a chassis with a

The new grilles on the three last versions (PV444HS, PV444K and PV444LS) altered the appearance sufficiently to encourage buyers to 'trade up' every year.

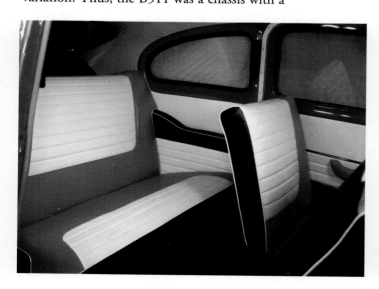

4.1–m wheelbase (which was never actually built), while the B512 and B513 had wheelbases of 4.7 m and 5.2 m respectively. These were followed by the B514, in which the driver was seated further forward to enable the front door to be located ahead of the front axle, mainly to facilitate one–man operation, in which the passengers passed the driver's station and paid their fares as they boarded. (For the sake of convenience, the third digit will not be used in the remainder of this book.)

The major news on the commercial front was the development of the VDA direct–injection diesel engine, which was intended for use in the B51 bus and LV14 truck series. Basically a redesigned and reinforced FA engine converted to run on diesel, this had a cubic capacity of 6.13 litres and an output of 95 hp. However, this first diesel unit was not yet ready for series production and, as it transpired, was never produced due to a variety of teething problems. As a result, a new VDA unit with a precombustion chamber was introduced a year later and, from mid–1945 on, was installed in a small number of B51 chassis, initially to provide experience of the company's new diesel–powered vehicles.

The 5.63–litre, 105–hp FE petrol engine (a unit used in the LV14 trucks) was adopted as an alternative to the diesel to facilitate immediate deliveries of the B51 bus chassis.

Negotiations had been under way for several years between Swedish and German interests concerning the manufacture, under licence, of one of the best aircraft engines of the time, the Daimler–Benz DB603, a powerful and reliable unit with liquid cooling. Although the Germans were interested in the project, they initially imposed completely unrealistic conditions which threatened to defeat the entire venture. Happily, however, this problem was resolved in time.

Production of the unit (now the DB605) commenced in 1944, enabling the successful Swedish B18 bomber (which, until then, had been equipped with the 14–cylinder, 1,200–hp STW C3 radial engine) to be fitted with considerably more powerful engines of higher performance. Final development of the J21, the new Swedish fighter with pusher propellers and an ejector seat (a world first) was also undertaken around this time.

Production of the DB605 under licence was a challenging task. The German inspection procedures and the scope of drawing documentation were such that a high standard of organisational ability was essential to ensure a successful outcome.

The results were satisfactory. The last Swedish aircraft engine to be series–built before the jet engine appeared on the scene was the best of the lot, serving the nation well during the still–tense postwar period.

A unique component! The lower filler cap was designed by Sigvard Forsell in 1944. The upper (identical) cap is still used today (1995), proving that functionality stands the test of time!

The B51 series bus (facing page, top) and L14 series truck (below and facing page, bottom) shared many components. The bus pictured on the facing page was the first light–alloy bus built by the Höglund company of Säffle (now Säffle Karosseri AB and part of the Volvo Group).

1945 WAS A DIFFICULT year for Volvo. Although the war was nearing its end, materials were in very short supply and delivery of the first of the new, peacetime PV444s and PV600s appeared remote. However, one division of the company was fully occupied and was receiving extremely favourable treatment from government departments.

Svenska Flygmotor, which had now been a member of the Volvo Group for a number of years, had worked feverishly throughout the war to produce aircraft engines as quickly as humanly possible. However, the units built during this period – the old Bristol version of the My XXIV and the STW C3, which had been copied from the American original – had both become obsolescent.

In its search for new peacetime projects, the company decided that light private aircraft offered a highly promising market, and a small, four–cylinder, air–cooled, opposed–piston engine called the 'Troll' was developed for this application, representing Svenska Flygmotor's first attempt to complement its substantial defence orders with civilian products.

The Troll was not a major commercial success. As their colleagues in the car sector had discovered years before, its makers found that quality Swedish products could not compete on price with high–quality, mass–produced American products. Continental and Lycoming, the North American giants, completely dominated the private aircraft market and even the other new Swedish entrant in the field, the Saab 91 Safir, was equipped with an American engine.

The failure was mitigated somewhat by the production of a couple of series of engines based on the Troll – for the Swedish army!

These units were supplied for installation in combat vehicles, for which the light, compact design, with its relatively high output, was particularly suitable. The first of the 150–hp engines (designated B42) were delivered to Landsverk for installation in a series of light tanks (IKV103).

A further series of Troll engines (B44) was delivered some years later, in 1961. These were used in the Swedish army's first tracked armoured personnel carriers, which were essentially m/41 tanks converted for the purpose by the firm of Hägglund & Sons in Örnsköldsvik.

Strikes had an adverse effect on Volvo's activities in 1945. Apart from a few taxis, the few vehicles manufactured during the year were mostly commercial vehicles (trucks, buses and tractors).

Difficult post-war problems

Rejoicing over the end of the Second World War in May 1945 was slightly subdued in the Swedish engineering industry. The reason was that a nation-wide strike broke out on 5 February, bringing practically the whole country to a standstill. As far as Volvo was concerned, this industrial dispute meant that development and production of prototypes for testing and trials was put back several months.

Another major problem which hung around for many months after the end of the war was the shortage of rubber for tyre production.

Yet another problem which hit Volvo was the difficulty in procuring sheet steel for its car bodies. At this point in time it was only American steel works which could supply sheet steel in the right widths. As demand for new cars had risen enormously more or less all over the world, Volvo found it difficult at first to assert its interests and keep up with the competition. It was the same story when it came to the supply of other parts from overseas suppliers.

These problems meant that deliveries of the PV444 could not get underway until the spring of 1947, two and a half years after the model was put on show in the Royal Tennis Hall in Stockholm.

An English edition of the Volvo customer magazine 'Ratten', which was started up back in 1930 – and which with its current circulation of a million copies is one of Sweden's biggest magazines – was printed and distributed in 1945. Export manager Rolf Hanson, who was the first editor of the magazine, wrote a rather humorous explanation and apology to the magazine's Swedish readers.

"As you well know, we have always been quite 'cocky' about and conscious of the splendid qualities of our company and our vehicles. Therefore, we feel a strong sense of conviction that Ratten is one of the most widely read and enjoyable magazines around, and that readers count the days to when they can receive the next issue, and putting aside all thoughts of time and place can sit back and absorb all the words of wisdom contained therein."

That is how Hanson began his article and explained that the special issue in English was intended to provide all Volvo salesmen around the world with information. These same salesmen had been kept in the dark about what Volvo had been doing during the war years and what was being planned for the future, especially with the PV444 as the main attraction.

It must have been quite frustrating for the Volvo management to see the enormous demand for vehicles, but not being able to supply at the desired rate. But there was one consolation: all Volvo's competitors were facing the same problem.

IN 1946, THE PRODUCT range was expanded with the addition of a small agricultural tractor which was to be of key significance to Volvo's success in the area. Known as the T2, the model was considerably smaller than the earlier T4 and, unlike its bigger relation, was designed to enable owners of small and medium–sized farms to replace their horse–drawn machines. The T2 series, which was characterised by its more modern, rounded styling, was to remain in production, almost unchanged, until 1959.

Volvo's tractor production (which was carried on alongside car production in Göteborg) was to expand enormously over the next couple of years, completely overshadowing the car sector, which was still operating at low capacity.

The first variant in the series, the T21, was also the smallest and lightest, and was available only in a petrol–engined version.

The T2 series had been further developed by the time tractor production was transferred from Göteborg to the Bolinder–Munktell works in Eskilstuna in the early 1950s. This included the introduction of a 2.2–litre engine known as the C22.

T2 series tractors were powerful for their size. The robustness, weight and higher ground clearance of the model made it much suitable for heavy duties, such as timber haulage, than its highly successful competitor, the Massey–Ferguson 20.

Volvo introduced its first large diesel bus, the B53, at the end of 1946. This was a relatively advanced, front–engined model with the completely new VDB precombustion chamber engine, an 8.6–litre unit developing an impressive 130 hp and driving a double–reduction final drive through a five–speed K2 gearbox installed midway along the bus. An expensive and exclusive design, the gearbox was used only in the B53.

Although primarily a powerful city bus, the B53 also acquired some popularity as a luxury touring coach. Among other applications, it was used by Linjebuss on its new international routes to central Europe and its services to cities such as Paris.

A few examples of Volvo's first L15 diesel truck were built in 1946.

The Volvo emblem on the PV60 was of a unique shape (the car itself is pictured opposite).

The big new B53 bus was introduced at the end of 1946.

AT THIS TIME, the coffers of the Swedish state were being swelled by fuel taxes. This was one of the main factors which stimulated the development of smaller, more fuel–efficient cars and created the conditions for the success of the PV444. However, it also increased the level of interest in the diesel truck, a type which was then fairly rare. Volvo foresaw the breakthrough with impressive precision, selling a small number of diesels to the Swedish Roads Authority at the end of 1946. The vehicles were probably intended as a final test series in preparation for a serious attack on the civilian market.

Diesel trucks of two different sizes appeared in 1947, the L15 (actually an L14 with a longer front to provide space for the bigger 6.13–litre, 95–hp VDA engine), and the L29C (for commercial applications) and L29V (for the Swedish Roads Authority), both modified L29s extended at the front to accommodate the powerful VDB unit (as used in the B53 bus).

Both series achieved popularity. The L15 quickly became the highest–selling large truck in Sweden, while the L29C and L29V were soon taking on their powerful and reputable Scania–Vabis counterparts in every area from heavy site work to snow–ploughing and tough long–haul service, often in a bogie version and hauling a single–axle or twin–axle trailer.

The first diesels underwent major modifications during their relatively short production life. In 1949, the LV15 was superseded by the almost identical L24, which was easily recognisable by its ten wheel nuts (the L15 had six initially, then eight). The new model was also equipped with the VDA engine, now of a much higher quality and with a slightly higher output (100 hp), and was available either with a four–speed, unsynchronised gearbox or with the new K1 synchromesh, five–speed unit.

Whereas the L15 had been available almost from the beginning in a three–axle version, it was not until 1949 that the big, heavy L29C was built in this configuration, usually for service as a long–haul truck towing a trailer.

Both the L15/L24 and L29C/L29V were produced until 1951, powered by precombustion chamber diesels which, although easily started, were fairly thirsty. From 1951 on, the L24 was normally equipped with the direct–injection VDC which, although of the same 6.13 litre/100 hp specifications, had been basically redesigned. Although a few L29Cs built in 1950 were fitted with the new direct–injection VDF (9.6 litre/150 hp), these were basically test vehicles for the forthcoming Titan model. Nevertheless, a series of L29V3s was supplied to the Swedish Roads Authority as late as in 1951. These were probably built because of the high reputation which the

Right: An LV291V2 operating under severe Swedish winter conditions.

'Longnose' had acquired during its short life (1946–51).

The diesel–engined version of the old LV29 with the 95–hp VDA was a remarkable cross between the L15 and the L29C. The engine was not installed at the plant but was supplied separately – making the only model which Volvo had ever supplied in kit form! This particular truck, (which was available only in a three–axle version) was recognisable by the fact that it had the same extended front as the original L29, with a 'Diesel' emblem on the grille.

Svenska Flygmotor was undergoing a period of change. The era of the piston–type aircraft engine was coming to an end and the need to develop a jet engine was obvious. To this end, the military authorities encouraged both Svenska Flygmotor in Trollhättan and STAL in Finspång to undertake the development of a Swedish model.

Known as the R–102, Svenska Flygmotors's relatively small jet engine was tested in January 1947. However, it soon became apparent that the development programme would be both long and comprehensive, and the production of British engines under licence was undertaken in the interim. As events transpired, the Swedish jet engine never became a reality (largely due to the caution of the defence authorities, who preferred the safer option of a tried–and–tested foreign design to an unproven Swedish model).

By 1948, VOLVO HAD become a tractor manufacturer to reckon with. During the first six months of the year, the company sold about 1,600 of its large T4 model and about 2,500 of the smaller T21/T22.

It was natural that the company should now seek to provide its farming customers with a wider range of service facilities, not just in terms of maintenance, but also by marketing improved implements.

The light T2 tractor, in particular, was used on small farms, often in fields which were both small and stony. For this application, the company developed an hydraulic lift of the same type as the Ferguson 20 'Grey Horse', an implement which greatly facilitated ploughing. Since the lift absorbed some of the plough force, it increased the pressure on the otherwise lightly loaded rear wheels of the tractor.

The device also simplified driving from field to field and on the road when the tractor was fitted with an implement.

The hydraulic lift became available as an accessory in mid–1948 and as standard equipment on new tractors a short time later.

A wide range of other accessories was also available, including a comfortable cab (although not yet of the reinforced, safety type), a fruit tree spraying unit and a front–mounted loader.

Rubber–tyred wheels were now standard on almost all tractors (having superseded metal wheels about a decade before), enabling the vehicles to be driven on the road. To improve mobility in fields, in forests and in the terrain generally, the rear wheels could be fitted with steel 'tread rings' to improve the traction or with loading weights to increase the downward pressure on the tyres.

Tractor production in Göteborg increased steadily during the late 1940s as the model range grew and the selection of implements was expanded. This 1948 photograph shows the 10,000th tractor built at the plant.

THE B51 WAS a medium–sized, all–round bus with a relatively small 95–105 hp engine. The B53, on the other hand, was a large, heavy model with a large passenger capacity and was powered by a big 130–hp unit. The natural compromise between these two, the B62, was introduced in 1949.

The new model was built on a medium–sized chassis with a B51 transmission and the large, powerful VDB engine used in the B53, creating a fast, medium–sized bus with an average passenger complement. The B62 was not developed by chance; it was purpose–designed for postal delivery service in the north of Sweden, often carrying passengers as well as mail and, in some instances, goods.

The B62 designation (rather than B52) indicated that Volvo was on the brink of introducing a new generation of buses.

The PV444 had proved to be a real stroke of luck for Volvo. The only fly in the ointment was that production was running well below demand although, happily, the car was now selling at a higher price than the original 1944 price of SKr4,800, at which the company had been obliged to sell the model for a considerable period.

Whereas chassis versions of the cars had always been available, production of a pure PV444 chassis was more difficult since the monocoque body was not mounted on a frame.

However, the PV445 introduced in 1949 was built on a conventional frame, with the PV444 front end and instrumentation, and was available as bare chassis which could be finished as a van or light truck.

A small van with a side–hinged back door, but without rear seats, was also shown at the launch. The estate version was soon appearing in greater numbers – most of them built by the Gripkarosser company of Västervik, which commenced regular production of estates based on the PV445 chassis soon afterwards. The PV445 became the basis for many different and attractive variants, ranging from ambulances and hearses to elegant convertibles, with bodies by several different coachbuilders. A number of the chassis were even furnished with special bodies by Italian firms.

Volvo tractors had become a real success story, particularly the little T2, which was now increasingly overshadowing the ageing T4. However, it was clear that the T2 needed a 'big brother' with more modern lines and an hydraulic lift to enable heavy, unwieldy, towed ploughs to be replaced by modern implements (an important consideration since fields at that time were not as large or open as today).

Introduced in 1949, the T3 was available in a number of variants: the T31 (which ran on paraffin), the T32 (petrol), the T33 (also paraffin–burning, with an adjustable track width and higher wheels for furrow cultivation) and the T34 (a petrol version of the T33). Although very similar to the little T2, the T3 was bigger and heavier in all respects.

The bigger D4 engine (the 'D' denoted the fourth four–cylinder petrol engine since 1943–44, not 'Diesel' as might be assumed) now developed slightly more than 30 hp. In fact, the T3 was almost as powerful as the T43 (the last version of the T4) which, with its Hesselman engine, could burn less expensive – and less heavily taxed – heavy fuel oil.

The T3 series was also the first Volvo tractor to be equipped with half–tracks (by ÖSA of Alfta), making it an efficient forest work vehicle.

Production of the first series–built jet engine, the RM1A, was commenced in Trollhättan ('RM' stood for 'ReaktionsMotor', the Swedish for 'jet engine'). Then (as now), the unit was a foreign design adapted for Swedish conditions and aircraft by the Trollhättan engineers. Based on the De Havilland Goblin, the RM1A was used in the Saab A21R as well as the De Havilland Vampire, the two twin–tail aircraft which were the first jets to enter service with the Royal Swedish Air Force.

The tractor range was widened in 1949 with the introduction of a larger, more powerful series similar to the little T21 (on right in the picture).

Harald Wiklund.

Harald Wiklund

When the War ended, a Dalecarlian by name Harald Wiklund was enticed to Volvo by a close friend, Helmer Pettersson. Helmer Pettersson is a legendary figure in Volvo's history and was the man behind Volvo's concentration on generator gas during the war years. He was also the father of the subsequently well-known Swedish car and boat designer Pelle Pettersson.

Harald Wiklund came to Volvo rather reluctantly to become responsible for marketing Volvo spare parts, and tried on several occasions to leave the company. But each time he was persuaded by Assar Gabrielsson to stay. The last time was in 1949. Then he was given the chance to head Volvo Penta and was given the title managing director. He could hardly resist such an opportunity, even though he was offered a better paid job somewhere else.

He obviously enjoyed his new challenge at Volvo Penta because he stayed on as managing director for 27 years right up until he retired in 1976.

Harald Wiklund has summed it up nicely in his own words: "*Volvo Penta – that was me!*"

He soon appreciated the significance of service and putting the customer in the centre. Wiklund would say that "*The worst boat in the world will become a decent one with good service. And the best boat in the world will become a poor one without service*". He recalls how difficult it was to achieve a breakthrough for the fantastic invention the Aquamatic after it was introduced in 1959, even though everyone appreciated its advantages. It was a question of 'buying oneself' onto the market, sometimes with the help of the highly respected name of Volvo.

One of Harald Wiklund's chief merits was that he succeeded in making production substantially more effective, started to 'marinise' car engines, and achieved some really outstanding success on the service side. Wiklund is also well-known for the 'garden-fence' engine. One day, he went out to take his dachsund dog for a walk. At the same time his neighbour, Lars Malmros, the head of the Truck Division, was also taking his dachsund for a walk. They stopped to talk by the garden fence. While the two dogs attended to their business, the two neighbours discussed the possibilities of developing a small diesel engine to power both boats and trucks. The result was the '40-engine' – the 'garden-fence' engine.

After retiring from the company, Harald Wiklund remained faithful to Volvo Penta by purchasing the company's products for the popular Nimbus boats which he and his sons produce and sell on the market.

100,000 Volvos

The 100,000th Volvo came off the assembly line at the Lundby plant on 25 August 1949; it was a black PV444. As it was an important celebration, all 68 'first-year employees' – in other words, all those who had been employed by the company since the start in 1927 – were invited to an extra crayfish dinner together with the Volvo management.

The ordinary crayfish dinner held each year to commemorate Gabrielsson's and Larson's first dinner at the Sturehof restaurant was held in 1949 for the 25th time.

On this celebration occasion, the magazine Ratten calculated that, up until that date, Volvo had contributed 762 million kronor towards improving Sweden's currency exchange situation by increasing exports and decreasing imports – a fantastic sum of money.

The production of the 100,000th Volvo was the occasion of lavish celebrations.

The PV445 was built in many different forms – as a small truck, an estate, a van and a convertible.

Production of the RM1, the company's first jet engine, at Svenska Flygmotor in Trollhättan proceeded at a high pace.

THE LITTLE PV444 had proved a success. However, Volvo's concern for its customers extended beyond the private motorist to the group which, perhaps more than any other, had contributed to the company's survival as an automaker – the taxi owners.

Since the PV800/820 series was still regarded with something like reverence by taxi operators, its basic features were retained when a revamped version was introduced in summer 1950. While the spacious interior, with room for the driver and six to seven passengers, was unchanged, the model was provided with a more elegant front which, in fact, was an exact copy of the PV444 on a larger scale. A touch of luxury was provided by the horizontal chrome trim along the body, while the rear end boasted a new boot lid and new lights. In keeping with the current trend, the model had 15" wheels.

The PV830 (as the new series was called) enjoyed a successful life in more or less unmodified form until 1956. A more luxurious version known as the 'Manager' with features including a more elegant dark blue or maroon finish (the basic model was black), twin spotlamps, a more lavish interior with plush upholstery and a radio as standard equipment, was introduced in 1953. Around the same time, the comfort and roadholding of the model were improved by adopting a new, up–to–date design of independent front suspension.

The L34, a medium–sized truck with exactly the same front end as the new PV830, was introduced almost concurrently. Neither was this 'new' model absolutely new since the chassis and mechanical components were those used in the last models of the LV10 and LV20 'Sharpnose' series. The L34 was to be the last bonneted delivery truck produced by Volvo.

The buyer who found even the L34 too big had the option of buying a PV830 chassis, which could be finished, for example, as an ambulance or as a light truck for delivering laundry, bakery products and other light goods.

The haulage trade was strictly regulated in the Sweden of the 1950s. Any driver without the official licence plate on the front of his vehicle found business difficult to obtain.

By 1950, Volvo was entertaining serious export ambitions, as indicated by the plethora of advertising brochures produced in various languages. Note the contrast between the typically Swedish text and the French title on the cover.

Facing page: The BM20 became part of the Volvo range following the takeover of Eskilstuna–based Bolinder–Munktell.

The PV830 was essentially the same as the old PV800/820 series with a new front (the same as the LV34 truck and resembling an enlarged PV 444).

In 1950, Volvo took over Bolinder–Munktell of Eskilstuna, which had previously been wholly owned by Svenska Handelsbanken. Since only two parties were involved, the deal was completed quickly and easily since. At the time, the BM range included two tractors (BM20 and BM10) which traced their origins all the way back to 1913, when the company began to manufacture tractors, or even to 1832, when Johan Theofron Munktell established his mechanical workshop in the town, leading, before long, to the manufacture of Sweden's first locomotive.

In actual fact, the BM20 was the same tractor as the Volvo T4, but with a different front section and a hot–bulb ignition engine with side fuel injection. It was easily distinguishable by the front which, although similar to the Volvo, had a particularly characteristic 'sad' appearance. In reality, the BM20 was an anachronism since the diesel was coming into its own and the days of the hot–bulb ignition engine were numbered. Nevertheless, its simplicity and reliability made it popular with Swedish farmers.

In 1951, the model was modified slightly and equipped with an overhead injection engine, becoming known as the BM21.

The BM10 was an even greater success than its larger sibling. Featuring the same rear section as the Volvo T2, but with a narrow front affording excellent visibility, and powered by a reliable and economical hot–bulb ignition engine, it was used for general service on small and medium–sized farms. Some individual models were even used in specialised applications, fitted, for example, with a rear–mounted excavator shovel or with half–tracks by ÖSA of Alfta for hauling lumber from the Swedish forests.

Car numbers increased dramatically in the early 1950s. The days when every family could afford its own car – not to mention the unheard of luxury and convenience of two cars – were still far off. However, people were now becoming more mobile, partly as distances between work and home became longer and partly as holiday travel (both in Sweden and abroad) became more commonplace. One result of these major social changes was to increase the importance of the bus, especially as the relatively short heyday of the tram in Sweden was drawing to a close. During the postwar years, up to and including 1952, Volvo committed a high proportion of its development resources to designing a completely new and improved generation of buses, from medium–sized to genuinely large models.

At about the end of the 1940s, Stockholm Tramways was preparing to invest heavily in the renewal of its bus fleet. Although the company had historically favoured Scania–Vabis models, Volvo was – for the first time – invited to tender on (theoretically) equal conditions for the supply of a

The little BM10 tractor was Bolinder–Munktell's best–seller, even following the Volvo take-over. The model was largely similar to the Volvo T21.

huge number of city buses, which were to be a feature on the streets of the capital for the rest of the decade. However, the technical director of SS did not favour conventional models (such as the Scania–Vabis H30) of the type which the company had been buying until then.

Front–engined buses were out; the new models were to be rear–engined, mainly because the same gentleman was highly impressed with the rear–engined Mack buses which had proved such a success in North America.

Scania–Vabis successfully negotiated a licence to build this particular Mack model. In return, Mack received access to the diesel technology which the Swedish company had been developing for 15 years since its type 16641 engine was introduced in 1936. The end product was the famous Scania–Vabis Metropol, which the company produced in large numbers for Stockholm Tramways, but which was otherwise disappointingly received by other customers.

It was clear from the outset that Scania–Vabis would receive the order; however, Volvo did submit its own city bus design under the designation B64, a model with a powerful rear–mounted engine and an automatic transmission. In fact, this was not a

Bolinder-Munktell

Bolinder-Munktell, a company steeped in tradition, had started to cooperate with Volvo during the Second World War. In principle, all models produced by the two companies had the same constituent parts, the exception being specific parts and components required for a BM tractor to work with its compression-ignition engine, and a Volvo with its petrol, paraffin or Hesselman engine.

In 1950, Volvo acquired the Bolinder-Munktell trade mark, plant facilities, and production range, thus gaining access to the production capacity that was required for the automotive operations to develop in Göteborg. The agricultural side of the business could expand in Eskilstuna without interfering with the main operations.

The manufacture of tractors and other agricultural machines (and a few years later also the manufacture of construction and forestry equipment) proved to be highly profitable from the outset. Between 1942 (when a few trial tractors were released) and 1987 (when the last Swedish-designed tractors left the plant in Eskilstuna), more than a quarter of a million tractors were to leave Volvo's plants.

For most of the 1950s, practically all tractors from Volvo and BM were delivered alongside each other from various competing tractor dealers all over Sweden, all of them similar in engineering, but clearly identifiable not only by their badge designation, but also by their dark green (for BM tractors up until 1958) or red (for Volvo tractors, and for BM tractors as from 1958) colour.

Volvo tried to create different market niches for BM and Volvo by stipulating that petrol-engine tractors were to be produced by Volvo, while compression-ignition and diesel engine tractors were to be marketed under the BM name. In theory, this division prevailed until 1956/57 when it was gradually erased, and Volvo tractors were equipped with diesel engines and BM also introduced petrol-engine tractors. On export markets it was more important that prospective customers could recognize and depend on the trade mark than that this fabricated difference was maintained meaninglessly.

The product range was soon broadened by a wider range of agricultural machines, chiefly under the BM badge.

completely original design; the first prototype was built on a B53 chassis powered by a transversely mounted 9.6–litre VDF engine developing 150 hp (as used in later versions of the B53 and in the L395 truck). The engine drove the rear wheels through an angle gearbox, which was the weakest link in the transmission chain.

In all, only five B64s were built. Nevertheless, the model is of interest as evidence that Volvo examined every conceivable design option before deciding on the front–engined configuration for its medium–sized and large interurban models, and on the pancake configuration (in which the engine was installed horizontally under the floor at the mid–point of the vehicle) for its large city buses.

In 1951, THE PUBLIC transport authority in the Danish city of Odense decided to close down its tramway system and introduce buses (although it already had a small bus fleet, including at least one Volvo B51). On the basis of its limited experience of bus operation, the authority approached Volvo to order a number of vehicles of a completely novel type – large city buses, mainly for standing passengers and built on a very short wheelbase (only 5 metres) to negotiate the extremely narrow streets of the old city. The engine was to be a horizontal diesel unit installed amidships (popularly known as a 'pancake' unit).

Since Volvo's chief bus design engineer, Sigvard Forsell, had visited Leyland in 1948–49, precisely to study the production of buses with pancake engines, the company was already somewhat familiar with the type.

At the time, new model development was not a long drawn–out process despite or, perhaps, because of the fact that resources were limited. As a result, responsibilities were clearly defined and duplication was avoided. Thus, Forsell was able to demonstrate the new B65 chassis to municipal transport managers from all over Sweden by December 1951, conducting a continuous series of test drives around the company's premises. In fact, the engineers were pressed for time and this was practically the only form of testing carried out before the chassis were shipped to Denmark for bodyworking by coachbuilders Aabenraa (a company acquired by Volvo Bus Corporation at the beginning of 1994).

The rest is history. Volvo delivered the vehicles on time and the trams – sadly –disappeared from the streets of Odense. The first series (B656) on a 5–metre wheelbase were unique; experience subsequently showed that the new chassis, with its wide lock, was sufficiently manoeuvrable to permit the use of larger vehicles with a 5.5–metre wheelbase and a slightly bigger interior.

The B65 underwent continuous development throughout its production life from 1951 to 1964. Power steering was soon available as an option, while air brakes were introduced successively as standard equipment. Several different automatic transmissions, including Volvo's own DRH–1 VolvoMatic, were available towards the end of the production period as alternatives to the all–synchromesh K1 gearbox. Air suspension became an option in the early 1960s, although only as an ancillary to the conventional spring–based type, which still accommodated some of the suspension forces.

Although the city bus version of the B65 was adequately powered, buyers of the tourist coach version complained that the model's 150 hp was on the low side –especially since an 180–hp, eight–in–line unit was available from the company's arch–competitor, Scania-Vabis (albeit in limited

The legendary B65 mid–engined bus was a familiar sight in most Scandinavian towns and cities. In Göteborg, it was to dominate the public transport scene for two decades, both in scheduled and charter services.

numbers). However, the D96AL ('D' denoted 'Diesel', '96' the cubic capacity in decilitres, 'A' the version and 'L' 'Liggande', or 'horizontal') was obsolescent and there was little reason to modify it by adding a turbo since a new generation of engines was just then under development. When its slightly modified successor, the B75, was introduced in 1964, customers were disappointed to find that it was not available in a turbo version. On the other hand, the radiator had been relocated further forward and the fan was driven from the engine by a long shaft, a change which improved the cooling and eliminated one of the few points of customer complaint. (This type of fan drive had been proposed in the original 1951 plans, but had been rejected by Gustaf Larson.)

Although the buses were the main focus of product development around 1950, the company was still making its living from trucks and, by this time, cars. The ageing L29 series (which dated from 1937) and the L29C/L29V diesel version were several years old and in need of renewal. The result was unveiled towards the end of 1951 in the form of the L395 (later known as the Titan when trade

mark restrictions on the use of the name were lifted). The model was far from being brand new (the complete L29C chassis had been used); however, the front end was of a gently rounded shape, and the exaggerated distance between the very front of the vehicle and the front wheel axis had been shortened, greatly improving the weight distribution and increasing the platform length within the same overall length. During the remainder of the 1950s and the early 1960s, this impressive model was to undergo continuous and comprehensive improvement, making it the true forerunner of today's ultra–powerful Volvo trucks.

The L395 Titan Turbo with the TD96AS engine (in this case, the prefix 'T' stood for 'Turbo' and the suffix 'S' for 'Stående', or 'vertical') was introduced in 1954. This unit was the product of herculean work by the Volvo design team under the legendary engine designer, John Stålblad. Despite a 25–kg increase in weight, the engine delivered an additional 35 hp at a very slightly higher fuel consumption. The TD96 unit was developed successively into the final (1964) TD96C version with a rating of 230 hp.

The L395FDB, a tandem–drive version with twin driving rear axles for heavy haulage and construction site applications, was introduced in the mid–1950s. Known as the Hendrickson type, the bogie suspension was of American origin (although its designer, Magnus Hendrickson, was Swedish–born, he had emigrated to the USA at an early age and was not part of Swedish motoring history). In the event, it was to be some time before Volvo achieved success with the tandem bogie, mainly because the Hendrickson design, with its four springs, was far from reliable.

In the late 1950s, buyers were offered the options of power steering (which eased the task of drivers who were not particularly athletic) and air brakes (which greatly improved harmonised braking between truck and trailer). Hub reduction was introduced as an alternative to a double–reduction final drive in 1964.

Also in 1964, the L395 was succeeded by the L495 Titan, which was modified in a number of details, and further improvements were made a year later, including the location of the instruments in front of the driver rather than in the centre of the dashboard. While Volvo was still delivering cabless chassis, growing numbers of trucks had been equipped with cabs by Nyströms Karosserifabrik of Umeå (later Volvo, Umeå) since the second half of the 1940s. By now, Åtvidaberg had ceased production and although many customers still preferred the comfortable cabs built by the BeGe and Floby companies, Nyström introduced its first impact–tested 'safety cab' in 1959–60, a unit designed mainly for Volvo and marketed as the 'Volvo safety cab'.

Volvo's first motorised combine harvester increased farmers' yields as well as augmenting the Bolinder–Munktell product range.

The Volvo Titan became well–known around the world, except in North America (although the company did have advanced plans to market trucks there). The picture shows two L495 Titans which underwent trials in the USA. However, it was to be another fifteen years before American sales began in earnest.

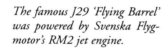
The famous J29 'Flying Barrel' was powered by Svenska Flygmotor's RM2 jet engine.

The MST–91, Volvo's first self–propelled combine harvester, was introduced in 1951. This machine was powered by an industrial version of the ED engine, converted to run on paraffin.

The self–propelled harvester was easier to operate than a towed type and saved more of the crop. Several new models and generations appeared up to the end of the 1970s. All of these became highly popular, and several are still in service on small and medium–sized farms to this day.

Aircraft engine development proceeded at a fast pace. In 1951, Svenska Flygmotor commenced deliveries of the new RM2 jet engine, which was based on the De Havilland Ghost, for installation in both the J29 'Flying Barrel' and the J33 Venom night fighter.

In 1951, Volvo Penta unveiled its BB4 engine, which consisted simply of a B4B (as used in the PV444) modified for marine applications. Marketed at a competitive, but profitable price, this powerful little tried–and–tested unit paved the way for the most successful years ever experienced by Volvo Penta, a period characterised by enormous sales, international expansion and highly rationalised production in coordination with the rest of the Volvo Group. Attributable solely to Harald Wiklund's efforts, the development of the BB4 undoubtedly saved Volvo Penta from extinction as a marine engine manufacturer. Without it, the company would probably have been reduced to the role of a mere producer of engines for Volvo vehicles.

The BB4 was to be followed by several marine versions of the B4B and other vehicle engines.

To complete the renewal of the company's bus range, the Volvo designers modified the design of the conventional front–engined models in 1952. The B51 and B62 became the B61 and B72 respectively, models with a new design of front suspension and the direct–injection VDC and D96 engines as standard equipment.

Customers could no longer buy a petrol–engined bus even from Volvo, which had been the most obstinate of all European vehicle manufacturers in its opposition to the increasingly popular diesel. The big front–engined B53 was replaced by the B63, which was much better suited for rationalised production than its exclusive predecessor. The B63, in which the gearbox was mounted immediately beside the engine, was used more and more as a tourist coach as the B65 made its triumphant progress in the cities, mainly in Sweden (it was to be some time before the pancake engine became accepted in tourist models). The B63 made history when a few vehicles of the type were equipped with turbochargers, although this version was featured in the sales brochures only that year.

Until 1952, Volvo was equipped to sell petrol or Hesselman tractors only, two types which were far from up–to–date. Meanwhile, the Bolinder–Munktell subsidiary was producing vehicles with hot–bulb ignition engines which, although reliable in operation, could not match the modern diesel–engined models coming from the USA, Britain and Germany.

It was with pride that Volvo introduced its BM35/BM36 and T35/T36 diesel tractors in 1952, proclaiming that customers now had the opportunity of buying the first Swedish–built diesel tractor. Furthermore, the model was in an extremely popular class with an engine rating of 40–50 hp.

Unsurprisingly for Volvo, the models were not entirely new. In terms of appearance as well as design features, they bore many similarities to the BM31–BM34/T31–T34 models introduced back in 1949.

The three–cylinder diesel engine was of the direct–injection type. In the simplest terms, it consisted of half a D67 truck engine (which had been introduced in the Viking truck and the B615 bus). Known as the 1053 (denoting a unit with a stroke of 105 mm and three cylinders), it was subsequently produced in versions with one, two and four cylinders.

The BM35/BM36 and T34/T35 achieved immediate popularity. Both these and later developments of this class of tractor were sold to large numbers of Swedish farmers over several decades.

In Skövde, Volvo Penta introduced a new, robust, low–speed inboard engine for small workboats. Since a couple of other Swedish makers

The BM36/T36 tractor became an immediate favourite, not only in Sweden, but also in Brazil, where it helped to enhance Volvo's reputation.

At Christmas 1952, all Swedish children born in 1945 received a book of fairy tales from Volvo. The stories described the adventures of 'Willie Volvo', a courageous little PV444, and were beautifully illustrated as exemplified on the facing page.

(Albin and Solo) were still specialising in this type of unit, Penta could no longer rely on modified car engines for its marine applications.

The Penta C2 was a two–cylinder, side–valve engine designed to burn petrol or paraffin. It now boasted the classic 84.14 mm bore (the same as the EC and ED units, as well as the later B18) and developed 11 hp at its low maximum speed of 1,500 r/min.

Comfortably quiet and vibration–free, the C2 helped Penta to maintain its competitiveness in this class of workboat engines. A few years later, the company permanently regained its status of Swedish market leader with its small, direct–injection diesels.

ALL COMPANIES SEEK to expand their product ranges and increase their production volumes by adding closely related products. Volvo was undoubtedly surprised to note the steadily growing number of vans and, on occasion, estate cars which were being built by independent bodybuilders on its PV445 chassis. This led to the introduction, in 1953, of one of the most beloved Volvo models ever made – the Duett.

Vans were the main variant at first; small commercial firms found them ideal for long as well as short runs to deliver finished goods or collect raw materials.

The company was quick to see the opportunity of combining the dual functions of private and commercial motoring in a single vehicle (although, in truth, it should be said that the Duett bore little resemblance to fast, comfortable and safe estate models of today). Nevertheless, the PV445 Duett was a roomy and powerful little van. Although modest, the speed afforded by the first 44–hp engine was considered acceptable on the roads of the time. The engine rating was increased successively, first to 51 and then to 60 hp (in the USA, the PV445 Duett was actually available for a time with the 70–hp B14A unit!).

Three different variants were available in addition to the bare chassis version of the PV445 Duett. These were a van without side windows behind the front doors, a van with a primitive rear seat and with side windows behind the front doors, and the most 'luxurious' version, which boasted a proper (folding) rear seat and full side windows. The Duett was refined successively in parallel with the PV444 saloon, although a successor to the PV445 was not introduced until two years after the PV544 had replaced the PV444.

The Duett was produced, not in Göteborg, but under contract by a company in Oskarshamn, where it was assembled from standard components manufactured in Göteborg and special body parts supplied directly from Olofström.

Whereas the PV444 and Duett were relatively simple, medium–class cars, Volvo was also entertaining grander ambitions, as demonstrated particularly by the 'Philip' project. A large, luxury model with a V8 engine (and an unashamed copy of the American Kaiser/Frazer), this was intended for production at around this time.

The Philip was to be equipped with the Volvo–designed B36AV V8 engine, a modern 3.6–litre OHV unit developing 120 hp. However, like so many others, the project was abandoned when company management had second thoughts. The single model built was used for many years as a company car by Bolinder–Munktell in Eskilstuna and is now in the Volvo Museum in Göteborg. The powerful V8 engine was adapted for use in the L42/L4201 Snabbe ('Speedy') truck.

The L385 Viking, one of the most popular trucks ever built by Volvo, was introduced in 1953 as the successor to the L245 'Roundnose' diesel of 1949. In reality, the model consisted of the chassis and mechanical components of the L245, with the styling of the L395 Titan. However, the Viking did not become really popular until the following year, when it was equipped with the more powerful (115 hp) D67 engine (the first version of the VDC developed only 100 hp). The 'Viking' name was not used until 1954, when the designation L385A was formally adopted.

The demand for terrain vehicles became urgent as the Swedish Defence Forces were steadily motorised. Volvo met the demand for a four–wheel drive staff car with the TP21, which immediately became known as the 'Sow' (perhaps because of its rotund rear end!). The model was based on a light truck frame, with a driven front axle, and was fitted with a body based on the PV830 taxi, shortened slightly to increase the off–road mobility.

The TP21 complemented the now–obsolescent TPV (which dated from 1944) and was completely superior to the latter as regards off–road operation,

The Duett was a best–seller right from its introduction. Production of the model was maintained at a high level.

The elegant Elizabeth I was built on a PV445 chassis, with a body by Michelotti.

The standard of driver comfort in the Duett was fully comparable to that of the 'ordinary' PV444.

'Spetsbågen'

Volvo had achieved its increasingly successful truck sales by virtue of modest car production levels. But when the PV444 was sold and exported in increasing numbers, the need for a new truck assembly plant became even more acute.

The problem was solved (for the next ten years at least) when a special truck assembly facility was built on the 'Spetsbågen' site immediately adjoining the 'Jägmästaren' plant at Lundby.

At that time, the new truck plant was enormous, more than 250 metres long and more than 50 metres wide. More than 250,000 trucks were to be assembled here up until the turn of the year 1991/92, when the plant was closed and all remaining truck assembly operations were transferred to the Tuve plant.

thanks to its bigger terrain tyres, higher ground clearance and shorter wheelbase. The front end was similar to the small TL11/TL22 military vehicles of the same period.

The Royal Swedish Air Force developed rapidly during the 1950s. New, modern jet aircraft (with engines built by Volvo Flygmotor in Trollhättan) were introduced at intervals of a few years. In 1953, Volvo made the first deliveries, to the air force, of the TL11 tractor ('TL' was an acronym for 'TerrängLastbil', meaning 'terrain truck') which, although equipped with four–wheel drive, was actually used exclusively for towing aircraft, mainly the J29, as part of airbase ground operations.

Few tractors were more sought–after than the BM55/T55. This large model, which had proved a worthy successor to the earlier BM21 and T43, was powered by a modern diesel engine consisting simply of two–thirds of a D67 – in effect, the same unit as in the BM35/T35, but with an extra cylinder.

The BM55/T55 quickly became a best seller in the agricultural industry. Some models were even fitted with a dumper trailer for site applications, presaging the appearance, a decade or so later, of the articulated dumper which was to make Volvo the world's leading manufacturer in that field. One of the companies to use the BM55/T55 with a heavy dumper trailer of its own design was Lihnell Vagn AB (LIVAB), which was eventually acquired by BM Volvo and became the basis for its successful entry into the earthmoving plant (or construction equipment) industry.

In 1953, BM introduced a small petrol–engined tractor, which replaced the BM10 and was built almost entirely from T2 series components. However, since the company was unwilling to market a BM tractor with a Volvo petrol engine, it was decided to use a British Austin engine in the small, green BM Teddy 200 (petrol) and 210

Independent firms created extremely powerful, diesel–driven 'tandem tractors' by coupling together two Bolinder–Munktell units.

(paraffin). This proved to be no more than a stopgap solution; the Teddy never achieved the same fantastic reputation as the T2, which is still used by farmers and holiday–home owners to this today.

The rear view of the TP21 shows quite clearly how it obtained its nickname of 'The Sow'.

The BM55 with a dumper
body was a forerunner of the
world–famous articulated Volvo
dumpers.

In the 1950s, the TP21 was one
of the leading vehicles of its
kind in the world. It was to be
used for over three decades by
the Swedish Defence Forces.

VOLVO UNVEILED TWO new cars in 1954. These represented two extremes, one being the smallest and simplest car the company had ever built and the other being the most unusual ever to enter series production.

The PV444 Export was launched during the production life of the PV444H. Although the label 'Export' sounded exclusive, the car was actually a 'poor man's' variant. While the demand for cars in postwar Europe was high, the level of hardship caused by the devastating war was even greater, and even the middle classes were forced to tighten their belts. As a result, the 'Export' was actually cheaper and more austere than the 'standard' version. Outwardly, it was recognisable by the fact that the trim, which was normally chromed, was silver–painted. The interior was frugal, with seats of the simple, tubular–frame type common in small French cars.

The 'Export' never became a success and was discontinued – quite unlamented –after a year. Although some cars were sold in Sweden, few status–conscious Swedes were disposed to buy a model which was so basic compared with their neighbour's.

The new Volvo Sport, which was first unveiled as a concept car prior to series production a couple of years later, was the direct opposite of the PV444 Export. This was the brainchild of Assar Gabrielsson, who was anxious to demonstrate that the Volvo marque was not only reliable, but could also be sporty and exclusive. Visiting the USA, Gabrielsson had been fascinated by the new Chevrolet Corvette, with its glass fibre body, and had decided that Volvo should produce a car of the

The prototype of the glass fibre–bodied P1900 was unveiled in 1954. Models built to different scales were built during the development phase.

same type. While the body styling and development were being carried out in the States, the engineers at home were busily planning for production by designing a modified tubular frame and boosting the output of a PV444 engine to 70 hp.

Transported on the platform of a Titan Turbo (the major truck development of the year), the Volvo Sport was exhibited to the Swedish public in the course of a nationwide tour.

The Titan Turbo was launched simultaneously with the other new additions to the Volvo range (the original Titan model, then with a 10–litre engine, had appeared in 1951). Although it was clear that a few more horsepower would be an advantage, it was equally apparent that a bigger unit would be expensive to develop, heavier and less economical, while the range of potential applications for it would be quite small.

There was, however, another – although as–yet unproven – solution which offered an exciting prospect to the engine design team (which was headed by John Stålblad and included the legendary Bertil Häggh, later known internationally as 'Mr. Turbo').

The Volvo team had become aware that the German company, Eberspächer, had designed a turbocharger sufficiently compact for installation in a truck (until then, turbos had been used only in stationary applications, on ships, in large aircraft and in rail buses).

Testing was carried out over a couple of years and a small series of test vehicles was launched in autumn 1954 when the engineers were satisfied with the results. A test fleet of only 200 Titan Turbos was envisaged initially; however, the trucks performed so well that production was continued without interruption, with the result that Volvo now has over 40 years of experience of building turbocharged vehicles –a unique tradition unmatched by any other maker.

More and more Volvo trucks were equipped with turbos as time went on, the last normally–aspirated model being produced a quarter of a century later, in 1980.

Compared with the Titan Turbo, the L37 represented both a major and minor development. Although a completely new truck, its long–term importance to the transport industry was in no way comparable to that of turbo technology.

The styling of the L37 was based on the PV444 and the PV830, but on a much larger scale. In other words, the model was extremely modern in appearance, with sweeping lines and flush–mounted headlamps.

Introduced to take the place of the now obsolescent 'Roundnose' models, the L37 was available in two basic versions, the L370 Brage (named after a Norse god), with the same A6 engine as the L230, and the L375 Starke ('Mighty'), with a 4.7–litre diesel engine developed concurrent-

ly with the A6. The L375 was to prove a long–lived best–seller, which was to survive in further developed form as the L465 Starke and L475 Raske ('Swift'), which were introduced at the beginning of the following decade, and (equipped with a new engine) as the N84 from 1965 to 1972.

The L37, L46, L47 and N84 were all characterised by their extreme ruggedness and – despite the fact that they were medium–sized models – they all became renowned as genuinely multi–purpose vehicles. In Sweden, the models were normally used for regional transport purposes or as light construction site vehicles. In export markets, however, they were used both as heavy long–haul vehicles and as timber trucks.

The L36, a series of the same basic design as the L37, but with lighter axles and chassis components, was introduced the following year. This series was designed specifically for regional distribution applications but never achieved particular success. The petrol-engined L360 Friske ('Lively') was equipped with the ageing ED side–valve engine, which fell far short of customers' expectations (even in the 1950s), while the L365 diesel, although powered by the same modern D47 unit as the L375 Starke, was not only too expensive, but appeared at a time when most buyers in this segment still favoured petrol engines.

The last truck to be introduced by Volvo in 1954 was the TL22, a fast, light military truck for carrying troops and matériel in extremely difficult terrain. Equipped with six–wheel drive and outsize wheels, it was almost impossible to stop with a fearless and competent driver behind the wheel.

The TL22 was a modern terrain vehicle with a safe and comfortable cab by Nyström of Umeå and the same powerful OHV A6 engine as the L37

The medium–sized L37 Brage and Raske trucks were used for a variety of applications. One example was the tanker seen here refuelling a Supermarine Spitfire and a Messerschmitt 109 at Säve airfield.

The TD96AS turbocharged engine was a worldwide sensation, delivering an extra 35 hp for a small increase in weight and almost unchanged fuel consumption.

Brage. The main characteristic of the engine was its ability to develop maximum power at low torque, even at very low revs, an extremely valuable attribute when negotiating tight spaces on poor surfaces in rough terrain.

Two developments which were to be of crucial significance to Volvo's fortunes were announced by Bolinder–Munktell in Eskilstuna. Neither was related to agriculture, although one was based largely on the tractor range.

Today Volvo BM is one of the world's leading makers of earthmoving machinery, its principal product being the wheel loader. This was a late

development of what was a fairly unremarkable product, the BL loader which, at a later stage and with certain modifications, as well as a different finish, became known as the H10. The model was developed originally by the independent firm of Lundberg Brothers in Skellefteå.

The H10 was a conventional agricultural tractor with a unique cab in which the driver was seated back to front (in other words, what was 'forward' in the tractor was 'backward' in the wheel loader). The lifting unit, with its lever action, was powerful, while the rear–mounted engine and the extra counterweights combined to provide stability. The rear–wheel steering afforded an extremely small turning circle, making the machine very easy to manoeuvre by the experienced driver.

Based on the BM35 tractor, the standard version of the H10 was equipped with a three–cylinder engine. However, a lesser–known alternative version based on the four–cylinder BM55 tractor was also produced.

Another machine which was to prove highly significant to BM's success was the new VHK55 road grader. This was built initially in response to a request from the roads maintenance authorities for a bogie suitable for Swedish road graders, followed later by an order for a complete machine. The VHK55 was the first of a long series of graders developed by BM.

A few of the original tractors built by Munktell in the 1920s had been converted for use as graders. By contrast, the machines developed now were unique and differed completely from the tractors.

The VHK55 was a rugged machine which, with substantial weight and powerful VDC diesel (of lower output than the units used in Volvo's trucks and buses), was suitable for road maintenance work in the summer and snow–ploughing in the winter.

Seated in a high cab, the driver had a clear view of his work, the large windows enabling him to operate the machine to a high degree of precision.

The grader was to be one of Volvo's most profitable products for many years. One reason for this was that a high proportion of Swedish roads were still unpaved and required continuous maintenance using fast, powerful machines.

In 1953, Svenska Flygmotor launched its most advanced product ever in the shape of the RM2B jet engine. Although based – as before – on the De Havilland Ghost, the new engine was equipped with an afterburner of the company's own design.

The new feature endowed the J29F (the last version of the 'Flying Barrel') with a completely new level of performance. particularly in terms of climbing capability (although the fuel consumption was increased enormously).

Svenska Flygmotor remained a world leader in the afterburner field for many years and its designs were sold to foreign manufacturers for production of this Swedish innovation under licence.

Unlike most machines of the type used in Scandinavia until then, Volvo's first road grader, the BM VHK55, was developed specifically for the application. The model was powered by a downrated version of the D67 truck and bus diesel.

Six–wheel drive and generous differential locks gave the TL22 excellent mobility.

Bolinder–Munktell H10.

The problems of the PV warranty

In November 1954, Volvo introduced a 5-year car warranty – the PV444 warranty. Volvo undertook to cover the costs of damage resulting from collision totalling more than SKr 200.

The Swedish Insurance Inspectorate took a dim view of this. Instead, it claimed that Volvo was guilty of breaching the law relating to insurance business, and started legal proceedings against Volvo.

The State prosecutor in Göteborg investigated the matter and in the summer of 1955 decided that no further action would be taken. In his lengthy report, the prosecutor uses exactly the same words used by Volvo when it introduced the warranty – 'significant benefits for car owners".

All would have been well but for the insurance companies. They were definitely opposed to this 'competition', so it became an issue for all the courts to decide upon.

While the legal process proceeded – first with Assar Gabrielsson as the principal person, then Gunnar Engellau – the warranty continued to be valid. It later covered even more models.

In September 1958 the Supreme Court issued a verdict in Volvo's favour. Gunnar Engellau and the whole of Volvo breathed a sigh of relief and an even greater effort was put into action.

That year there were 170,000 cars with the warranty (the Amazon was also covered by it, of course, immediately following the Supreme Court's verdict). More than 12,000 damages claims were settled the same year.

Just a few days after the historic verdict, Volvo submitted an application for concession to start up its own insurance company, Försäkrings AB Volvia. This company was set up to sell insurance to cover damages for those cars for which the PV car warranty had expired.

It was not until 18 December 1959, a month or so after the warranty period for the first cars had expired, that the Swedish government approved Volvo's application, and Volvo started up operations with Olle Keyling as General Manager.

The business operations of the new and small company soon grew, and the number of Volvo car-owners who took out insurance with Volvia rose rapidly. Volvo was also soon able to offer insurance to cover things like fire, theft, windscreen damage, vehicle recovery, and legal protection. The company now also offers third party insurance in cooperation with the Dial company, which was taken over from Skandia. Insurance is also offered for Volvo trucks, as are also all Renault cars. Moreover, Volvia has started up a drive on the European market in cooperation with local insurance companies, chiefly in Norway, Finland, Belgium, the Netherlands, and Great Britain.

THE MOST POPULAR vehicle introduced in 1955 was the legendary BM Victor tractor, which had been designed simply by taking the components of a T24 tractor and replacing the petrol engine with a two–cylinder version of the direct–injection diesel used in the T35 and T55.

The Victor was the right product at the right time. Small and medium–sized farms were now ready to abandon the horse in favour of the more efficient tractor (happily, the horses were usually pensioned off and allowed to live out their days in leisurely retirement). In addition, petrol was becoming increasingly expensive, making it common sense for the farmer to spend the extra money on a diesel rather than a petrol or paraffin–burning vehicle.

The 1052 engine was half of a T55 diesel with a longer stroke, a feature which endowed the unit with exceptional low–speed torque and made it more powerful than suggested by its size and service weight (the two–cylinder configuration also gave the unit a highly characteristic sound).

The Victor was more than a new model of tractor. The first little green model (a red Volvo version was introduced later under the much more mundane designation T230) was soon the fastest selling tractor in Sweden and became a legend in the course of time. Today, the model is much sought–after on the secondhand market by summer house owners. In France, however, the model could not be marketed as the Victor, but was known by the French equivalent of 'The Yokel'!

The export of cars to the USA commenced in 1955.

The J35 Draken, powered by the Volvo RM6 engine, made its maiden flight in 1955.

Apart from the Ferguson 'Grey Horse', the most beloved tractor of the decade was the BM Victor, which was built in both the green BM and red Volvo versions.

The Stora Holm test track

Perhaps the most important Volvo news item in 1955 was not a product but the new test track at Stora Holm, close to the Tuve area on Hisingen Island. This enabled more organized tests to be carried out. Volvo could now seriously begin to check the validity of its laboratory tests on complete vehicles.

Stora Holm was a rather small facility consisting of a number of road sections with different surfaces and hill sections with various gradients. But it provided invaluable help in the work being carried on to create cars of a high quality and reasonable weight.

Previously, durable cars had been created simply by introducing more powerful frames or thicker panels. In the long term this was an unsatisfactory method, especially when there was a strain on car prices and the price of petrol started to rise.

Of particular importance to Volvo were the greater possibilities of performing quality and durability tests when the company launched its PV444 in America, and when the P1200 Amazon was in the final stages of development. This was a new car and it was vital it did not become a failure.

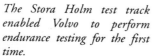

The Stora Holm test track enabled Volvo to perform endurance testing for the first time.

The 100,000th PV444 to be produced (in early 1956) was a PV444K, the version introduced towards the end of 1955.

A hundred thousand celebrations 1955 and 1956

On 29 June 1955, the 100,000th B4B engine left the production line at the Volvo Pentaverken in Skövde. Most of the engines were used for powering PV444 cars, but some were also fitted in the Volvo 445 van and Volvo Duett models. A few were sold as marine engines, and some as truck engines.

The anniversary engine also signalled the opening of a new workshop.

Just after that it was time for an even bigger celebration. This was to commemorate the 100,000th PV444. Ahead of this milestone the magazine 'Ratten' announced a competition. The person who could guess correctly when car number 100,000 would be built would also win the car. The car was built on the 24th of January 1956 and left the production line at 7.52 in the morning. The car was won by an engineer from Skönsberg, Thure Nylander.

Volvo flooded the US market

Some names are for ever firmly associated with Volvo's car sales drive in America – Sefeldt, Hirsch, Engellau… The story has several key characters.

C A Lindblom was the very first. He travelled to the USA in early 1947 with a prototype PV444. He arrived in Pittsburgh, where the car attracted a lot of attention. Lindblom even won an award for his and the car's safe performance in town traffic.

Following the special appearance in 1947 it was to take up until 1955 before the American venture got seriously under way.

Some years later Gunnar Engellau wrote an article for the house journal 'Luftrenaren' in which he described the USA venture. In it he gives credit for the initiative to one person in particular: Director T G Andersson.

We can only assume that he was the man who convinced an otherwise hesitant Assar Gabrielsson to commence shipping cars across the Atlantic to the 'car's own promised land'.

When Engellau succeeded Gabrielsson in 1956 the USA drive had already begun. But Engellau had expressed his profound belief in exporting cars to the USA long before he became Managing Director.

When it comes to pioneering Volvo cars in the USA, two names stand out: Nils Sefeldt and Leo Hirsch.

In 1955, Sefeldt was an aeronautical engineer who was extremely interested in cars. He also nurtured a desire to sell a Swedish car in seven southern states in the USA. He borrowed money, packed his wife, three children, and masses of luggage into a trimmed dove-grey Volvo PV car, and sailed for New York. From there he drove the car to Fort Worth in Texas, where he intended to set up his importer agency.

The journey was an adventurous one. Not even hurricane 'Diane' could prevent the car continuing its journey, sometimes through water half a metre deep covering the hub cups and exhaust pipe.

At the end of the four-day trip, Sefeldt calculated that, in spite of the heavy load on-board and the high speed at which the car was driven, the fuel consumption was 0.76 litres/10 km. This impressive figure became one of the PV's best sales arguments. Nonetheless, he found it difficult to sell the car.

Sefeldt soon received five cars to sell. but sales were sluggish. He received another five. They were just as difficult to sell.

He almost gave up, but in the spring of 1956 sales suddenly started to pick up. Sefeldt later moved to Houston, where you can still see the Nils Sefeldt Volvo sign in several places.

In 1955, Leo Hirsch was a businessman from Los Angeles visiting Sweden on business to buy nails. He travelled by taxi – a Volvo, of course – and was so impressed he got himself an importer contract to sell Volvo cars in eleven states in Western USA. There he built up his empire thanks to devoted salesmanship.

STABILITY HAS ALWAYS been a Volvo characteristic. Thus, when Assar Gabrielsson handed over to Gunnar Engellau after 30 years at the helm, his successor carried on the traditions of the previous three decades.

However, 1956 was notable, not only as the year the company acquired a new head, but as the most exciting year in its history in terms of product launches.

With the PV444, Volvo had finally become a successful automaker, even though Sweden was still its biggest market. Having produced expensive, medium–class cars for the first 20 years, the company had become a manufacturer of small cars, supplemented by big, solid taxi models. Now, however, there was a demand for a medium–class model which would appeal to the PV444 owners anxious to trade up to a bigger, more comfortable car.

For this reason, the P12/P1200 Amazon attracted considerable attention when it appeared at the beginning of 1956, although some time was to elapse before customers could take delivery of the new model.

The 1956 Amazon was available only in a single four–door version. Although more powerful than

The P1900 was a much–admired, although rare car (only about 70 examples were built). Most of these still survive in the tender care of their owners.

the B4B/B16 used in the contemporary PV444, the 'new' B16 engine was simply a bored–out version of that unit. The output had been increased from 51 to 60 hp, while Swedish buyers soon had the choice of a 'sports' version rated at 85 hp (until then, twin–carburettor sports engines had been reserved for PV444 buyers in the USA). The original idea of equipping the Amazon with a small 2.5–litre V8 was abandoned in favour of the more conservative option of a four–in–line engine.

The work of Jan Wilsgård, the new chief design engineer, the styling of the Amazon was clearly inspired by Italian as well as American sources. The two–tone finish – especially the striking red and white combination which found immediate favour with the public – was particularly reminiscent of American models. The front, with its twin grilles, was one of the most characteristic features and was retained (albeit in a more discrete form) on the 144 introduced a decade later.

The Amazon offered a fairly high standard of comfort, even though the rear seat was designed to assist entry and exit, and gave only moderate support to the two outermost passengers when occupied by three people.

"I doff my hat as a mark of respect for all that has been achieved in the past – and roll up my sleeves to tackle the future."

These immortal words were spoken by Gunnar Engellau on the day he took up his post as President and CEO of AB Volvo on 13 August, 1956. He came from a position as President of Svenska Flygmotor AB in Trollhättan, a post he had held for 13 years.

Just one year previously, 50 Volvo cars had been shipped over to that promised land of motoring, the USA. Gunnar Engellau immediately threw himself wholeheartedly into the job of continuing this trend. In 1956, Volvo exported 5,000 cars, in 1957 the figure rose to 10,300, and so it went on.

One of the people whose job it was to put the Volvo badge on roads around the world was Bertil Brattberg. When Bertil Brattberg passed away in 1994 he was a legend in his own right. One of the many stories told about him also put the spotlight on his mentor Gunnar Engellau, who made a point of inviting about 20 of his closest colleagues home for a lavish dinner every Christmas. On one of these occasions in the early sixties, Brattberg found himself sitting opposite Gunnar Engellau, who caught sight of Brattberg's elegant, slim wrist-watch, and asked to have a closer look at it. Brattberg mentioned that he had received it from an importer, upon which Engellau simply pocketed the watch and said *"you have no right to accept such beautiful gifts in the course of your work."*

Brattberg was understandably less than happy over this turn of events, but got his own back before the evening was out. Standing in the doorway bidding his host goodbye, he espied a rich oriental rug adorning the wall. Quick as a flash, he pulled it down, rolled it up and tucked it under his arm. Engellau rushed to defend his property and directed a few well-chosen words to his colleague, who stood his ground and insisted that it was he who had introduced Engellau to the person who had given him the rug in the first place. And of course he rounded it off with *"you have no right to accept such beautiful gifts in the course of your work."*

Engellau naturally burst out laughing and exchanged the watch for his precious rug. Brattberg later saw to it that Engellau received a watch similar to his own, but a few extra millimetres thicker than his own. As he

GUNNAR ENGELLAU

explained: *"After all, you've got some time to make up!"*

Volvo expanded considerably during Engellau's 15 years at the helm. The turnover increased tenfold from 600 million kronor to 6 thousand million. The number of cars produced increased from 31,000 in his first year of office to 205,000 in the year he vacated his seat.

The introduction of the F88 truck in 1965 signalled an export drive overseas. In 1969, the heavy-duty sector was separated from the rest of Volvo.

Volvo's growth in the 1950s meant the original plant in Lundby, Göteborg, was now bursting at the seams. A large area on the outskirts of Göteborg, but still on Hisingen Island, near Torslanda Airport, was acquired. The foundations were laid for a new plant. The investment was enormous and the inauguration ceremony on 28 April 1964 was attended by King Gustaf VI Adolf, Finance Minister Gunnar Sträng, and several thousand guests.

In his speech, Gunnar Engellau once again showed his immense respect for the company's two founders (Gustaf Larson was present, but Assar Gabrielsson passed away in 1962). "It took Volvo 23 years to produce its first 100,000 vehicles, which is less than we now make in a single year. However, making those first 100,000 units was a far more impressive feat than churning out the same amount every year today. All we are doing is to build on the foundation they laid, but let us never forget that it was they who laid the foundations. As Swedish poet Tegnér once wrote: *"Where would we have been if they hadn't been?"* Assar Gabrielsson and Gustaf Larson have left an indelible mark on Swedish industrial history."

Today, the world can also add Gunnar Engellau's name to the roll of honour in that same history book. Following the spirits of Volvo's two founders, he made Volvo a household name, both through an immense export drive and by establishing facilities within the EEC, in Ghent in Belgium. He made the Volvo name synonymous with safety, quality, durability and value for money. So it was a healthy company facing continued expansion prospects which Pehr G Gyllenhammar took over in 1971.

Gunnar Engellau remained chairman of the board until 1978 and passed away on 5 January, 1988 at the age of 80.

The P1200 Amazon (the car in the right–hand picture is a prototype).

The Amazon was shown at a dealer conference early in 1956 together with the new L42/L4201 Snabbe truck. Introduced to replace the elderly L34, the Snabbe was the first (and last) truck to be equipped with a Volvo V8 engine (not, it should be noted, an original truck engine but the V8 designed for the Philip luxury car, which never entered production). This unit bore the designation B36AV ('B' standing for 'Bensin' or 'petrol', '36' for '3.6 litres', 'A' for the version and 'V' for the V8 configuration).

Helmer Petersson, who had previously worked with Erik Hjern on the PV444, was chief designer for the L42 project. Under his direction, the cab was designed entirely of steel – a first for Volvo since the larger trucks were still sold without a cab.

The first Volvo forward–control truck to be produced in numbers, the Snabbe became especially popular as a delivery truck and as a shop on wheels, due to its low frame. Since the frame was also arched over the rear axle, the model could be built with the lowest section of the platform close to the ground.

The L4301 Trygge (or 'Trusty') – a similar model with a heavier (straight) frame, heavier axles and a higher payload – was introduced the following year. Although any model with this particular cab is nowadays generally referred to as a 'Snabbe', most of the L43/L4301s were Trygges which, in reality, superseded the short–lived L36 Friske.

The powerful 3.6–litre, 120–hp V8 engine (which, for a couple of years in the 1960s, was also available in a 120 or 180–hp marine version, with or without an Aquamatic drive) was a thirsty beast. Fortunately, this was not a major consideration, given that most of the vehicles were delivery trucks operating over short runs, often amounting only to some tens of kilometres daily. In time, however, the fuel cost became a more important economic factor

The forward–control Snabbe and Trygge trucks became popular delivery vehicles, especially because of their low platforms and lively V8 engine.

Facing page, bottom: Together with the Ferguson 'Grey Horse', the petrol–engined Volvo Krabat/BM Terrier contributed to the mechanisation of even small Swedish farms.

and customers were offered diesel engines as an alternative. The first of these was a Ford engine introduced in 1963/64 under the designation D36. This was later replaced, in the renamed F82 and F83 trucks (formerly the Snabbe and Trygge), by a Perkins diesel with the designation D39. These two units (whose lack of power unfortunately had an adverse effect on driving enjoyment) were the only non–Volvo engines ever to be used in the company's trucks outside North America.

Neither were the farmers neglected in 1956. In early summer, Volvo introduced the T15 (and the Bolinder–Munktell version, the BM15), a small. light petrol–engined tractor with a downrated PV444 engine known as the B14C (the suffix 'C' was henceforth reserved for tractor engines). The tractor was now taking over to a growing extent, even on small farms, and the marketing experts at the Volvo plant in Eskilstuna were, perhaps, troubled to see the enormous success enjoyed by the Ferguson 20 'Grey Horse'.

While the BM15/T15 was a light tractor, its relatively long wheelbase gave it a high tractive power despite its low service weight. It quickly became popular, especially when it was equipped with the more powerful B16C engine after about a year. The model, which was then renamed the BM425/T425 ('T' standing for 'Tractor', '4' for 'four–cylinder' and '25' for the horsepower) and was produced without modification until its replacement by the T320 Buster (although it was equipped with a five–speed instead of a four–speed gearbox towards the end of its production life). Initially, the T15/T425 and BM15/BM425 were easily distinguishable by their colours (the Volvo was red and the BM green); however, the BM version was also finished in red (although with the compromise of a green engine) after a couple of years in production. The Volvo and BM variants of the model were also named the 'Krabat' (which translates roughly as the 'Rascal') and 'Terrier' respectively.

The 1950s were dominated by the cold war between east and west, and the Swedish Defence Forces were heavily armed 'just in case'. The standard of equipment was improved even further when deliveries of the Volvo TL31 commenced in 1956. This rugged terrain vehicle (which is still in service almost 40 years later!) was based essentially on the L395 Titan truck. Equipped with a heavy–duty frame and all–wheel drive, it boasted impressive performance. The rounded Titan front was replaced by functional styling with straight, no–nonsense lines, while the steel cab by Nyström of Umeå was unique.

The TL31 (in the versions used to haul anti–aircraft and artillery pieces) was normally equipped with a 9.6–litre diesel engine with an output of 150 hp. However, a 185–hp turbo version was also built as a fire–engine for the air force.

The turbo engine had become popular in Volvo trucks and Penta also introduced turbocharging in its TMD96A engine from 1956 on. As an alternative, the KMD96A was available with a mechanical supercharger instead of a turbo. The TMD96A and the little–known KMD96A were the forerunners of the KAD42, Penta's market success of the 1990s, which actually boasts both features!

The B16 engine was used in the PV444, Amazon and P1900 cars, as well as in the BM425/T425 tractors and P2304 terrain vehicle. The unit was actually a modified B4B.

Actually a reinforced, all–wheel drive Titan, the powerful TL31 terrain vehicle possessed exceptional mobility.

JUST AS VOLVO experienced explosive development in the mid–1950s, Sweden itself underwent a transformation during the 20 years immediately following the Second World War. Once a country with a highly developed agriculture and a well–populated countryside, it rapidly became – for good or ill – a modern industrial society.

As agriculture declined in importance, forestry developed and took over some of its role. In this situation, it was hardly surprising that Volvo expanded the activities of its Bolinder–Munktell subsidiary to take advantage of developments.

Until the mid–1950s, mechanisation was practically non–existent in the forests. Although the unwieldy motorised saw had replaced the manual saw, the felled trunks were hauled out by horse and no worthwhile processing was carried out until the lumber reached the mill. This was the situation when the agricultural tractor was first used for forestry work, mainly during the winter when farming activity was at a low level generally.

However, since the tractor was not as mobile as a trained horse, vehicles with a high degree of mobility were needed. The four–wheel drive tractor was still a novelty, while the tracked type (in its original form) was too big, too heavy and too expensive.

In the early 1950s, the Swedish company, Östbergs Maskin AB (ÖSA) of Alfta, developed a

The Bolinder name was famous long before Volvo became a world marque and continued in use even after Volvo took over the Eskilstuna company. This photograph is from an exhibition held in Paris years before Volvo cars became common in France.

'half–track' which could be mounted on an ordinary tractor, greatly increasing its usefulness in the forest and enabling it to haul heavier loads than a horse in almost equally difficult terrain. One of the first tractors to be fitted with ÖSA half–tracks was a BM10. This was followed in rapid succession by growing numbers of BM and Volvo tractors, making them equally useful in field and forest. However, ÖSA was looking even further ahead and was already planning the next step towards the development of more efficient forest harvesting.

What, in effect, was the world's first purpose–built forest machine – the BM B230

The VISTA symbol is well–known. This version represents the competition for Volvo car technicians.

Championship for mechanics

1957 saw the introduction of the Volvo Championships for Mechanics, which was later to become an annual event throughout the whole of the Group. After being a 'Swedish championship' for a few years, the competition soon spread to include other markets.

Today, the competition is known as VISTA. It is held every second year within the car organization and every second year within the commercial vehicles organization. Several thousand mechanics take part in each round of the competition, and the winners from each country meet up for a study visit with the 'VISTA Club'.

Bamse ('Bear') – was unveiled in 1957. This was a comprehensively modified version of Sweden's most popular diesel tractor, the two–cylinder BM Victor, which had been introduced as a conventional wheeled model two years before. The ÖSA project was carried out in collaboration with and with the full support of Volvo, which supplied the chassis. The tracks were not mounted rigidly, but were carried on a number of spring–loaded support wheels, providing the driver with a more comfortable ride and ensuring that almost the entire track remained in contact with the surface, even when the ground was uneven. The arrangement afforded low ground pressure, optimum tractive effort and minimum ground damage.

The Bamse was normally equipped with a simple, yet efficient timber grapple, while a safety frame was fitted to protect the driver if the machine overturned.

The BM B230 was a major success and was to remain ÖSA's main product for many years to come. The long goods trains carrying Victor chassis to the ÖSA plant in Alfta left again with finished Bamse tractors, over 1,000 of which were built in six years.

That the Bamse was built exclusively for forest applications did not prevent it from gaining acceptance and becoming popular in other areas. In agriculture, for example, it proved ideal for ploughing when fitted with a three–point lift. The model also had a measure of success in export markets. For instance, it was used as a tractor unit in canal works in Holland, where ground conditions were particularly difficult.

The Bamse was available in two versions. The model was finished in 'BM green' until 1960, when a wide range of improvements was made. At this time, the chassis was lengthened and reinforced, while the ÖSA crane – normally an extra until then – was included in the standard specification and the model was finished in red (a change made to the BM tractor range about a year earlier).

Collaboration with ÖSA and Bolinder–Munktell was expanded in step with the success of the Bamse. In the years ahead, this was to culminate in the development of increasingly sophisticated machines for more efficient forestry work.

The BM Bamse was the world's first, small, purpose–built forest machine. Although built on a two–cylinder Victor chassis, it was equipped with tracks and finished in either green (earlier versions) or red (later versions). The Bear symbol used in the publicity for the model is shown at the top of the page.

ALTHOUGH THE PV444 enjoyed success throughout the 1950s, its freshness was beginning to fade after almost 15 years and public opinion was suggesting that the Amazon introduced two years before should now be followed up by a smaller Volvo in the lower price class.

However, when the PV544 was introduced in autumn 1958, it was obvious that Volvo's priorities in developing its 'new' car had been to limit the development costs and minimise the risk of teething troubles.

The PV544 was almost identical to the last and best version of its predecessor –the PV444L. Although the PV544 had a single–piece windscreen – a feature which distinguished it immediately from the earlier models – the front was the same as on the PV444L and the body styling was otherwise identical.

Some interior changes had been made to accommodate five passengers legally.

For several years, Swedish lovers of speed had envied the fact that their American cousins could buy the PV444 with the 70–hp B14A engine, and later with the 85–hp B16B. Now, at last, the sports engine was also available in Sweden, where the standard engine was the same as in the last version of the PV444 (and in the Amazon).

The PV buyer now had a choice of no less than four versions of the model. The standard version was equipped with a 60–hp engine and a three–speed gearbox, while the 'Special 1' featured the standard engine and a three–speed box, chrome trim on the sides, opening rear side windows and a choice of wheels. The 'Special 2' was identical to the Special 1 except for its four–speed transmission and, apart from its twin–carburettor sports engine, the 'Sport' version was identical to the Special 2.

Volvo had spent the three decades since it produced its first bus (based on a truck chassis) developing ever–bigger models. The type of small bus built on a small L34 or L42 chassis and fitted with a bus body by the customer himself had been neglected to some extent.

In the mid–1950s, the company was requested by one of its customers to supply a small bus suitable for service in suburban areas with light traffic. Development work on the model (nicknamed 'Sigvard' in honour of Sigvard Forsell,

Like all cult models, the PV544 provided the inspiration for a wide range of model cars.

The PV544 was an immediate success, despite the fact that the basic design was fifteen years old. Its popularity was largely attributable to the PV544 Sport which, with its powerful B16 engine and high performance, greatly enhanced the model's image. In the photograph on the facing page, the model is pictured in an idyllic setting at Vadstena, on the Göta Canal.

Volvo Employees' Association formed

In 1958, the Volvo Employees' Association was formed with the aim of providing food and other necessities to employees. With a staff of 50, the association was responsible for running 14 canteens and two central kitchens.

Shares for long-serving employees

For many years there was a celebration feast in August for 'those employees who had been with the company since its formation'. The first time this was held was in 1948 when the company 'came of age' – that is, when it celebrated its 21st anniversary.

The dish on the menu was, of course, crayfish.

In time, the Volvo management agreed that long-serving employees should receive additional rewards, so it was decided to give them shares.

The first shares were handed out at a celebration on 18 August 1958, when Assar Gabrielsson presented shares to each of the employees who had been with the company from the start. Finally, Gabrielsson himself was presented with shares from the hand of Gunnar Engellau.

Several years were to pass before these pioneers would receive five shares for 35 years of service, and another ten years before they were suitably rewarded for 45 years of service.

The record number of years of service is shared by the very first Volvo employee, Henry Westerberg, and Rune Hansson. Both these 'faithful servants' gave 55 years of their life to Volvo.

the company's chief bus design engineer) was initiated, resulting in the appearance of the B705 model in 1958.

A miniature version of the larger Volvo models, the B705 was built on a chassis designed in every respect to ensure a high standard of comfort. The mechanical components – the D47A engine and the unsynchronised, five–speed gearbox – were taken from the medium–sized L375 Starke truck.

The model became a valuable addition to the range, although not in its original form as a suburban relief bus. By the time it was finished, the customer had changed his mind and had decided to operate the routes in question with bigger buses which could double as simple, spacious tourist coaches at the weekend, providing transport to the beach or other recreational centres for people without cars.

Launched in a blaze of publicity, the little B705 bus never achieved real popularity. The picture is of Volvo's own test model, which was demonstrated to numerous bus companies.

Aquamatic from Aquavit

Volvo's pioneer in the USA, Nils Sefeldt, tells a story that, in the late 1950s, he received a visit in Houston from Volvo Penta's John Järnmark. Järnmark told Sefeldt about a fantastic invention which was soon to be launched – but it needed a name.

Sefeldt thought for a second or two, took one look at the bottle of aquavit on the table, and exclaimed: "Aquamatic!"

The year's only other engine development – the single–cylinder, direct–injection MD1 marine diesel – was minor. Production of the unit was located in Skövde for the first few years, then transferred to the company's plant in Flen, where the manufacture of small marine diesels continued until 1993.

The MD1 was a major success. Compact and light, its fuel consumption was minimal and the use of diesel made it much cheaper to run than a petrol engine. New versions of this significant unit, in single and multi–cylinder configurations, were introduced over the years.

In 1958, the powerful 10–litre turbo marine diesel became the first Volvo engine to be equipped with an intercooler (or charge air cooler), which enabled the output to be increased and the combustion temperature reduced, extending the life of the unit. However, the TIMD96A did not develop a significantly higher output than the normally aspirated TMD96A; in this case, the purpose of the intercooler was to permit continuous and reliable operation at a high power level.

The most important item of engine news came from Trollhättan. The RM6 engine built by Svenska Flygmotor for the Draken jet aircraft was a further developed version of the original Rolls–Royce design. The thrust delivered by the afterburner was now such that speeds well above the sound barrier were routine to the pilots flying the most powerful Volvo engine to date.

Svenska Flygmotor also introduced the VR3, a powerful liquid–propelled rocket which never reached the production stage. However, a refined version (VR35) was to be used some years later in a military robot.

The Penta MD1 direct–injection engine was revolutionary. The unit delivered the same or even better performance than its petrol–burning equivalents, at much lower fuel consumption.

With his many rally triumphs in the PV444/544, Gunnar Andersson did much to create the exciting Volvo image. He also competed later in the Amazon. In this photograph (taken during an event in Greece), he is pictured (right) with navigator Valter Karlsson.

Gunnar Andersson – the Champion

One of the most significant sales arguments to support the Volvo PV car following its introduction on the US market in 1955 was the fantastic achievement of the Swedish car on various race tracks in the USA. The Volvo PV car was entered in both durability and speed races and achieved such good results that competitors sometimes refused to take part if there was a Volvo in the starting line-up.

But it was not as easy to win car races in Europe, where the rally was a popular form of competition.
One of the most famous of all drivers in that particular discipline was Gunnar Andersson – affectionately called 'Volvo-Gunnar'. He had an outstanding season in 1958 when he became European champion. He achieved this through overall victory in the Swedish 'Midnight Sun Rally' and the Adriatic Rally in Yugoslavia, and by winning his class (in 3rd place overall) in the Acropolis and German Rallies.

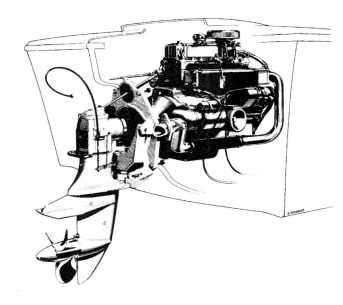

THE AQUAMATIC 80 was to be to Penta what the PV444 California had been to the car sector, the initial launch in the USA being followed by a period of fantastic sales growth.

The glass fibre boat industry had just been born and, with it, the opportunity of mass–producing leisure craft. However, the engine problem had not been solved. On the one hand, a big inboard engine with a fixed propeller and a separate rudder was too cumbersome and heavy an arrangement; on the other, the outboard engines of the day, although powerful, were extremely thirsty and noisy two–stroke units.

James R. (Jim) Wynne was the man who devised the solution of combining the inboard engine with an outboard drive, although he received little encouragement from the North American marine engine industry, which was committed to the outboard.

The world's first inboard/outboard (I/O) drive, the Aquamatic 80, became a huge success and established Volvo Penta on a firm footing in North America.

The P1800 was shown in North America in 1959, although it was to be another two years before series production commenced. Elegance rather than sportiness was the model's main selling point.

Following a meeting with John Järnmark, President of Volvo Penta USA, Wynne got in touch with Penta boss Harald Wiklund. As a result of their discussions, Penta acquired sole rights to the new 'I/O' (Inboard/Outboard) drive.

Penta unveiled its unique innovation at the 1959 New York Boat Show, using a modified 80–hp B16 engine as power source. It was the start of an era.

Volvo's image had changed appreciably between 1956 and 1959. Formerly a producer of modest–sized family cars (the PV444), the large four–door Amazon and, in particular, the PV544 sport, with its string of rally victories, had transformed the company into a manufacturer of products which many people dreamed of owning.

The P1900 is usually regarded as having been a major disaster. Although this was true of the technical and quality aspects of the model, the

Races helped to sell the Aquamatic

In exactly the same way as with the PV car some years earlier, races were used as a means of marketing Volvo Penta's Aquamatic in the USA.

Victories in various boat races were used as a springboard for sales of engines and transmission drives. For instance, the plastic catamaran 'Miss Aquamatic' won the Miami-Nassau Ocean Power Boat Race, which was generally regarded as being the world's toughest ocean-boat race. The margin of victory was 11 hours.

The engine, a BB70 developing 65 hp, also powered the boat which won the Orange Bowl Regatta, and in doing so set four new world records.

'plastic sports car' had actually been an outstanding success in PR terms. In the advertising campaign, the expensive (about SKr25,000) open sports car was featured in attractive colour pictures adorned by beautiful and more or less lightly–clad young ladies.

In discontinuing production of the P1900, Gunnar Engellau also decided that Volvo should build a new (second–generation) sports car, this time with a conventional steel body to enable Volvo to control and guarantee the safety and quality of the model. The Scandinavian climate, as well as the safety and comfort aspects, were major factors in the decision to develop a covered model.

Since Italy was the world leader in sports car design, the choice of an Italian designer, Frua, was a natural one.

The P1800 received its premiere in 1959, although it was to be another two years before series production commenced (at the time, Volvo was enjoying considerable success with its other models and spare production capacity was not available). As a result, the first models were built by Jensen in Britain.

Rather than a genuine, high–performance sports car, the P1800 was a special sports body mounted on a shortened Amazon chassis. Although the B18 engine (initially with an output of 100 hp) was bigger and more powerful than the B16, it was soon to be used in the Amazon and PV544 also. The gearbox was the same four–speed, all–synchromesh unit as before; however, the P1800 version was also available with a fifth gear in the form of electrically operated overdrive, affording a relatively high top speed while ensuring satisfactory acceleration in the four lower gears.

Although the P1800 was a sports model, it was equipped with two 'emergency' rear seats for two children or – on very short trips – for two adults. Although small, the boot was sufficiently big for the driver's and passenger's weekend luggage.

The P1800 received a major publicity boost as the car driven by 'The Saint' (played by Roger Moore) in the television series of that name based on the famous Leslie Charteris thrillers.

With the opening of Volvo's new plant at Torslanda, outside Göteborg, for production of the other models in the range, production of the P1800 was transferred from Britain to the company's older facility at Lundby.

The engine output was increased successively from the original 100 hp, first to 108 hp and then to 135 hp (in the 1800E powered by the B20 with mechanical fuel injection).

At the other end of the product range, BM introduced its new T350 Boxer and T470 Bison agricultural tractors. These two models were to become legendary; the basic design and components of the machines laid the foundation for the

The three-point seat belt – first in the world

In the mid-fifties, Volvo began to take serious interest in safety matters. A seat belt was produced in cooperation with Vattenfall, and from 1957 onwards this was sold on the market as an accessory. It was also fitted as a standard feature in the sport versions of the PV544 and Amazon car models.

In the summer of 1958, Volvo employed Nils Bohlin to become responsible for the development of safety features. Bohlin brought with him a wealth of experience of working on safety in the aircraft industry.

Just one year later in 1959, Volvo became the first car manufacturer in the world to offer a three-point seat belt as a standard feature in all its car models.

With its three–point seat belt, the Amazon was one of the world's safest cars.

Ewy Rosqvist – a ladies' champion

Being a vet driving about 30,000 miles a year on gravel roads in and around Skåne was obviously the right sort of background to have to become European rally champion in 1959. At least, that was the conclusion Ewy Rosqvist drew when she won the ladies' European rally title driving her Volvo PV car.

But Ewy brought more than experience of rally driving to the competition, she was also experienced in car orienteering and speed races on track and ice, as well as stock car racing.

The newly developed 'Terra–Trol' tractor hydraulics, with a pump capacity of 40 l/min and a lifting force of almost 4,000 lb, represented the most significant innovation in the Boxer. The system afforded automatic depth control in ploughing work.

Although the T350 Boxer replaced the BM35/T35, it featured a basically new chassis and a three–cylinder engine with a longer stroke (now 111 mm compared with 105 mm before).

The T470 superseded the BM55/T55. In this case, the engine had the same longer stroke but was a four–cylinder unit. (The designations of the new models were comprised of the number of cylinders followed by the approximate horsepower. However, this was only a temporary system introduced with the T425 Krabat/Terrier and was abandoned on later models.)

Initially, the two models were sold under both the Volvo and Bolinder–Munktell names. By now, however, all tractors were finished in red and the familiar BM green was a thing of the past.

Both models became multi–purpose vehicles. Apart from their agricultural uses, they were employed in modified form (sometimes painted yellow) as tractor units for dumpers, under the designations DD1015/630 and DD1520/1524 respectively.

The H10 wheel loader had been equipped with a crude body with the same front as the BM35/BM55. Now, the machine which was to provide Volvo with its real breakthrough in the building and construction site industry was introduced. This was the LM218, a model with an angular and highly distinctive body shape, and a much more ergonomic operator's station. Although based on the Boxer tractor, the LM218 was equipped with reinforced components.

The LM218 was succeeded later by the LM222/LM225, which were also based on the Bison.

Whether on the farm (above) or the construction site (below), the T470 Bison (left) and the T350 Boxer (right) were powerful models for their time.

A little known hybrid of the T350 Boxer and the LM218 was introduced a few years later. Known as the T675 transport tractor, this was designed mainly for heavy, slow–speed transport duties on industrial estates.

The T470 Bison was succeeded by Volvo's first four–wheel drive tractor, the T471 Bison. However, the new model was not a great success; the retrospectively designed all–wheel drive system lacked the robustness and reliability required to withstand rough handling by careless drivers.

Volvo trucks also underwent further development, the L385 Viking and L395 Titan becoming the L485 and L495 respectively. However, the modifications were minor and were only introduced successively as existing components were used up in production. Apart from the engine developments, the most significant changes were the improved engine and cab mounting arrangements.

Military vehicle production was prospering. Nils–Magnus 'Måns' Hartelius, the man in charge of this sector of the company's activities, foresaw that the Swedish Defence Forces would need a successor to the ageing Willys Jeep, which the

More than any other model, the LM218 provided Volvo with its admission ticket to the earthmover market.

The 15 longest-serving employees

Assar Gabrielsson and Gustaf Larson wanted to reward in some way those employees who had been with the company a long time. So the idea of giving shares after 25, 35 and 45 years of service was born.

The two founders also wanted to give a little extra reward to those who had been longest with the company. They believed that the 'Volvo team' consisted not only of employees, but also of supportive wives and husbands. For that reason, wives and husbands were invited to the celebration to mark the formation of the '15 longest-serving employees club' on 1 December 1959.

This club has lived on ever since. The active part of the club comprises the 15 employees who have given longest service and who are still active in the company. Today, it takes at least 42 years of service to become a member of this exclusive Volvo club.

When a member retires, he/she remains a member of the club with the right to attend the various functions which are organized – lectures, excursions, etc. Just under one hundred Volvo pensioners are members today. The two longest ever serving Volvo employees, Henry Westerberg and Rune Hansson, were active in the club, of course. Rune Hansson was the chairman for many years in the 1980s and early 90s.
Both achieved 55 years service as Volvo employees.

The first members of the exclusive 15 longest-serving employees club were:
Henry Westerberg
Gunnar Olsson
Gustaf Rhodin
Rolf Hansson
Axel Olofsson
Johan Härdin
Edvin Bäck
Frey Berg
Hugo Hansson
Nils Hellgren
Erik Larsson
John Krantz
Gösta Käck
Sven Johansson
Nils Palmquist

military had bought immediately after the war as a light terrain personnel carrier. To With this in view, he designed a light cross–country vehicle without a bonnet which, with its flexible suspension, short front and rear overhangs, and large, low–pressure tyres, could negotiate the terrain better than any comparable vehicle. Differential locks also contributed to the vehicle's excellent mobility.

In mechanical terms, the new vehicle was based largely on the Amazon. The B16, B18 and B20 engines were used in the different versions together with the standard, four–speed gearbox which, combined with a transfer gearbox, afforded eight forward speeds.

Known officially as the Laplander and popularly as the Cub, the new vehicle was produced as a small trial series (L2304) in 1959. Actual series production of the final version (L2314) did not commence until two years later and was to continue throughout the 1960s.

The Laplander was bought in large numbers by the Swedish and Norwegian defence forces. It became familiar from its service with the United Nations, with its distinctive white finish and blue 'UN' markings.

The Swedish Defence Forces acquired a worthy successor to the Willys Jeep with the introduction of the P2304/ L3314 in 1959. The 'Cub' was not only superior to all other terrain vehicles of the day, but is still holding its own after more than 35 years in service.

1960 WAS A YEAR of recovery for Volvo. The Amazon was selling in growing numbers, while sales of the ageing PV544 were steady and preparations for series production of the P1800 were proceeding. The heavy truck range had undergone a series of improvements the previous year.

As the only major product innovation of the year, the PV445 (now almost ten years old) was finally revamped (the PV544 had been updated in 1958).

The P210 was introduced at the beginning of 1960 and was favourably received. Although the Duett was now more than seven years old, its most successful period was still to come.

Although the single–piece windscreen was the most obvious change, the modifications under the skin were quite comprehensive. All of these improvements made the estate model more comfortable and a little more like an 'ordinary' car.

Volvo was now beginning to acquire a more well– defined safety image. Seat belts had been standard equipment in all of its cars since 1959. In 1960, the 'Volvo safety cab' – the components of which had actually been available on the market the previous year – was launched in earnest. Built by the Nyström company of Umeå, the cab was more than just a response to the new Swedish cab safety legislation, which came into force in the mid–1960s.

Gösta Nyström, founder and owner of the Umeå company, had long been lobbying for the development of a safer cab capable of withstanding an accident without deformation. Since his company's steel cabs were superior to competitive products in this respect, he naturally had a commercial interest in the introduction of the new regulations, which promised his company an opportunity of eliminating a number of its competitors.

In all, cabs from three manufacturers – Nyström, BeGe of Oskarshamn on the east coast of Sweden and the Floby company in Västergötland province – met the standards. Since then, innumerable truck drivers have escaped with their lives or avoided serious injury thanks to the unique Swedish legislation. In addition, the regulations have contributed to the enormous success in export markets enjoyed by both Volvo and Scania–Vabis (now Scania) since their introduction.

Svenska Flygmotor in Trollhättan continued its efforts to lessen its dependence on military contracts. In 1960, the company undertook the manufacture of turbochargers – a logical step since Volvo was the industry leader in turbo development and had considerable experience of turbine blade manufacture from its aero engine activities. However, it proved impossible to compete commercially with the huge central European manufacturers, who enjoyed the benefits of large–scale production. Thus, Volvo remained a user rather than a producer of turbochargers.

The Volvo P210 Duett van was a real workhorse. The orange–painted Swedish Telecommunications vans were familiar to a whole generation of Swedes.

The Swedish UN forces favoured white–painted Duetts as staff cars.

Arvika-Thermaenius

In 1959, Volvo acquired all the shares in Arvika–Thermaenius AB (AVA), a company whose main operations were the manufacture of combine harvesters and agricultural equipment. The company had factories in Arvika, Hallsberg, and Skurup. It was merged with Bolinder-Munktell in 1960. After that, the manufacture of combine harvesters was concentrated to Hallsberg, while the Arvika plant took over more and more of production of construction equipment. BM's combine harvester assembly plant in Flen was taken over at the same time by the Volvo Skövdeverken, and the overhaul of car engines was transferred there.

THE SWEDES ARE a peculiar race. While motorists in other countries have traditionally favoured practical four–door cars of standard type or exclusive coupés, the Swedes had long had a preference for impractical, standard, two–door models.

The P130 Amazon (the name was used only in a few markets for copyright reasons) was introduced in 1961. The basic models were now fairly closely grouped, with the new two–door Amazon between the worthy but obsolescent PV544 and the four–door P120 series.

Compared with the PV544, the main advantages of the new model were its greater roominess and more attractive appearance. However, neither the handling nor the performance had been greatly improved.

The performance of the Amazon had, admittedly, been significantly improved by the complete redesign of the B18 engine, which was now 2 dm3 bigger and had been modernised by the addition of features such as a five–bearing crankshaft. However, since the Amazon was heavier, its performance was only marginally better than that of the lighter PV544 (even the version equipped with the B16 engine).

In hindsight, it is easy to see that Volvo should have exploited the slimmer lines and more elegant appearance of the new version compared with the solid, four–door P120. This was not done for a number of reasons. Firstly, the new, exclusive P1800 (in effect, an Amazon with a sporty exterior) was due to appear shortly. Secondly, it was necessary to fill the gap at the lower end of the market to prevent manufacturers of small foreign cars (and Saab, with its updated 96 model) from taking advantage of the growing obsolescence of the P110.

As a result, the P130 Amazon was introduced only in a single–carburettor version with a 75–hp engine, while the four–door P120 was also available with twin carburettors and a 90–hp unit. It was to

Two elegant machines – a two–door Amazon and a twin–engined Piper aircraft (note the familiar symbol on the tail). The red finish indicates that the car was not built in the first year of production.

The B18 engine, one of Volvo's most durable products ever, appeared in 1961.

A period photograph from the early 1960s, showing a British–built P1800 at a BP filling station.

be two years before those buyers who yearned for a two–door Amazon Sport were afforded that option. Initially the P130 Amazon was available only in standard colours; the bright red finish was only introduced later at the same time as the Sport engine, as was the five–speed overdrive gearbox, which was available only with the B18D.

It was widely expected that the PV544 would also be equipped with the new, more powerful engine – and this expectation was duly fulfilled in what was to be the final version of the model. The 90–hp Sport featured in many duels between rally drivers such as the renowned Tom Trana and the legendary Erik Carlsson, his counterpart at Saab.

A new tractor known as the Buster – a model destined to become extremely popular in its size class – was unveiled in Eskilstuna. One of Volvo's notable successes had been the BM425/T425 Terrier/Krabat. A light, inexpensive vehicle powered by the reliable PV444/PV544 engine, this had proved ideal as a second tractor on large estates and as the main tractor on farms which had formerly been the domain of the horse. However, the Terrier/Krabat was a petrol–engined model –and most customers were now demanding diesel tractors in every class from the smallest to the biggest.

In reality, the Buster was merely a diesel version of the last petrol–engined model with the five–speed gearbox. In appearance, however, the

original grille was replaced by a divided, vertical mesh type.

Since the Buster Diesel replaced the previous petrol–engined model, a new petrol version known as the Buster Bensin ('bensin' being the Swedish for 'petrol') was introduced at the same time. Identical in appearance to the diesel, this was powered by the bigger B18C engine which, in reality, was an ordinary PV544/Amazon engine with a restricted speed and, as a result, an extremely low output.

The Buster Bensin was never used as an ordinary tractor, but was bought mainly by the Swedish Defence Forces, which had a long history of suspicion of diesel–engined vehicles, especially those of the lighter class.

The Buster Bensin was first to enter production (in 1961). The Buster Diesel followed a year later.

Development of the new RM8 engine for the Viggen fighter commenced in Trollhättan. The most powerful powerplant yet produced by Volvo, this enabled the aircraft to reach a speed of Mach 2. For the second time in Svenska Flygmotor's history (and the first time legally, since the company did not have a licence agreement on the first occasion), a US Pratt & Whitney engine provided the basis of the design. As before, Volvo used an afterburner of its own design, firstly because the company was (and still is) the world leader in the field and secondly, since the original Pratt & Whitney unit was a commercial aircraft engine without this power–boosting feature.

The B18 became popular as a competition engine and specially tuned versions were produced by many well–known firms. Ellemann–Jakobsen of Partille was perhaps the most famous of these.

The Volvo T320 and T400 Buster models became best–sellers among small farmers who wanted a small, modern, diesel tractor.

The Saint

Nowadays, car manufacturers will pay almost any amount of money to have their cars as a centre of attraction in a television series. Mainly as a result of a huge slice of luck and skilful use of an opportunity which presented itself, Volvo gained enormous publicity for its P1800 car in the early 1960s, just when it was most needed.

When the television series 'The Saint' (based on Leslie Charteris' books) was to be filmed with Roger Moore playing the leading role, the E-Type Jaguar had just hit the car scene. It was expected that 'The Saint' would drive such an attractive car.

But for various reasons there wasn't any E-Type car available for delivery and Jaguar couldn't produce a mock-up interior for indoor filming.

An enquiry was therefore made to Volvo, who quickly produced both a P1800 car and a couple of mock-up interiors. Thus Volvo's success was assured.

How much did Volvo have to pay for this television advertising worth millions?

Answer: Not a penny. On the contrary, the TV company paid the full price for both the car (more were to follow) and for the mock-up interiors.

The fact that 'The Saint', played by Roger Moore, drove a P1800 was a major factor in the model's international success.

P220 Amazon Estate.

VOLVO WENT UPMARKET in the early 1960s, when it began to concentrate more on the production of comfortable medium–class cars rather than small family models. Although the P210 Duett was popular and durable, it was far from ideal in terms of comfort and status. In short, a more luxurious model was needed.

The P220 Amazon estate was introduced in 1962. Unlike the Duett, it offered the same standards of comfort and roadholding as the corresponding saloon version (P120).

The new estate was American–inspired in its design. The rear doors were unique with their large side windows and straight top edge, while the tailgate was divided exactly as on US models, enabling long objects to be carried on the open lower half. As a further advantage, each half of the tailgate was only half the height of a conventional, single–piece tailgate hinged at the top.

Since the estate was very little heavier, it was almost a match for the saloon in terms of performance. Initially, customers had to be content with the B18 engine. Later, however, customers (Swedish as well as foreign) were offered the option of twin–carburettor sports engines. Since the model had a considerably higher load capacity than the P120, it was fitted with bigger tyres.

The Amazon estate had a fairly short life; the 145 – which was bigger, more comfortable and safer – appeared in 1967, only five years after the launch of the P220. Thus, the model actually disappeared sooner than the Duett, which was produced for a couple of years in parallel with the

145 as a more rugged and cheaper alternative for buyers who used their estates as work vehicles.

The L4751 Raske TIPTOP was introduced towards the end of 1962 for those commercial customers who required bigger trucks. Although based essentially on the established Starke/Raske models, the new truck was equipped with the very latest forward–control cab, which reduced the overall length, increased the cargo space and equalised the axle weights, all with the aim of maximising the legal payload.

The main innovation was that the cab could be tilted forward and upward (a facility which had been a feature of American cabs for decades),

affording greatly improved access for carrying out service in a rational and ergonomic manner. At a single stroke, one of the reasons for buying a bonneted truck was eliminated and the development of efficient forward–control models given a decisive boost.

The Raske TIPTOP cab had been developed jointly by Volvo and Nyström of Umeå. Although Nyström was still an independent company and would continue to be for a number of years to come, it was now working very closely with Volvo and the number of Volvo trucks fitted with Nyström cabs was diminishing fast.

The L4571 was well–equipped for its size. Power steering and turbocharging – two features which were still only options on the corresponding normal–control versions – were standard equipment.

Delivery and public service duties were the normal applications of the Raske Tiptop, although some of the vehicles were used as light construction site trucks.

Sweden was preparing for the changeover to right–hand traffic, which was to take place five years later, and Volvo realised that this would create a boom in bus sales. The doors on all existing Swedish buses were on the left–hand side and a high proportion of the national fleet was too old to justify expensive modification.

Launched as a 'right–hand traffic' bus, the B71 was to be a best–seller for many years to come. The 'right–hand' version with doors on both sides was especially popular since it could be used both before and after the changeover on 3 September 1967.

The B71 was a conventional bus bordering almost on the old–fashioned in its basic design. The 7–litre engine was at the front beside the driver.

L4751 Raske TIPTOP

However (for the first time in a mass–produced model), it was available with a turbocharged engine. The passenger capacity was extremely large, while the long front overhang provided adequate room for entrance doors at the front to suit one–man operation.

The first safety award

Over the years, Volvo has won many awards in recognition of its work in the field of safety. The first such award was presented to Gunnar Engellau in Copenhagen on 10 December 1962. This was when the Danish Road Safety Board awarded its special prize to a vehicle manufacturer for the first time – and it was also the first time the prize went 'overseas'. The prize was in a form of a statue by the Danish sculptor Anker Hoffmann.

The citation accompanying the prize quoted Volvo's unyielding efforts in developing the seat belt, even though there were many people then who believed that it would be more difficult to sell cars fitted with belts than those without.

The next award was won in 1964, when Gunnar Engellau was presented with the Swedish National Association for the Promotion of Road Safety's gold medal.

'Volvo På Väg' magazine

As time went by, Volvo felt there was a need for Swedish heavy duty truck owners and operators to be provided with information specific to trucks. To meet this need the company launched the (Volvo on the road) magazine alongside the Ratten magazine. The first issue was dated October 1962, which means it has been in existence more than 30 years. It also has an impressive circulation – almost 100,000 copies published four times a year.

OVER THE YEARS, Volvo has manufactured all kinds of remarkable vehicles possessing more or less total mobility. In this respect, the new tracked vehicle introduced in 1963 was in a class of its own. Probably no other Swedish vehicle has ever displayed the same unique capability of operating in every type of terrain as the BV202 ('BV' standing for 'BandVagn' of 'tracked vehicle' in Swedish).

Although Volvo had developed a tracked off–road vehicle two decades earlier, this had been a pure copy of a German model. However, the new model was an original design, which resulted in a substantial order from the Swedish Defence Forces and, subsequently, in several major export orders.

The BV202 was not equipped with steering in the true sense. Like the modern dumper, it was articulated, providing it with exceptional manoeuvrability and the ability to 'turn on a sixpence' about its own axis.

Conceived originally for the northern infantry divisions of the Swedish Defence Forces and designed for operation in snowy conditions, the BV202 was extremely light and equipped with wide tracks, affording an extremely low ground pressure and superb mobility over snow–covered ground, as well as in boggy and marshy terrain.

However, the designers of the vehicle (including Måns Hartelius in the early stages) also realised that an amphibious version could be built, provided that the weight could be minimised and the problem of sealing the underside of the craft solved. Their efforts were successful; the series–built BV202s were able to negotiate watercourses of all types, including lakes, carrying an infantry troop or a squad of commandoes on reconnaissance missions.

Since the project was to result in a serial order and the vehicles were to operate in the field for many years under difficult conditions, simplicity took precedence over complexity. Thus, the designers resisted the temptation to equip the vehicle with a propeller or water–jet system, relying on the tracks themselves for the necessary forward propulsion. As a result, the speed through the water was no more than a few knots. However, this was sufficient since the purpose of the craft was to negotiate the waterway rather than to operate at speed.

Since the light, twin–carburettor petrol engine was that used in the P1800 sports car, the 100 hp which it developed was more than adequate. However, the transmission was unique, consisting of differential brakes which assisted the driver in manoeuvring the vehicle.

The vehicle was built at the Bolinder–Munktell plant in Arvika.

The BV202 became well–known, especially from its service with the British army in the Falklands invasion in the early 1980s.

The Swedish National Defence Matériel Administration (FMV), the body responsible for

The L3304 anti–tank howitzer carrier – the lightest 'truck' ever built by Volvo – was developed to meet the needs of the Swedish Defence Forces. Although a direct development of the Laplander, it was equipped with an open body.

the purchase of defence materials for the Swedish Defence Forces, was already planning to introduce a new series of tracked vehicles in the late 1970s. At this time, regional employment was a major consideration and the Hägglund company of Örnsköldsvik, in the north of Sweden, was selected to build the new generation (BV206), with Volvo supplying some of the design documentation from the first series.

Production of yet another military vehicle, the 9031 anti–tank howitzer carrier (or 'Pvpjbil 9031' to use the military designation) commenced in 1963. This was not a completely new design, but was based on the L2304/L3314 Laplander, which had been in production since 1959.

The new terrain vehicle was armed with a light, Swedish–made, recoilless, anti–tank cannon. Since it was essential to provide a clear line of sight in front of the weapon and a free path for the blast at the rear, a rudimentary (although roofless) body

Nothing but wins in rallies

In 1963, Volvo drivers achieved the Grand Slam in rally competitions. Gunnar Andersson and Sylvia Österberg became European champions. The final event of the European Championship, the RAC International Rally, was won by Tom Trana.

The car all three drove? The PV544, of course.

These successes led to Volvo setting up a special competitions department in 1962, in which six people were employed on the development of racing engines and cars to be sold all over the world. The department was headed by Gunnar Andersson. He gave up racing with the PV car in 1963 to compete in the Amazon car, and this proved just as successful from the word 'go'.

Other 'names' who became linked with the Volvo racing stable were Carl-Magnus Skogh and Bengt Söderström.

was designed to protect the vital components. In the course of time, the L3304 was provided with a heavy anti-roll bar to protect the occupants from injury when operating in especially rough terrain.

Highly mobile terrain vehicles were by far the most interesting items of news in 1963. To coincide with its fiftieth anniversary as a tractor manufacturer, Bolinder–Munktell unveiled the prototype of its new multi–purpose vehicle, the Lisa, which was designed for three specific applications: as a military tractor unit, as a forest vehicle and as a powerful tractor for the increasingly mechanised farming sector.

The Lisa was an articulated implement carrier which was highly adaptable for a range of tasks. The engine was a type D50, six–cylinder truck unit mounted asymmetrically in the chassis.

Neither the agricultural nor the military sector had the resources to invest in an advanced machine like the Lisa at this time; however, a series of a few hundred machines, including a short version, or 'skidder', equipped with a crane and a longer, articulated version, also with a crane, for hauling logs, was built for forestry duties.

Penta expanded its marine drive range with the addition of the Aquamatic 180 – its most powerful I/O unit yet. The drive consisted of the tried–and–tested B36AV V8 engine used in the Snabbe and Trygge trucks, with a reinforced Aquamatic unit. The output was increased from 120 to 180 hp to provide boat owners (particularly in North America) with adequate speed resources.

Neither land, snow nor water could stop the BV202, the amphibian built by Bolinder–Munktell in Arvika for military forces in Sweden, Norway and Britain.

The Amazon was the mainstay of production at the Nova Scotia plant during the first few years.

Car production plant in Canada

On 11 June 1963, Volvo started up car production in Dartmouth, Nova Scotia in Canada. An old plant building was acquired and it took just three and a half months to refurbish it before being officially opened by Prince Bertil of Sweden. Volvo thus became the first European manufacturer to start up car production in North America.

When fully completed, the plant would have a final assembly capacity of 5,000 cars a year.

By setting up operations in North America, Volvo would also avoid having to pay at least some of the high duty charges imposed on imported cars and parts in Canada.

Sales of Volvo cars were successful in Canada and in April 1967 a new plant was opened, this time in Halifax, also in Nova Scotia. Capacity at this plant could be expanded to 10,000 cars a year. When the first Volvo plant in Canada was opened in 1963 it was the company's first own assembly plant outside Sweden. Prior to that a number of general agents had set up assembly of Volvo products – in Chile and South Africa (cars), and Morocco, Iran, Portugal, Holland and Belgium (trucks).

Two EVENTS IN the truck sector provided the most exciting news from Volvo, Göteborg in 1964.

The 'new' L4851 Viking TIPTOP was, in fact, not completely original, but consisted of the chassis from the normal–control Viking, together with the tilting cab from the L4751 Raske Tiptop introduced at the end of 1962.

The Viking TIPTOP quickly became popular and paved the way for the introduction of the F86 the following year.

The L4951 Titan TIPTOP proved a sensation when it was launched in 1964. Not only was the model the first European, forward–control truck with a longer cargo space and better weight distribution than its normal–control equivalents; it also boasted even better service access than the latter.

As a further advantage, the standard of safety was as high as in models with a long bonnet in front.

The L4951 Titan TIPTOP had actually been developed (under the designation P2859) for the US market, where tilting cabs had been common since the early 1950s. However, having decided to postpone its attempted entry into the US truck market for the time being, Volvo opted to launch the new, heavy, forward–control model in Europe instead.

The twin–axle L4951 and three–axle L4956 achieved success beyond the company's expectations; however, their greatest significance lay in the fact that they were the forerunners of the brand new F88, which was to appear the following year and which – although almost identical in appearance – was entirely new in mechanical terms. Since the Titan Tiptop cab had suffered from a series of teething troubles, the F88 was equipped with a high–quality cab from the outset.

Volvo's forward–control trucks with tilting cabs made an immediate impact. The L4851 Viking TIPTOP was the forerunner of the best–selling F86 (above), while the L4951 Titan TIPTOP (top) paved the way for the famous F88.

With a full trophy cabinet, Tom Trana in his Amazon (right and above right) was the most successful Swedish rally driver of 1964.

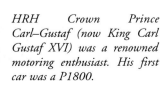

HRH Crown Prince Carl–Gustaf (now King Carl Gustaf XVI) was a renowned motoring enthusiast. His first car was a P1800.

Tom Trana European Champion

Volvo's domination of the European rally scene continued into 1964. The season ended with Tom Trana repeating his previous year's victory in the RAC rally driving his PV544. This time the win also meant he was European champion. He was also awarded the Swedish RAC gold plaque, which he received from the hands of Prince Bertil, the chairman of the club.

The Torslanda and Alsemberg plants

Volvo was never the same after 1964. Until then, Volvo had been a domestic manufacturer with almost all its assembly operations housed in the old premises in Lundby, Gothenburg, premises previously discarded by one-time parent company SKF.

With the completion of the new Torslanda plant, Volvo had secured a production capacity which would give the company a world ranking in car production. The fact that it took several years to build is some indication of the size of the plant, which was erected on virgin soil on Hisingen Island far from the hustle and bustle of Gothenburg city.

The inauguration ceremony on 24 April 1964 was one of the most impressive to have taken place in Sweden. Former Technical Director Gustaf Larson was one of the guests of honour (Assar Gabrielsson had passed away two years previously), together with King Gustaf VI Adolf. They travelled the length and breadth of the new plant with Gunnar Engellau in a restored Volvo ÖV4, the very first car produced by Volvo.

If the Torslanda plant was important, then the new truck plant in Alsemberg, Belgium, was an even stronger pointer towards Volvo's ambitions for the future. The EEC – forerunner of today's EU – became increasingly insular and Volvo was becoming increasingly keen to establish a local presence in Central Europe. The answer to the problem was Volvo's truck assembly plant in Alsemberg near Brussels, and it marked the final shift of Volvo from a position as Swedish to European manufacturer. The new operation in Belgium was organized as a separate company under the 'Volvo Europe' banner, together with the car assembly operation which was to open shortly in Belgium.

The Torslanda plant (above) provided Volvo with the production capacity which it needed for future expansion. The completion of the huge plant on Hisingen Island, outside Göteborg, took several years to complete. The picture on right was taken during the construction.

Below: The commencement of assembly at Alsemberg in Belgium was the start of Volvo's triumphal worldwide progress. The plant was inaugurated by Prince Bertil (below left).

Bolinder–Munktell of Eskilstuna was intent on complementing its product range with earthmoving machines of various types. While tractors remained the company's main product, these were now being used not only in agriculture, but also as motive units in small earthmovers.

The tractor–excavator – an agricultural tractor equipped with a shovel at the rear and a loading bucket at the front – was an exceptionally versatile unit which could be used not only for digging and loading, but was also extremely useful as a snowplough in winter. As a result, it was generally felt at Volvo, Eskilstuna that the company should produce a vehicle of this type.

The GM611 introduced in 1964 (the designation stood for 'GrävMaskin' or 'excavator') was basically a Boxer tractor equipped with an excavating shovel supplied by the established independent manufacturer, Vaggeryd. The standard fitting was a 250–litre bucket (a common size at the time). The GM611 was the first complete, series–built tractor–excavator produced by BM, although another company, Hymas, had commenced production of this type of vehicle four years earlier.

The next model, the GM612, still fitted with a Vaggeryd shovel but mounted on the more rugged LM218 truck chassis, appeared only a year later.

The last of this generation of three–cylinder excavators was the GM614, which was produced from 1964 to 1972. Although basically similar to its predecessor, the shovel (which could be angled to facilitate excavation along the walls of buildings) was now made by Hymas. The bucket capacity had been increased to 300 litres.

The road grader – which was sold in relatively large numbers – was one of Volvo's most profitable products ever. The first BM model (VHK55) was ten years old in 1964, an occasion which was celebrated with the announcement of a new generation. Known as the VHK310, the new model boasted a more spacious cab and better visibility, an improvement achieved by angling the windscreen, providing the driver with a view of the area almost directly below his station, underneath the shovel. The engine was still the familiar 6.7–litre diesel; however, the operation of the machine had been simplified by installing an hydraulic transmission.

Volvo's range of marine engines was expanding steadily. The revolutionary little, direct–injection, single–cylinder MD1 had become successful as an auxiliary engine. A version with an additional cylinder (named the MD2) was introduced in 1964, providing owners of open workboats or medium–sized sailing boats with the option of an efficient and economical power source/auxiliary unit.

The legendary GM611–GM 646 excavator–loaders broadened the product range of the growing Bolinder–Munktell Volvo company. The picture above is of a GM614.

Above right: The first articulated vehicle in the range, the SM667, paved the way for the almost identical DR631 dumper introduced a couple of years later.

Nyström's in Umeå

Once trucks had become more and more of a complete unit instead of just a chassis, there was a great need for close cooperation between the chassis producer and cab manufacturer. And when the forward control truck became generally accepted, the truck and cab were no longer two separate entities, but a single integral product. (The TIPTOP cabs had been developed in cooperation between Volvo and Nyström's.)

During the 1950s, the number of Swedish cab manufacturers had declined. And when the safety regulations with impact test came into force in 1960 there were only three body plants manufacturing truck cabs. Volvo worked closely with Nyström's in Umeå, while Scania-Vabis had close cooperation with Be-Ge in Oskarshamn. Floby was an independent manufacturer but soon concentrated on manufacturing special cabs which did not compete directly with those produced by the other two manufacturers.

It was a natural step for AB Volvo, therefore, to acquire the assets of Gösta Nyström's Karosserifabrik in Umeå in 1964. The company soon changed its name to Umeverken and became Sweden's biggest body plant.

The company;s wheel loaders became increasingly popular. Based on the T400 Buster tractor, the little LM422 was produced to meet the demand for smaller types.

LARS MALMROS

Lars Malmros has devoted almost his whole life to the automotive industry and closely-related industrial operations. He was born in 1927 and grew up in the Dutch Indies (Indonesia). When he was 12 years old he was given a scrapped car, an early 1920s Fiat, which he dismantled and partly put together again.

He graduated from college in Kalmar, and in 1951 he gained a Master of Science degree at the Royal Institute of Technology in Stockholm.

He managed to obtain various summer jobs, first working with construction equipment in the USA, then at Scania's drawing office, and then at Renault in Paris. After doing his undergraduate thesis – which was on the subject of MTM – he got his first job, as a methods engineer at the Volvo Pentaverken's foundry in Skövde.

In 1955 Lars Malmros was offered a job at Ford in Detroit, and he became responsible for building the company's first foundry in Sao Paulo in Brazil. In 1959 Lars Malmros received a letter from Volvo director Svante Simonsson, and this resulted in the Malmros family returning once again to Sweden. Here, up until 1963 he helped Swedish and Norwegian suppliers to rationalize their operations and expand in pace with the strong expansion which the car industry in particular was experiencing at the time.

Lars Malmros then carried out a survey which not only attracted a great deal of interest, it was also vital to Volvo's future. The issue at stake was whether Volvo should start producing cars and trucks within the new EEC, in which tariffs of up to 22-25 per cent were imposed on imported cars? And if so, where?

Lars Malmros calculated the transport and freight costs and found that train transport was too expensive. The products would have to be transported by sea, so any plant built would have to be close to a port. He visited every port between Hamburg and Dunquerque and found that neither the Germans nor the French were interested in Nordic competition. But the Dutch and Belgians were.

Lars Malmros finally found the place he was looking for in Ghent, Belgium; a not too costly site which many people thought was far too big. But he found someone sympathetic to his plans in the representative of the local council, van den Daele, who later became mayor of Ghent.

"*On one occasion we drew up an agreement on the back of a menu*", Lars Malmros recalls.

"*During the 1970s there were problems in Göteborg with labour disputes, high turnover of personnel, and many hours lost through sickness. Another assembly plant was needed. This was set up in Oostakker, outside*

Ghent, and this has been a worthy sparring partner ever since, not least when it comes to quality."

Lars Malmros also remembers how many people doubted that Belgian employees could live up to Volvo's standards. But history has undoubtedly confirmed his optimism, even though when the plant was opened wages and salaries costs were 60 per cent of those in Sweden, as opposed to 120 per cent today. Lars Malmros was appointed the first general manager of the plant in Ghent. He led the start of production of both the Amazon cars and the N (normal control) trucks.

By the late 1960s Volvo had designed and developed a new generation of diesel engines for trucks, and had also become the first European manufacturer to build forward control trucks. But there were many problems along the way and the truck operations were soon in a crisis situation. So it was decided to reorganize them into a separate division with its own responsibility for all business and industrial areas. Lars Malmros was brought home from Belgium to be the first general manager of the Truck Division, a position he held from 1969 until 1976 when he was succeeded by Sten Langenius.

In 1974 he was appointed Executive Vice president of AB Volvo and deputy to the chief executive officer with particular responsibility for the commercial vehicles sector within Volvo. Lars Malmros was instrumental in the development of Volvo's first medium duty truck range in the so-called 'Club of Four', in which Renault, DAF, and Magirus also took part. He also helped to set up Volvo's truck and bus operations in Brazil, and in the acquisition of the truck assets of White in the USA.

Under his chairmanship, Volvo BM ceased production of agricultural and forestry equipment to concentrate on developing and producing construction equipment. Today, this company, after ten years cooperation with the Clark-Michigan company, has now returned to the Volvo fold, and it is now called Volvo Construction Equipment, VCE. This company is a world leader in its segment.

The year 1984 saw Lars Malmros return to Ghent, where the operations now had a workforce of 5,000. He retired from the management of the company in 1988 to start up his own consultancy firm in Belgium together with his wife. Lars Malmros took an active part in the discussions surrounding the proposed merger between Volvo and Renault, and together with a friend from his youth, Håkan Frisinger, played a significant role in Volvo remaining an independent manufacturer.

The one millionth car and gearbox

In September 1964 there was a double celebration at Volvo. The one millionth car – a black, two-door Amazon – left the assembly line at the Torslanda plant. At the same time, the Köping plant celebrated delivery of the one millionth gearbox. The entire Köping workforce accompanied the crate carrying the gearbox to Göteborg to witness the installation in – quite naturally – the one millionth car.

IN 1965, THE TRUCKS underwent a degree of renewal never since repeated.

'System 8' was an ambitious renewal programme which, however, was also born of necessity since the products to be replaced had originated as far back as 1930s.

New features of a vehicle are usually more obvious from the outside than the inside. On this occasion, the opposite was true; almost every component of the heavy trucks had been basically redesigned, whereas the lighter models remained unchanged to a greater extent. In appearance, however, the new models resembled their predecessors.

More than just a marketing slogan, 'System 8' indicated that the changes concerned eight component groups. Thus, the engines were new, as were the gearboxes in the heavier models, while the rear axles had undergone further development, and the frames, steering, brakes, suspension and some of the cabs were all of new design.

The most important components were the new 7 and 10–litre engines, together with the modified 5–litre unit. Now twelve years old, the existing engines had reached the limit of their development and performance. This had been demonstrated embarrassingly in the course of an unsuccessful US launch in 1958–60, which had to be abandoned when the engines proved unable to cope with the uniquely North American conditions, including constant operation at maximum power and rough treatment from drivers.

The most radical innovations were made to the gearboxes, which subsequently became legendary. Volvo's gearboxes (all of which were produced in Köping) had always been noted for their durability rather than their sophistication.

The completely new R50 and R60 units were all-synchromesh, range–type units which were later copied by many competitors with varying degrees of success. The range configuration provided the driver with eight forward and two reverse speeds using just four lever positions. The eight speeds contributed to the large difference in ratio between

Compared with its contemporaries, the F86 boasted an ergonomically designed interior which contributed to the model's international success.

Facing page: The most powerful Volvo truck of the 1960s was the 6x4 tandem–drive N88, which was also available with an hydraulic torque converter (however, the unit shown inset is a later version of this transmission).

In Britain, Volvo grew from a newcomer into one of the leading truck marques in the space of a few years.

top and bottom gears, enabling the models to be used in applications which, in theory, were too diverse for a single truck. The new gearbox enabled the truck to be driven either slowly under difficult conditions or fast in long–haul traffic, on the flat or in mountainous terrain.

The F88 and F86, both forward–control models of the heaviest class and powered by 10 and 7–litre engines respectively, were the most famous System 8 models. Both models were highly successful in a number of export markets, making a significant contribution to Volvo's development as a leading truck marque in countries such as Britain, France and Australia.

The F85 (which was similar to but less powerful than the F86) and the N84 (a development of the 'old' L465 Starke) became relatively popular in Scandinavia and in certain other markets, such as Switzerland, as well as in countries outside Europe. Although bearing new designations, the F82 and F83 were actually identical to their predecessors, the L4251 Snabbe Diesel and the L4351 Trygge Diesel.

The numerous customers who preferred large, normal–control (N–type) models had the choice of the N88 (with a 10–litre engine) or the N86 (7 litre). Under the skin, these were basically similar to the F88 and F86. In appearance, however, they were identical to their predecessors, the L495 and L485, apart from the big new Mars symbol impressed in the grille.

Two years earlier, Penta had introduced its first high–powered Aquamatic model (the 180). Based on Volvo's own V8 engine, this was a heavy unit which was not suitable for use in leisure craft.

The company now introduced a new I/O package designated the Aquamatic 150 and powered by a Buick V6 engine. In time, this was followed by several, increasingly powerful Aquamatic drives, usually powered by six or eight–cylinder V8 units.

The last PV, and a new Favourite

The Volvo PV car was without doubt the car model which laid the foundations for Volvo to become the major car manufacturer it is today. The PV turned out to be the true 'people's car' on its domestic market, and it flooded the market, not least in the USA.

When asked which car model IS Volvo, all old Volvoites readily answer 'the PV'.

The last PV544 came off the assembly line in Göteborg on 20 October 1965. The Amazon had been around for nine years and had taken over the title of 'best seller'. There was still less than a year to go before Project 66 – the Volvo 144, that is – was launched.

The PV had played its part.

With the discontinuation of the PV, 21 white PV54S were put up for lottery among the personnel at Volvo's production plants in Göteborg, Skövde, and Köping, and also at Svenska Stålpressnings AB in Olofström.

The PV444 was replaced by a 'boarding step' model with a rather low purchase price: the Amazon Favourit. This featured a black finish, rubber mouldings around the windscreen and windows instead of chromium strips, and a three-speed gearbox. Thus Volvo made another attempt at creating a budget model. But customers said 'no' this time too. They bought cars not only for their own sake, but also to impress their neighbours.

New diesel engine plant in Skövde

During 1965 a new diesel engine plant was finally opened in Skövde. This secured the necessary levels of quality and manufacturing capacity ahead of the introduction of the new generation of engines which was perhaps the most important part of 'System 8'.

The new plant also relieved the pressure on car engine production, which had become stretched to the limit by the growing number of Amazon cars produced, together with the anticipated success of the forthcoming 144 model.

The workforce at Olofström celebrated the production of the last PV544 by decorating the body in bright colours and humorous messages.

The P1800 was built in Sweden from the mid–1960s on, with a vast improvement in quality.

Commended Amazon seat

The 1965 Assar Gabrielsson 100,000 kronor grant was awarded to Nils Bohlin. Bohlin not only introduced the three-point seat belt as a standard safety feature in Volvo cars, he also made a significant contribution as chief interior designer to making Volvo one of the recognized safest cars on the market.

The seat in the Amazon car, for example, was considered to be so safe that this was a major reason why Bohlin was awarded this prestigious grant.

Volvo Europa N.V. in Belgium

After Lars Malmros' search in the early 1960s in many parts of the EEC for a suitable location, the Volvo management decided in 1963 to produce both trucks and cars in Belgium.

Ever since 1951, Volvo's general agent in Belgium and Luxembourg had assembled cars and trucks at its factory in Alsemberg, south of Brussels. Up until 1963 more than 10,000 cars and 7,000 trucks had been produced there. Now, the plant would have a capacity of 3,000 trucks a year and 150 employees, and it would only produce trucks.

In Ghent, where the port, as was also the canal system, was extended out to the sea, a site covering 250,000 square metres was purchased. On this site, the capacity would be increased to 14,000 cars a year after just a couple of years of operation, and it would employ about 600 people.

The new plant was opened by Prince Bertil on 3 November 1965.

There was some measure of doubt as to whether the Belgians would be able to match the Swedish quality requirements, so key personnel were first trained in Göteborg, and subsequently the rest of the workforce in Ghent.

The personnel at the Ghent plant were obviously very quick and ready to learn, as the standard of quality at the Belgian plants has been and is still is at least as good as the standard at the Swedish production plants.

The victory of the PV544 in the famous East African Safari Rally was a major news item which greatly enhanced the car's reputation as a competition model.

The F88 made Volvo an international heavy truck marque.

Volvo – world champions

Success followed success for Volvo in rally competitions all over the world even in 1965. Several wins led to Volvo being hailed as world champions.

The most notable achievement was that of the Kenyan Joginder Singh in winning the East African Safari Rally. Other victorious Volvo drivers were Carl-Magnus Skogh in the Acropolis Rally, Tom Trana (for the second year running) in the Swedish Rally, and Klaus Ross (also for the second year running) in the world's longest rally, the 3,900 mile long Shell 4000 Rally in Canada.

Volvo succeeded in confirming its leading position as a rally car in many other national competitions all over the world.

Volvo City

From being pure countryside, a large area on Hisingen Island became the site of a car production plant in the early 1960s. A head office and other facilities were also built on the site.

As many thousands of people would be working at the plant and offices, Volvo wanted to build a shopping and service centre there. The Torslanda local council said 'no' at first, but in 1965 a decision was taken to build 'Volvo City'. By this time Torslanda no longer had its own local council as it had become part of the Municipality of Göteborg. So building permission was granted.

However. it was to take a few years more before the building was completed, and it was finally opened in March 1970. Volvo employees now had their very own supermarket, banks, post office, and dentist's surgery just a stone's throw from where they worked.

The first part of Volvo City, the 'Bilbiten 1' service workshop, was opened already in August 1968 though.

IF ANY ONE CAR may be regarded as a model for the concepts of active and passive safety in practice, it was the 144. Despite this, the 144 was not radically different in design from a model such as the Amazon, but was a comfortable four–door family car with a four–cylinder engine, designed for conservative buyers rather than those looking for a fast or exciting model.

However, the 144 was designed from scratch and was characterised by austere styling which was certainly not copied from any other model. In fact, the distinctive rear quarter light and clean lines of the model made the overall effect severe.

The braking system was one of the most distinctive features of the new top–of–the–range model. The Amazon had already been equipped with front disc brakes for several years. Now, the 144 was equipped with disc brakes all round – a radical advance at a time when this exclusive system was used mainly on racing cars or high–powered sports cars.

For maximum safety, the hydraulic system was split into two separate circuits, each acting on three rather than two wheels to maintain the necessary braking capacity in the event of an otherwise disastrous leak in the system.

The 144 was more spacious than the Amazon. A high standard of comfort was maintained by installing the same ergonomic seats which had been introduced a year earlier in the latter (and are still among the best on the market).

The 144 immediately became known as a safe and attractive family car (the picture shows a late version).

The 144 was reasonably fast – particularly when powered by the 95–hp sports engine. Nevertheless, Volvo had lost a little of its reputation for supplying 'more speed for your money' – an image which it had cultivated successfully with the sports version of the PV544 (although equipped with the same B18B unit as the new 144, the 544 had a lower kerb weight). The performance of the 144 was enlivened after a couple of years by the introduction of the B20 engine; however, it never became a really sporty model.

A new generation of buses was launched in 1966, paralleling the 'System 8' truck programme implemented the year before.

Undoubtedly the most important development was the launch of the B58 which, although based on the experience gained from the earlier pancake–engined B65 and B75, was a 'reborn' model of higher power.

Due to lack of resources, Volvo had never before developed a turbocharged pancake engine. As a result, the mid–engined bus had never become a competitive alternative for tourist coach applications; in short, the engine power was too low to deliver the high cruising speed desirable in large, luxury vehicles of this type.

At this juncture, Volvo had a stroke of luck. The Swedish Defence Forces were just then developing a new generation of tracked armoured cars (the PBV302, which was very similar to the American M113) and required a six–in–line, pancake–type, turbocharged engine for the purpose. To meet the need, Volvo was invited (at the expense of the military) to convert its new, vertical TD100 unit to a pancake configuration, providing it – practically free of cost – with a unit which was suitable for use in a mid–engined bus.

Comprehensively modified, the B58 was to become one of Volvo's most versatile and most popular buses ever.

The high–capacity, front–engined B57 was the conservative complement to the B58. The engine

This x–ray illustration of one of the last 144s shows the safe, rugged construction of the model.

The design of the conventional, front–engined B57 bus was based on over thirty years of experience of the type. The model became especially popular in the developing countries.

The Amazon 123GT was a fast, well-equipped car with the same performance than the P1800, but with considerably more space.

used in this model was the new 'System 8' 7–litre unit from the F86 truck, which was available both with and without a turbo.

The third – and last – new bus was the B54. However, this was not a genuine bus, but an adapted F85 truck powered by a six–litre engine and of relatively simple construction.

One of Volvo's most important tractors ever, the T800 superseded the earlier Bison model. Its

The mid–engined B58 was a modernised version of the classic B65 bus, with a powerful turbocharged engine of new design.

'The safest car in the world'

The Volvo 144 car was presented and regarded as being a car built with fundamental safety.

An all-welded, monocoque body with unequalled torsional rigidity achieved by the use of box section beams and reinforcements, as well as sturdy bottom and cant rails, were all safety arguments, as was also the rear wall of the luggage compartment that had been extended upwards.

Robust beam sections made of steel surrounded and protected the passengers, and a 'roll-over bar' was incorporated into the car roof to provide protection in the event of the car rolling over. Volvo's American organization made startlingly great play of this by producing a photograph showing seven Volvo 144s placed on top of each other – just to prove how strong the structure was.

Energy-absorbing front and rear sections – so-called 'crumple zones' – are even more important to safety.

The steering wheel was of the 'safety' type. The steering shaft was protected from being displaced in its upper and lower parts.

The magazine 'Ratten' wrote that 'the safety approach had influenced the appearance of the car right from the very first design stage'. This was a reference to the design of the driver area, in which the steering wheel was not allowed to be too close to the windscreen. The rear seat passengers would also be protected from being knocked against the rear window by the shape and design of the rear shelf.

Demands had been made in the USA for safety-type door locks. Accurate figures had been calculated relating to the forces the locks should withstand without the doors flying open during a collision.

The Volvo 144 met these demands by a wide margin. Ratten also carried a report of the exhaustive collision tests that had been performed before the model was presented.

In the issue prior to the introduction of the Volvo 144, Ratten presented 'Oscar', the test dummy which had been used for the tests. The rest of the issue was devoted to the Amazon, which was celebrating its tenth anniversary. This proved to be a smart 'campaign' for the older model before the new one was introduced.

Perhaps the most important safety feature of the Volvo 144 – which also won for Volvo the Swedish Motormännens gold medal – was the dual, triangular braking system. This car also had disc brakes all round. Prizes and awards positively rained over the car. It received praise in the press, and was voted 'Car of the Year' in Norway, Sweden, and Holland. The German magazine Der Spiegel chose it as 'Das Spiegel Auto des Jahres'.

Here are a few headings taken from press cuttings:
- The new Volvo is timeless and safe.
- The new Volvo is a triumph for road safety.
- The Volvo 144 'Car of the year' is a carefully designed medium class car.
- Quality, safety, and economy.

powerful six–cylinder diesel engine (the same as in the N84 and N85 trucks, but in a normally aspirated version only) made it an extremely high–capacity vehicle.

Characterised by straight lines and sharp corners, the forceful styling of the T800 was a departure from the softer lines of earlier Volvo and Bolinder–Munktell models. This styling was to characterise all subsequent Swedish–built Volvo tractors (with the exception of the very last model, the 2005/2105, which was further developed in collaboration with the Finnish company, Valmet).

The same powerful six–cylinder engine was also used in the LM840, the company's most powerful wheel loader to date. Although developed on the same principles as the earlier, rearward–facing machines, this model was of a considerably higher capacity, while its four–wheel drive afforded excellent mobility on surfaces of all types and in all weathers.

Bolinder–Munktell of Eskilstuna had enjoyed considerable success with its dumper models, which consisted of a modified agricultural tractor and a rugged dumper trailer with one or two axles. The new model represented a further advance in that it was not equipped with conventional steering, but consisted instead of two rigid sections connected by

Volvo's progress towards its present status of a world leader in articulated dumpers commenced with the introduction of the DR631.

an articulated joint. Four–wheel drive afforded excellent mobility.

The DR631 replaced the small DR630 tractor dumper, which consisted of a T350 Boxer tractor with a single–axle dumper trailer and a payload of 10 tonnes. The larger DD1524 tractor dumper (a T473 Bison with a twin–axle trailer) continued unchanged and remained in production for a couple of years more.

The DR631 achieved some success on the domestic market, although it was to be several years before Volvo was to attain complete domination in world markets with its epochal articulated dumpers.

A modified version of the DR631, known as the SM667, was built for forestry applications.

The powerful Nalle '(Teddy Bear') forest machine had been introduced some years earlier with satisfactory results. A smaller version (popularly known as 'Little Teddy'), a three–quarter track version of the T400 Buster, in which the front wheels and conventional steering arrangement were replaced by articulated steering, was introduced in 1966. Equipped with timber rails and a timber grapple, this was an efficient machine for small and medium–scale forestry operations.

The G410 excavator–loader was yet another

machine based on the small T400 Buster tractor. This smaller model was designed for lighter duties than the bigger G612. The three–cylinder Perkins engine delivered sufficient power to operate the hydraulics when excavating and using the front loader, and when travelling short distances between work sites.

Above and above right: Two machines which were used in forestry applications were the 'Little Teddy' and the LM840 wheel loader. The former was based on the little T400 Buster tractor. while the latter was a relation of the T800.

Right: A much more efficient machine than its predecessor, the T470, the T800 Bison was to become a classic and was produced in various guises until the mid–1980s.

Below: The G410 excavator–loader was a popular machine for light construction work.

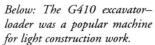

Volvo Bus Division

Volvo buses experienced an enormous upswing in the years immediately prior to 3 September 1967, the date when Sweden went over to driving on the right-hand side of the road.

What were previously rather peripheral bus operations suddenly found themselves in the spotlight in a way that was completely different to anything before. Following this rejuvenation the foundations were laid in 1966 for a separate Volvo Bus Division.

THIS WAS A YEAR of consolidation, in which all of the major innovations were a natural continuation of developments initiated in 1966.

The 144 soon proved to have been a fortunate development for Volvo. At home in Sweden it had been named 'Car of the Year' and owners of other makes in the same size class, as well as Volvo owners, had all taken the 1966 model to their hearts. It was now time to expand the range and to phase out those other models which were becoming long in the tooth.

Introduced in 1967 as a slightly cheaper and more popular model than the conservative four–door variant, the 142 quickly became the best–selling car in Sweden, bringing the era of the Amazon to an end. The P120 four–door Amazon was discontinued at the end of 1967, freeing the plant capacity which was urgently needed for production of the 140 series.

Introduced later the same year, the 145 estate was mechanically identical to the four–door saloon. However, the conventional estate body behind the rear doors (which were the same as in the saloon) afforded extremely generous cargo space. Unlike the P220, it was provided with a single–piece tailgate which opened upward, affording easy access to the goods in all areas of the cargo space.

The best–selling T350 Boxer tractor was superseded by the T600, which was similar in design, but smaller than the T800 introduced the year before.

However, there were relatively few new features under the skin since the T600 was basically a Boxer in a new guise. Nevertheless, the model remained a favourite, especially with Swedish farmers.

Long articulated buses were introduced on routes in the city of Göteborg, and as airport

The Viggen 37 fighter, which made its maiden flight in 1967, was powered by the Volvo RM8 engine.

28,000 accidents

'A dramatic vindication of the efforts of the Road Safety Board' was the comment made by a Swedish daily newspaper when the biggest ever traffic accident survey was carried out. Volvo presented the results of 28,700 accidents involving 42,318 vehicle occupants, and well and truly proved the worth of using a seat belt.

For several decades Volvo's accident research engineers were able to refer to the results of this impressive survey. It was found that the three-point belt prevented fatal injuries occurring at speeds as high as 100 km/h, while people had been killed at 20 km/h not wearing a belt.

This year, 1967, Volvo also started to fit belts in the rear seat.

And in 1968, head restraints were fitted to the front seats.

Gunnar Engellau presented the winner's prize in the competition to design the new Volvo head office.

'My Square Lady'

In 1967, as part of the major expansion of the Torslanda plant during the 1960s, Volvo presented a new head office.

A competition for architects had been announced in 1964, and the winning entry was submitted by Göteborg architects Rune Lund and Alf Valentin, who called their model 'My Square Lady'.

It was the first office premises in Sweden to be designed as an open-plan office from the outset, and it was the biggest open-plan office in Europe.

There has been heated discussion on the pros and cons of open-plan offices ever since. Many people find it hard to imagine working in any other type of office, while others would gladly move to another job simply to avoid being in such an office.

Nontheless, the model set the pattern for all office building within Volvo for many years. When the Car Corporation opened its Car Headquarters in the early 1970s, the open-plan offices in that building were twice as big as those in the Volvo Head Office.

Volvo's head office contained 20 open-plan offices, each with a floor area of about 1,000 square metres. The total floor area was 42,500 square metres. Several years later a fourth building– which was just as square as the original three– was added to the head office. Today, the office building is referred to as VAK, Volvo Administrative Office.

The 140 series was completed with the addition of the two-door 142 and the 145 estate.

Drivers – rather dirty people!

In 1967 a campaign was implemented under the banner 'Keep Skåne Clean'. This was followed by other similar clean-up campaigns along several roads and highways in the province.

The magazine 'Ratten' reported the campaign and made a number of calculations of all the rubbish and problems on the roads caused by drivers in Sweden. It also mentioned the enormous sums of money that were needed to clean up after drivers.

One of the most alarming pieces of information brought to light was that were as many as 100,000 cars dumped as scrap in the Swedish countryside.

Nation-wide warranty

Volvo's PV car warranty – and also later Volvia – had been so successful that Volvo decided that some sort of warranty should also be offered for used cars. A used Volvo car had a high trade-in value and more often than not cost as much as a new small car.

So, in early 1966, Volvo introduced its nation-wide warranty. This was valid six months for defects affecting road safety, six months for defects affecting functional reliability, and at least two years remaining of the PV car warranty.

coaches between Stockholm and Arlanda International Airport. These models were equipped with a steerable third axle, giving them the same excellent mobility as a conventional twin–axle city bus while carrying a considerably higher number of passengers.

In technical terms, the articulated models consisted of a B58 chassis with a shorter wheelbase, connected to its trailer by a joint manufactured initially by the Hägglund bodybuilding company (Volvo introduced its own completely new articulated models in the early 1970s).

The T675 industrial tractor and the redesigned T600 were two variations on the Boxer theme introduced in 1967. The styling of both was based on the big T800 model.

Volvo dealers have a wide range of products to offer, from cars to trucks and buses.

The right child seat affords protection for tiny passengers.

Most of the B58 articulated buses introduced in 1967 were equipped with the turbo pancake engine. However, trolley bus versions were also used in Switzerland.

Rearward-facing child seat

For the sum of 115 kronor, owners of Volvo Amazons and the new 144 were able to buy a revolutionary innovation – a rearward-facing child seat for children aged between 1 and 7.

This child seat had been developed by Volvo in cooperation with Bertil Aldman, a laboratory technician at the Swedish National Road Safety Board.
The child seat could be installed by unscrewing the entire passenger seat and turning it through 180 degrees. It was then fixed by means of special straps and a separate back plate in the turned seat.

Researchers had already demonstrated that children travel much more safely with their back facing the direction of travel, so it was natural for Volvo's technicians to concentrate on a child seat based on this fact of safety, even though it was not all that straightforward to install.

Even now, almost 30 years after the first child seat was introduced, there are many car manufacturers who do not invest in their own development of child safety accessories. Volvo, however, has consistently gone for developing child seats and cushions, fully in line with the company's safety policy.

Cooperation with Bertil Aldman continued for many years, even after he became Professor of Safety at the Chalmers Institute of Technology in Göteborg.

THE NEW, LUXURY 164 was a natural development of the safe, modern 144, which was now established as the leading model in the range. The passenger capacity, most of the body and the standard of safety were exactly the same in both the basic four–cylinder model and the luxury six–cylinder version.

However, the front end, including the grille and wings, was totally different. Although the rounded lines were not in complete harmony with the rest of the body, the styling gave an impression of power and status which reflected the character of this expensive model.

The major innovation in the 164 was the powerful, in–line, six–cylinder 145–hp engine (later equipped with fuel injection, the same unit developed 175 hp). Although the high–powered engine and, above all, the extremely high torque made the 164 a fast car, the heavy cast iron unit also made it heavy at the front. This luxury model was certainly not built for rallying!

Since the 164 was built largely from standard 144 components, the production cost was reasonable. As a result, the model sold at a competitive price which, although well above that of its four–cylinder sibling, was also considerably lower than those of its foreign (mainly German) competitors in the luxury class.

The four–cylinder model was equipped with a bored–out B20 engine at the time the 164 was equipped with the B30, making its performance comparable to that of the lighter Amazon before it.

The level of activity at BM in Eskilstuna remained high, new models for a range of applications being launched in rapid succession.

The new DR860 dumper was one of the most important BM products ever. In effect, this replaced the now–discontinued DD1524 model, which had consisted of a T473 Bison tractor and a driven bogie trailer. The earlier four–cylinder Bison was now replaced by a tractor unit which, like the T800, was powered by Volvo's six–cylinder, 5–litre

With the 164, Volvo added a genuine executive model to its range. The car boasted a powerful, six–cylinder engine, a luxurious interior and the same high standard of safety as the 140.

The B20 unit, which replaced the B18 in 1968, consisted of two–thirds of a 164 engine.

engine. The rear unit and dumper body were basically similar to those used in the DD1524.

As in the DR631, the front axle had been replaced by articulated steering, an arrangement which afforded unsurpassed manoeuvrability and superb mobility.

The DR860 quickly became a success, even in export markets (the DR631 had been sold mainly in Sweden), paving the way for the worldwide dominance which BM has since established in the dumper field.

Yet another legendary Volvo BM product saw the light of day in 1968. This was the SM668, an economical, high–capacity forest machine which replaced the familiar Nalle. Like several other BM machines of the same period, the new model (and its successor, the SM868) were articulated. The SM668 was developed in collaboration with Östberg Maskin AB of Alfta (which had been a

The Volvo plant in Brisbane has contributed to the company's strong position in the Australian market.

First truck assembly operations in Australia

In 1968, Volvo started up truck assembly on a modest scale in Australia, in a small workshop in Wollongong, New South Wales.

But this was not the first time Volvo had produced commercial vehicles in Australia. Two years earlier local production of the B38 bus had got under way.

Volvo plants in the Far East

Volvo's market drive in the South East Asia area began in February 1968 when a car assembly plant was opened in Kuala Lumpur in Malaysia. Initially, this plant employed 130 people, and the capacity was 2,500 cars a year.

Volvo opened an office to take charge of the operations in the area in Kuala Lumpur by forming a subsidiary company, Volvo Far East Ltd.

Later, other plants were opened in Thailand and Indonesia. A decision was taken in 1995 to start up assembly of Volvo 850 cars in the Philippines.

In 1993, bus production was started up in China, and in 1995 a bus plant was opened in Vietnam.

supplier to BM since the production of the BM B230 Bamse).

Volvo BM had a comprehensive and varied product range, the components of which could be combined in many ways, creating rational and efficient machines for areas in which Volvo had not previously been involved.

Although the MK690 mobile crane was based on the T600 tractor and the LM640 wheel loader, suitable modification and the provision of a long crane boom made it an economical and easily operated mobile crane of the lighter type.

Volvo cars were built alongside another make in Indonesia.

The mobile cranes manufactured by Volvo from 1968 on were among the company's least-known products.

A more powerful grader offering improved operator comfort was introduced in 1968, as was the landmark DR860 three-axle, articulated dumper – one of the vehicles mainly responsible for the prosperity of the present-day Volvo Construction Equipment company.

BOTH VOLVO and Bolinder–Munktell introduced new products during the last year of the decade.

The little Buster tractor had retained its old–fashioned rounded styling until 1969. The model occupied an important place in the range; at the time, however, Volvo did not have the resources to design either a completely new model or its own diesel engine in this size class.

Thus, like the T600 a few years earlier, the T430 was a revamped version of a current product.

Once again, the exercise was a success, the T430 gaining new customers and retaining the loyalty of existing ones. As the smallest tractor in the range, the model became popular both in the red agricultural version and in the yellow version for municipal and industrial applications.

BM signified its intention of becoming more deeply involved in the production of earthmoving plant when it took over the production of wheel loaders (and a large tractor known as the Parca) from the well–established firm of Aktiebolaget Svenska Järnvägsverkstäderna (ASJ).

The successor to the P1800, the 1800E, was equipped with the more powerful, fuel–injected B20E engine, making the model faster as well as beautiful.

The ASJ wheel loaders complemented the Volvo range ideally. Whereas Volvo's machines were derived from agricultural tractors, ASJ's had been developed originally as earthmovers.

Like their foreign counterparts, most of the ASJ machines (with the exception of the smallest model, the 654, which was soon discontinued) were articulated. The big 854 and 1254 loaders quickly became a valuable asset to Volvo dealers and were soon supplemented by the extremely powerful 1640.

Only one feature of the ASJ machines was not quite compatible with the Volvo range – they were equipped with Scania engines.

Intensive development work was undertaken without delay to refine and improve the various models, while the ergonomics and the standard of driver comfort were improved by modifications to the cabs. Volvo diesel engines built in Skövde and Eskilstuna were also introduced in all of the models, replacing the Scania units.

Volvo Truck Division

After long and difficult deliberations, the Volvo Truck Division was formed in early 1969. This created a decentralized truck organisation within Volvo which would be able to combine and stimulate the necessary resources, expertise and enthusiasm ahead of the expansion period in the 1970s.

Protest:
Volvo too good!

Wielding hammers and crow bars, eleven angry Volvo dealers attacked an eleven year-old Volvo PV544 in New York. They pushed the car over, and hammered and beat it until the sweat was running off them.

They did this because they believed Volvo to be too good. Yes, that's right – far too good. A car should not last that long. It should wear out and be replaced by a new one after a relatively short time. The profits to be made were too small if the car was of such good quality. The protesters were finally satisfied with what they had done. The car was in a terrible state. But one of them looked at it with some measure of doubt. He opened the door and crawled into the car, which by now was lying on its side.

Was it really done for?

He turned the starter key – and the engine flew to life.

Eleven dejected dealers shook their heads with a sigh of resignation. This unusual event was immortalized by the Sunday News in New York with the simple statement: 'Now you've seen everything'.

The SM868 forest machine introduced in 1968 became a market success the following year.

An 11 million kronor donation to Volvo's personnel for Sörredsgården

The Volvo Board first decided to donate five million kronor to AB Volvo's Personnel Foundation. The money was to be used among other things for building a conference and sports and recreation centre overlooking Volvo City. Before the end of 1969 the company had donated an additional six million kronor to the building of the 'Personnel House'. Planning and projection of the project got under way. The personnel magazine Luftrenaren announced a competition in 1970 to find a name for the building.

The winning name was 'Mobilen', ahead of names like Frida, Piggvaren and Volvogården. The winner, Ian Lundegard, won a stereo music centre.

Then followed a period of construction, and the house journal monitored every step that was taken. But for some reason the name Mobilen was never used again. Instead it was called 'Personnel House' up until the autumn of 1971 when it was renamed 'Sörredsgården'.

It was opened on 8 June 1972.

Accident Investigation Team and inertia reel belts

The biggest car news in 1969 was the introduction of inertia reel belts in the front seats. No-one could now complain that it was troublesome to put the belt on.

A major accident survey carried out in 1967 led to Volvo starting up on-going accident research in 1969. Initially, an accident investigation team for trucks was set up as a trial measure.

The following year Volvo's Road Accident Research Group was set up, of which the accident investigation team was a part. The group was divided up into sub-groups for each product group, but they cooperated closely with each other and shared their experiences.

The Road Accident Research Group investigates many thousands of accidents each year on a statistical basis. It studies photographs, damage claims, police reports, hospital journals etc – and interviews people who have been involved in the accidents. The accident investigation team is called out to all major accidents which occur within a certain radius from Göteborg.

Sometimes, crashed vehicles are taken to Göteborg for special studies to be made in the safety laboratory, and on other occasions Volvo's research engineers study serious accidents which have occurred far from Göteborg.

Reports are published regularly describing a special type of accident or damage, for example. All material is collected and analysed and all results are reported back to the design engineers.

Bolinder–Munktell was specialising more and more in earthmoving plant by the end of the decade – and yellow products were beginning to outnumber the red. Examples included the T430 industrial tractor (above and above right), the RM695 road maintenance machine (facing page) and increasingly bigger articulated wheel loaders.

Olofström part of the family

On 7 March 1969, Volvo purchased Svenska Stålpressnings AB in Olofström – which was then a subsidiary to Alfa Laval – and renamed it the Volvo Olofström Plant.

This company celebrated its 250th anniversary in 1985, which makes it the oldest company in the Volvo Group. Way back in 1735, merchant Johan Wilhelm Petré from Stockholm purchased the rights to build an iron works on the shore of the river Holje.

The operations there have undeniably varied over the centuries – agricultural equipment, coppersmith's workshop, paper mill, flour mills, saw mill, weaving mill, spirits distillery, liqueur factory, candle factory, and more.

In 1926, the company was owned by Separator. In addition to industrial separators, the company also started to produce kitchen sinks and other stainless steel vessels. Also that year, Chief Engineer Karl Granfors was in the USA to study the manufacture of enamel products.

Whilst there, he received a telegram from his managing director, Gösta Runnquist, demanding him to quickly find out all he could about manufacturing car bodies. Olofström had received a visit from two men, Larson and Gabrielsson, who had a serious mission. They were about to start up car production and wanted Swedish bodies.

Granfors came home to inform his superior that, in the USA, it took five years to produce press tools for a car. He was given six months to do the same.

He succeeded, and Volvo's car bodies, or most of the parts for car bodies, have been pressed in Olofström ever since. But it took until 1950 for the value of car bodies to exceed the value of kitchen sinks.

Karl Granfors and Assar Gabrielsson became very good friends and worked with a very open attitude – the first written agreement between Volvo and Strålpressningsbolaget was not written and signed until 13 years later.

The Olofström plant now houses the biggest pressing industry in Northern Europe, and it is by far the biggest employer in the region. It is a hypermodern company, with Volvo the dominating customer, of course. But it also sends a significant proportion of its production for export, particularly to the American automotive industry.

WHEREAS 1970 WAS marked by initiatives in the commercial vehicle sector, the car range underwent only the customary cosmetic changes.

The current truck models were equipped with more powerful engines towards the end of the 1960s, mainly to comply with the regulations governing the minimum permissible horsepower per tonne of train weight and to permit higher average speeds so that the vehicles were no longer a source of traffic jams. In this respect, Volvo was some way behind; its biggest engine was just under ten litres and the increasingly popular V8 was a type conspicuously absent from the range.

Volvo returned to the first division of truckmakers with the introduction of the F89 in November. Although the exterior of the new model was identical to the five year–old F88 (with the exception of the wider grille), it concealed a considerably more powerful 12–litre engine developing a gross 330 hp. The higher power once again enabled Volvo drivers to negotiate even steep climbs more quickly and to match the cruising speed of cars.

The new TD120 was an in–line, six–cylinder unit with a swept volume of 12 litres. The unit was actually part of the System 8 range introduced in 1965; however, it had been decided then not to introduce the new, more powerful truck until five years after the other products. At that time, Volvo had not decided whether to use a six or an eight–cylinder unit in the new model and was also unsure what the exact horsepower requirements of customers would be a few years down the road. Ultimately, it was decided to stick to the original plans and to make the engine a six–cylinder unit.

Developments since then have shown that the engine design team (headed by the legendary Bertil Häggh) had made the correct choice. While the V8

Volvo F89.

The last Amazon.

enjoyed a brief period of popularity in the 1970s, almost all new heavy truck engines since then have been straight sixes with swept volumes from 9 to 13 litres.

Powerful engines require powerful gearboxes. In 1969, Volvo had introduced a further developed generation of its range–type gearbox (under the designation '61') and these units were now made available, in 8 and 16–speed versions, in the F89. In practice, almost all F89s were sold with the 16–speed SR61 box since the engines of the day had a relatively narrow speed range and a high torque, requiring the driver to change gear fairly frequently.

The G88/G89 (in which the front axle was located further forward to comply with Swedish and Australian regulations requiring a longer

The last of the Amazons

On Friday 3 July 1970 Amazon car number 667,323 came off the Torslanda production line. It was pushed out by hand by, among others, managing director Gunnar Engellau and executive vice president Svante Simonsson.

Volvo featured in film on the environment

A film called 'Environment 70' was made for the European Environment Conservation Year in 1971. It was intended to be shown all over Sweden at symposiums and for educational purposes.

Volvo was chosen to be a good example in the film. One of the reasons for this was that Volvo was a forerunner in the field of emission control. Two years before legislation was brought in to limit the carbon dioxide content in exhaust emissions to 4.5 per cent, Volvo had already introduced emission control, which meant that the cars met the limit.

Volvo features included in the film were a 'bio-technological aid' in the paintshop, carburettor adjustment in the TC facility, apparatus for measuring air content, Volvo's boiler room and chimney stacks.

Open-plan offices were filmed as an example of a good working environment, as was also a selectograph – whatever that was – in the head office basement.

distance between the first and last axles) were introduced concurrently with the F89. Although the G series models won many admirers with their American lines, they were actually not as comfortable as the basic versions due to their shorter front springs.

Between 1965 and 1970, the F88 had been built with a sleeper cab only. Now, the F89, G89 and G88 were all available with the option of a sleeper or a short day cab without a bunk. In addition, the F88 was available with a short cab for those buyers who did not require an overnight facility or who preferred to maximise the cargo space.

The F89 and G89 were produced in almost unmodified form until 1977–78. The early versions of these models are recognisable by the absence of a roof hatch.

BM of Eskilstuna also unveiled a number of new products.

The three–cylinder, medium–class BM35–36/T35–36/T350 Boxer/T600 Boxer had been Volvo's most popular tractor for almost two decades. Agriculture had also become rationalised in that time; large–scale operations involving smaller numbers of more efficient personnel were common

The BB57 was developed to meet the need for easy–to–drive buses without a door ahead of the front axle. The model became popular in countries as far apart as Norway and Peru.

The two millionth car – Take two!

In the autumn of 1970 the two millionth Volvo car came off the production line.

The car, a yellow 144, was donated to the Red Cross, and was handed over to Secretary General Henrik Beer in Geneva by the then head of Public Relations Hans Blenner.

Shortly after, the magazine Ratten carried reports from Great Britain where the two millionth Volvo – yes, you've guessed it, a yellow 144 – was donated to an organisation engaged in building safe play-areas for children. The anniversary car was put up as first prize in a lottery, the proceeds of which went to the play-area organization. One cannot help wondering how cars were counted in the years 1970-71. Perhaps there was a third two millionth car? A yellow 144 in the USA perhaps?

and tractors offering higher standards of comfort were in demand.

Although the T650, which replaced the T600 Boxer, resembled its predecessor in appearance, it was largely of new design. The most important new feature was the considerably more powerful engine which, with its extra cylinder, was much smoother running. The T650 was a heavier vehicle which developed a considerably higher tractive effort and afforded more stable operation with various implements.

In terms of comfort, the new model was superior to its predecessor. This was due, in no small part, to the Volvo cab, which was now standard equipment (tractors were still being exported without cabs).

The T650 was ideal in size for most farms, although many users considered it underpowered for such an all–round vehicle. Some owners fitted turbochargers to boost the power. Since these non–BM units were not always ideally matched to the engine, BM introduced its own T700 with a turbocharged engine as standard after a couple of years. However, the demand for a four–wheel drive type was not pursued beyond the production of a few hand–built prototypes.

Since the new, four–cylinder D42 engine in the T650 was ideal for heavy earthmoving applications, it was also introduced the same year (1970) in the LM622/LM642 wheel loaders and, a year later, in the MK692 mobile crane.

Formerly a manufacturer of large tractors, Volvo now became involved in the production of smaller

The T650 (above and below) became famous for the 'odd' applications in which it was used, whether military, agricultural or industrial.

machines, for which there was a demand from farmers and local authorities alike.

However, the 'Mini' introduced by BM Volvo in response to this demand was not strictly a Volvo product, but was built by the Roper Corporation of the USA. Marketed through the ordinary dealer network, the model was available in both single–cylinder and two–cylinder versions, with a wide range of accessories, including everything from heated cabs to snowplough attachments, refuse collection units, and many more. As it transpired, the company's involvement in this area was of short duration. The dealers were un-accustomed to mini–tractors, while the comprehensive legal regulations applicable to 'real' machines applied equally to the smaller type, making the degree of adaptation required unacceptably high.

BM introduced its new LM845 wheel loader. Powered by the 112–hp Volvo D50B engine, this was the first articulated model designed and built by BM.

Safety training course on TV

In the spring of 1970, the Swedish Television Corporation recorded 15 traffic training programmes with Volvo cars and rally driver Carl-Magnus Skogh playing the leading role.

A survey had revealed that 90 per cent of car drivers considered themselves to be among the better class of drivers. In other words, there was (and surely still is) reason to question the judgement of car drivers. The training course surely had a vital function to fulfil.

The SM462 light forest machine (which was built from T430 components) and the LM 845, the first articulated loader of Volvo's own design, were two highly efficient vehicles.

Volvo unveiled one of its most famous cars ever, the 1800ES, in 1971. A refined version of the 1800E with an estate–type rear section, the 1800ES was actually a compromise developed to overcome the expense of designing, producing and launching a brand new sports car.

The 1800ES is often said to have been unique as an estate–type sports car. However, this is by no means true since several different models of the type were introduced around this time, especially in Britain, all exclusive and all (with the exception of the 1800ES) built in small numbers. The Reliant Scimitar and the Aston Martin shooting brake were two of the best–known examples and, like the 1800ES, were not particularly long–lived. Today, all of these models are highly prized as classic collectors' items.

The 1800ES was identical to the ordinary P1800 as far as the rear edge of the door. Behind this, Volvo's chief designer, Jan Wilsgaard, had added an estate–type rear section with a larger, opening tailgate. The rear seat in the two–plus–two seater could be folded down to create a long, low luggage compartment. In practice, the rear seat usually remained folded down since it was barely big enough for two children (or two very small adults).

Like the P1800, the 1800ES was extremely well equipped (leather upholstery was included in the standard version). In addition to the manual M46 manual gearbox, buyers had the option of a Borg–Warner three–speed automatic transmission.

Air conditioning was another accessory which was installed mainly in the high proportion of the cars exported to North America (for which the model had originally been developed). In Britain and Ireland, the car was often supplied with a retrofitted fabric sunroof.

Many of the 1800ES cars sold in Sweden were fitted with a tow hitch – an unusual feature in a sports car. It was undoubtedly the sight of the sporty model towing a small trailer which earned it the nickname of the 'fishmonger's car' – a sobriquet which was certainly not coined by Volvo's PR department!

Although popular, the 1800ES had a short life. In the event, it was a shortage of production capacity which decided its fate; the A Hall in the old Volvo plant was needed to produce the C300 terrain vehicle (production of which commenced in spring 1974), bringing the story of Volvo's only mass– produced sports car to a close.

Volvo Penta introduced a new, low–speed inboard engine for small boats. This unit laid the foundation for the production of the Albin O–11, an engine designed and built by Albin Motor of Kristinehamn. Volvo thereby took over the production of Albin's marine engines (although the latter continued in business as a supplier to Volvo).

Pehr G. Gyllenhammar.

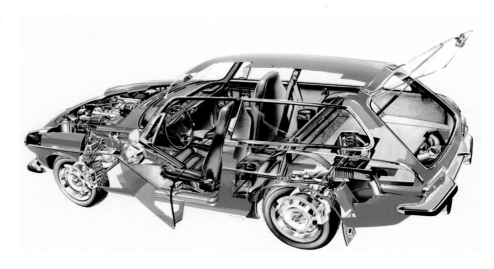

The 1800ES combined functional design with sporty lines and comfortable elegance.

PEHR GUSTAF GYLLENHAMMAR

Just 36 years old, Pehr G. Gyllenhammar came to Volvo in 1971 to succeed Gunnar Engellau as the chief executive of AB Volvo. Anyone who doubted the wisdom of choosing one so young, or the son-in-law of Gunnar Engellau, soon realised that Volvo's third managing director was the right man to take on this heavy responsibility.

In just a short time P G Gyllenhammar had won for himself a profound reputation as a business executive, not only in Sweden but throughout the world. He was voted the most popular person in Sweden year after year, and in the 1980s he instituted the European Round Table of Industrialists and was the first chairman of this illustrious group.

During the more than 20 years Gyllenhammar was at the helm at Volvo, many major business deals and ventures were implemented.

It all began in 1972 with the Dutch car manufacturer DAF. Initially this appeared to be a poor deal, especially in 1976 when the Volvo 343 was launched and got off to an unfortunate start. Also at this time Volvo was experiencing difficulties with its larger car models, where one of the major problems was corrosion. The entire car operations hung in the balance and were saved only by a brave decision to invest in a new model which was to be the Volvo 760.

Volvo's Kalmar plant, which was opened in 1974, received a great deal of attention at this time. This was well and truly a plant of the future. The principal feature of this fascinating assembly plant was that the focus was firmly on the people who worked there. A completely new way of producing cars was introduced at this plant and it attracted great interest from all over the world. This unique car production concept was developed still further with the announcement in the mid-1980s that Volvo was to invest in an even more modern assembly plant. This was to be built in Uddevalla, some fifty miles north of Göteborg. With the opening of both these new and progressive factories P G Gyllenhammar was praised for the faith he showed in people and their inherent capabilities.

Two 'deals' which attracted a lot of attention in the late 1970s, but which eventually came to nothing, were the agreement with the Norwegian government, which would involve extensive cooperation between Volvo and Norwegian industry, and a proposed merger with Saab.

Despite these setbacks, Pehr G. Gyllenhammar continued to have the backing of everyone. This was thanks in no small measure to his profound charisma. The early 1980s saw the next major 'deal' initiated by Gyllenhammar. This time it involved the take-over of Beijer Invest. Suddenly, Volvo had become a major player on the Northern European market in trading in oil, food, and pharmaceuticals. The deal also led to a power battle between Gyllenhammar and Beijer chief Anders Wall, a battle which Gyllenhammar won.

The next deal involved Fermenta, but before this could be implemented Volvo avoided being taken for a ride by the head of Fermenta, el-Sayed, by the skin of its teeth.

Volvo – and in particular Pehr G. Gyllenhammar – had enjoyed very good relations with Renault ever since the crisis in the car industry in the 1970s. That was when Renault acquired a minority shareholding in Volvo's car operations. These relations were developed upon, through the PRV joint venture, for example. This concerned producing V6 engines in France for Volvo, Renault, and Peugeot.

February 1990 saw the next deal to cause quite a stir in business and industrial circles; this time it was the alliance between Volvo and Renault. The idea was that close cooperation and a significant form of cross-ownership would eventually lead to a merger of the two companies. The decision to do so came in September 1993.

On 25 April 1990, P G Gyllenhammar handed over the job of managing director of AB Volvo to Christer Zetterberg, who also assumed the role of chief executive officer on 15 October 1990. This was to enable P G Gyllenhammar to have a better opportunity of working full-time on the alliance. He remained chairman of the Volvo Board.

Zetterberg himself was replaced by Sören Gyll on 12 May 1992, who had been brought in to steer the company through the alliance period and to tackle the difficult task of lifting Volvo from the depths of the recession in which the company found itself.

In late autumn 1993 there was increased opposition to the proposed merger with Renault, and this came chiefly from the engineers at Volvo who started to have doubts about the outcome of the venture. The main criticism came from former Volvo executives Håkan Frisinger and Lars Malmros as well as from a majority of Volvo's top managers.

At a meeting of the Volvo Board on 2 December 1993, the Board yielded to the massive criticism levelled at the proposed merger, and in front of an assembly of journalists from all over the world Pehr G. Gyllenhammar resigned as chairman of Volvo. Suddenly nothing had come of the merger which both companies had worked so hard over three years to achieve, and the top man at Volvo made a hurried exit from the arena, but with his head still held high. This brought the curtain down on Pehr G. Gyllenhammar's illustrious career at Volvo, a career which can be measured in terms of the increase in turnover during this period, from 6 thousand million to about 100 thousand million kronor. Another measure is the number of employees – from 40,000 to around 75,000.

The Albin O–11 acquired a high reputation and was perhaps the last representative of a long line of small, Swedish–built marine engines dating from the 1890s (not, however, by Albin or Penta).

Although Volvo Penta had already designed a small, two–cylinder, marine engine known as the MD6, this project was now shelved in favour of the Albin unit, which was produced at the Flen plant.

This was also the year that Volvo launched the direct opposite of the P1800 sports car in the form of the B59 city bus. The new model had an extra low entrance step to facilitate passenger boarding.

The B59 was the first Volvo bus since 1951 to be powered by a rear–mounted engine, an arrangement which was necessary to lower the floor level sufficiently and provide space for twin front doors beside the driver (the conductor was no more and passengers paid their fares as they boarded).

The rear–mounted engine was identical to the unit in the B58 and was installed horizontally, making the floor extremely low along the full length of the vehicle (apart from a slight upward slope at the very rear). All of the engine variants were turbos, with low exhaust emission and noise levels by the standards of the day. Thus, the B59 may be regarded as Volvo's first 'environmental' bus, although exhaust emission control did not become a matter of general public concern until after the major UN environmental conference held in Stockholm in 1972.

The chassis was of advanced design. The frame, which was extremely light, was not designed to support the full weight of the bus. Instead, it interacted with the rigid body so to minimise the kerb weight and maximise the passenger capacity within the axle weight limits applicable to twin–axle buses.

One of the B59's main characteristics – its wide lock and extremely small turning circle, which greatly facilitated driving in dense city traffic – was a function of the new design of front suspension. The wide lock was an essential feature since the B59 was invariably built as a long vehicle to carry a large complement of passengers.

An automatic transmission was usually installed to facilitate the driver's task. However, the model was also available (at least initially) with a Wilson gearbox made by the British company, Self Changing Gears (SCG), as an option for those operators of a more conservative nature or whose main priority was cost.

The B59 never became as popular as the pancake–engined B58, one reason being that it was designed specifically for city traffic and was unsuitable as a tourist coach (although a lone version of this type appears to have been sold to a French customer). As a result, it gained acceptance only in a small number of countries outside Scandinavia, mainly Belgium and the Netherlands. The B59 was built exclusively in Sweden, first at the Lundby plant near Göteborg and, from 1977 on, in the new busbuilding plant at Viared, outside Borås.

The early 1970s were prosperous years in the forest industry sector, with BM playing an active role in the development of new, more efficient forest machines. In 1971, it unveiled the first of a number of highly advanced machines known as processors, which enabled a single operator to fell and process trees, including crosscutting and delimbing.

Tailor-made in Italy

A car named 'Volvo Viking' attracted considerable attention at car shows in 1971.

Putting it slightly diplomatically you could say that this car would probably not be put on show today. But at the time it was considered to be a beautiful specimen of a car.

Based on a Volvo 1800ES, the Italian body designer Sergio Coggiola had succeeded in producing a different design for Volvo's sports car.

The Volvo Viking attracted considerable interest at the 1971 motor shows. It was one of the many designs proposed as a revamped version of the 1800E.

Volvo's first rear–engined model for twenty years, the B59, became a popular city bus in a small number of countries.

Volvokontakt

When the Volvo Staff Employees Union, VTK, was formed in 1939 it started to issue a magazine for its members. This was called 'Ljuddämparen'. To provide information about the 'Decathlon' competition which was organised by the union, a newsletter bearing the same name was also issued.

The magazine 'Ratten' had been in circulation since 1930. This was distributed to employees and other people interested in Volvo and its products.

August 1946 saw the two staff magazines merged into one with the new title 'Luftrenaren'. It was still produced for staff union members, but at the request of the Volvo management Luftrenaren became a house journal for all Volvo employees in Göteborg.

Yet another newsletter which provided news and information much quicker than Luftrenaren saw the light of day in 1964 . This was named 'Volvokontakt'. In 1971, Volvokontakt became the sole house-journal for Volvo employees in Göteborg. By this time, Ratten had developed into a customer magazine.

Volvo grew. The various companies achieved their own identity. The personnel needed more information, especially the type of information which Volvokontakt did not have the space or the capacity to provide. For this reason, local newsletters were produced. In the early 1980s, journals appeared at the Volvo Car Corporation and Volvo Truck Corporation. The question was raised as to whether Volvokontakt was needed or not.

The Volvo management was of the opinion that since there were as many as 35 journals and newsletters in the Swedish part of the Volvo Group alone, it was time to discontinue Volvokontakt.

A tough debate followed. The journal, along with 'Car News' and 'Truck Extra', went out of circulation in 1987 – only to reappear as 'Volvo Nu', a journal for Volvo employees in Sweden. But this was a time of drastic cost-cutting programmes, and Volvo Nu became the lone Volvo house journal.

When the economy started to recover again the cry went up for local information. Newsletters appeared at the various companies, containing information which never made it to the pages of Volvo Nu. Alongside Volvokontakt and Volvo Nu, a four-colour magazine titled 'Volvo Monitor' was published and distributed to employees in the latter half of the 1980s. A Flemish edition was published on a few occasions. Omnibus editions in English were printed every year.

In the early 1990s, a magazine 'Volvo Global' for all employees outside Sweden came into circulation. Another magazine 'The Leader' appeared at the same time, written for all managers in the Volvo Group. And there was an elegant magazine called 'Globetrotter' which was distributed to Volvo Truck employees.

Over the years, Volvo has always provided its employees with relevant information. There have been periods when the magazines and house journals have enjoyed considerable freedom of speech, but there have also been periods when they have been regarded as being the 'voice of big brother'.

The Club of Four

In November 1971, four European truck manufacturers, one of which was Volvo, announced that they
had entered into an agreement to cooperate on
developing, purchasing, and producing parts and
components for light duty trucks. Thus the 'Club of
Four' was formed.

This represented a step into a new market for Volvo,
as up until then it had concentrated chiefly on heavy
duty trucks. The members of the Club were the Dutch
manufacturer DAF (van Doorne's AutomobilFabrieken
N.V.) SAVIEM (Société Anonyme de Véhicules
Industriels et d'Equipments Mechaniques) a subsidiary
to Renault, and KHD (Klöckner Humboldt Deutz) in
Germany.

The first Volvo trucks to be produced in this joint
venture were the F4 and F6 in 1975.

Volvo carried out this test to demonstrate the unusual strength of the 140 body. The cars in the photograph had suffered water damage and were about to be scrapped before somebody suggested a better use.

The PRV co-operative

On 29 June 1971, Volvo, Peugeot and Renault made a
joint announcement that they were embarking upon an
extensive joint venture. The three companies had
planned to produce car engines in a jointly-owned
factory in Douvrin, not far from Lille in the far north
of France.

The investment was to total 400 million kronor, split
equally between the three companies. All other 'PRV
operations' were to be carried out on equal terms.
Development work was to be shared equally and
production carried on in a jointly-owned company.
The companies were, however, to cooperate whilst
remaining independent and competing with each other
on the market. They also agreed to take advantage of
other opportunities that may arise in the future
concerning joint projects.

After a few years, the plant would have the capacity
to produce 350,000 engines a year. In spite of this,
Volvo promised to increase the capacity of the Skövde
plant.As far as Volvo is concerned, the PRV co-
operative meant that there would be a concentration of
high-tech know-how and independent development of
certain engines and emission control. Another
advantage for Volvo was that it meant allocating part of
Volvo's considerable increase, and thereby the need for
more engines, to an area where there was assured
availability of manpower and which was closer to the
continental market areas.

The engine which the three companies had in mind
was a V6, manufactured partly from aluminium. The
first Volvo version, the B27 developing 140 hp, was
introduced with the Volvo 264 in the autumn of 1974.

The PRV co-operative continued up until 1990
when the Volvo 960 was launched with a new, in-line,
six-cylinder engine produced at Skövde, manufactured
entirely from aluminium and with a power rating of
204 horsepower.

A completely new generation of forest machines was developed in the early 1970s. In the event, however, only a few examples were built.

Works Council for employee participation

In May 1971, the newly appointed chief executive officer of Volvo presented his policy statement.

The introduction to that statement is worth repeating:

"We have been taught that it shall be difficult to bear adversity. I would claim that there is something that is even more difficult, and that is to bear success. Success makes us relax, makes us place demands, makes us forget that things can go against us, and makes us less watchful and less venturesome."

The rest of the statement contained some essential information on the subject of employee participation and right of co-determination. Pehr G. Gyllenhammar set up a Group Works Council comprising employee representatives, and these were granted quite considerable opportunities of participating in company affairs. The Council also included eight management representatives and twelve union representatives.

Volvo employees were also given the opportunity of participating in the work of the Volvo Board via their unions.

Gyllenhammar's initiative in this matter has since led to Volvo enjoying a good reputation for its open attitude towards its employees, and the company is often quoted as being a good example when it comes to employee participation.

In 1972, VOLVO ANNOUNCED that it was to acquire the car division of van Doorne's Automobiel Fabrieken (DAF) in the Netherlands. This was the first of a series of strategic acquisitions and joint ventures which Pehr G. Gyllenhammar had mapped out for Volvo over the next two decades.

The announcement caused surprise, not because of the proposed cooperation between the two companies, but because they were perceived to be so different, Volvo being a manufacturer of high–quality, medium–class cars and DAF a maker of small, functional models for use as suburban transport or as economical, all–round vehicles.

In fact, Volvo and DAF were not that dissimilar. Both were producers of trucks as well as cars, and both were based in relatively small countries, with a need to develop their export sales to finance rational, forward–looking product development on a sufficiently large scale.

Although less well–known than some of the industry's other innovators, Hub van Doorne (1900–79), the founder of DAF, was one of the true geniuses of the motoring world. He had founded his company in the 1930s to build trailers and had later expanded into terrain vehicles before unveiling his masterpiece – the DAF 600 car with Variomatic transmission – in 1958.

By the end of the 1950s, this small to medium–sized car was selling in increasing numbers and was a highly sought–after model. While the little bubble car was a thing of the past, Europe had not yet recovered from the war to the extent that there was any appreciable demand for larger models.

The 55 coupé was the most elegant and sporty model in the DAF range.

In effect, the DAF 33 was the last descendant of the ingenious small car which appeared in 1958.

Powered by a two–cylinder, 590 cm3 engine developing 22 hp, the DAF 600 was a spartan model, with space for the driver and three passengers. Its major feature was van Doorne's ingenious Variomatic transmission which, despite the simplicity of its design, was an automatic transmission providing an infinite number of speeds and minimal power losses, making the car extremely easy to drive in city traffic.

Variomatic transmission was used on all DAF vehicles, as well as on the first two generations of Volvo cars built at the Born plant.

However, it was not the ingenious design of the DAF car which attracted P. G. Gyllenhammar to

this relatively insignificant marque. Instead, it was a combination of Gyllenhammar's environmental awareness and the company's need to complement its product range which led the company to acquire 33% of DAF initially, a proportion which varied from a minority to a majority shareholding over the years.

When Volvo acquired its interest, the Dutch company's range consisted of the DAF 33 (the last development of the original DAF 600 and the more familiar 'Daffodil'), the DAF 44 (a larger model with the same two–cylinder unit as the DAF 33), the DAF 55 (a 44 with a four–cylinder Renault engine) and the DAF 66 (a 55 with a more powerful engine and a De Dion rear axle).

All of the models were basically two–door saloons, although the larger body was also available in an estate version. In addition, the DAF 55 was built as a luxury (at least in appearance) coupé with a low roof, while an open version of the four–cylinder model, known as the DAF 66Y, was also developed for the Dutch army around this time.

The company's truck designers were fully occupied with the development of several generations of new models for introduction in the late 1970s and early 1980s. Meanwhile, their aim was to maintain the existing models in a reasonably up–to–date and competitive state. As part of this programme, revamped versions of the L42 Snabbe and L43 Trygge (now bearing the suffix 'S') were introduced at this time. The F82S and F83S boasted a modernised front with a wide, black, plastic grille. The driving ergonomics had been improved by relocating the engine and gearbox so that the gear lever was beside, rather than slightly behind the driver, while the cabs were now impact–tested in accordance with the tough Swedish regulations.

Top: The DAF 66 estate was the most powerful and most practical of the Dutch cars.

Above: In appearance, the DAF 44 was the same as the 55 and 66 models. However, it was equipped with DAF's own two–cylinder engine (an uprated version of the unit used in the 33).

In other respects, the F82S and the F83S, with their fixed, forward–control cabs, were unchanged.

Although tractors were still an important part of its product range, BM was becoming increasingly involved in the production of earthmoving plant. The new LM1240 represented a decisive breakthrough for Volvo loaders. In terms of size, the model was in the upper medium class, the type bought by a large number of building and construction companies.

In the largest class, the LM1640 was replaced by the LM1641, whose most important feature was the Volvo 10–litre turbo diesel introduced instead of the earlier Scania 11–litre diesel.

Another heavy earthmoving machine introduced at this time was the powerful VHK510

The VESC signalled Volvo's intention of developing cars offering not only high, but the highest possible standards of safety.

Volvo Experimental Safety Car (VESC)

In 1969, several different countries had served notice that a whole range of safety legislation relating to cars would be forthcoming. Instead of studying the demands item by item, Volvo decided to build rolling-road laboratories, where most of the requirements could be applied to one and the same vehicle.

This work led to the presentation of VESC – Volvo Experimental Safety Car – in 1972.

This car was Volvo's answer to the ESV vehicles and ESV projects which were being built and started up in many places, particularly in the USA (ESV = Experimental Safety Vehicle).

VESC was not only a car filled with exciting safety features, it was also beautiful in design and was very similar to the Volvo 240 which was to be introduced two years later.

When the USA presented its ESV requirements in the form of 82 points, Volvo had equivalent or tougher requirements for 70 of these points. There was some uncertainty concerning nine points. In only four points were the ESV requirements tougher than Volvo's.

VESC was to withstand a crash barrier collision – as well as being run into from the rear – at 80 km/h, and also withstand a hefty roll-over. On that point Volvo's requirement was four times tougher than the ESV requirement.

The VESC had an engine design which is now standard in all Volvo cars, namely 'a force-steered engine. On collision, the engine is pushed downwards and under the car instead of being pushed into the occupant compartment.

Anti-lock brakes were included in the VESC, as were also automatic seat belts and air bags to provide protection in head-on collisions, and also protection behind the car occupants. The steering wheel was of a resilient construction which meant that it would be pushed in towards the engine compartment in a collision, and the front seats had head restraints with a pop-up function. So as not to obstruct vision during normal driving, these head restraints were recessed into the back of the seat where they could be folded up lightning fast in the event of a collision.

The success of its road graders prompted Volvo to introduce an extra heavy–duty model, the VHK510, with a 10–litre engine (the smaller models introduced before and after were powered respectively by 6 and 7–litre units).

Volvo's Environmental Declaration

At the UN Environment Conservation Conference in Stockholm in 1972, Pehr G. Gyllenhammar formulated Volvo's first environmental declaration. It stated that:

• Volvo has no intention of safeguarding the car at all costs or in all contexts;
• The car is, however, an indispensable means of transport;
• It is in Volvo's interest that the car is driven and used in such a way that it does not cause any damage or injury;
• Volvo now believes it is responsible not only for ensuring that its products are a functional means of transport, but also for ensuring that they function in a wider context – in our environment.
• Volvo cannot solve all the environmental problems associated with the car by itself. Society has main responsibility for developing our transport systems. But Volvo earnestly wants to and will actively contribute with viewpoints and proposed solutions;
• Volvo is convinced that a living and more human-friendly city environment can be combined with efficient transport resources. Society needs both.
• Volvo is of the opinion that utopian products of fantasy or a romantic return to nature will not solve the problems facing society. What is needed is simple and practical solutions that can be openly discussed and understood by everyone.

road grader. With a service weight of 16,600 kg, this was also powered by a 10–litre turbo diesel (earlier models were equipped 'only' with a 7–litre unit!).

Volvo Penta made considerable efforts to expand the range of applications of its large diesel engines.

The THAMD70B was actually a 1965 truck engine, now installed horizontally (a more convenient configuration in some instances) and equipped with an intercooler. The 7–litre engine was also combined (as the first big diesel used for the purpose) with an I/O drive in the Aquamatic DR70B/750. The '750' designation indicated that this was a completely new and more powerful drive, which expanded the range of applications of the Aquamatic far beyond its original capabilities.

Volvo's Technical Centre

The spring of 1972 saw the opening of Volvo's biggest single investment after the Torslanda production plant. This was the Volvo Technical Centre, known as VTC. The investment amounted to a then staggering 220 million kronor.

The building consisted mainly of several laboratories and workshops for research and development on Volvo cars. And not least important was the Safety Centre, where all types of collision tests, full-scale tests or simulation tests, could be performed outdoors under well-controlled forms.

There was also an ultra-modern emissions laboratory, test rigs for all types of material strength tests, a wind tunnel and a climate chamber, as well as a noise laboratory which was separate to the main building and built directly on the rock. All research, development and testing activities were supported by a state-of-the-art computer centre.

The engineers also needed space and they were housed in two large open-plan offices with a combined floor area of 19,200 square metres.

DAF – NedCar

During 1972 a deal was made whereby Volvo was to acquire on 1 January 1973 a third of the shares in the Dutch manufacturer DAF's car operations. The shareholding was increased in two stages. From 1975 the share was 75 per cent and the company became a subsidiary to Volvo; in early May 1975 the name was changed to Volvo Car B.V.

The small cars which were produced at the plant carried the DAF badge. But after a few years the main model was renamed the Volvo 66.

The extensive integration process of the European sales networks of the two companies had just been completed in February 1976 when Volvo launched its 343 model – the car Volvo really wanted when it decided to purchase the plant in Born in the far south of Holland.

The car was an immediate success and it was predicted to have a very bright future. But then came a succession of teething troubles. A large number of recalls had to be made, and its reputation was blighted for a very long time.

During these years the economics of these operations was not particularly good. More capital was needed. For some time the van Doorne family had retained part of its ownership but Volvo's shareholding was reduced to 55 per cent in 1978 by the Dutch government buying shares to give them a 45 per cent stake in the company.

There were two important goals for Volvo Car B.V. in the 1980s: to keep the Volvo 340 on the market for as long as possible, and to develop project Galaxy.

The Volvo 340 was further developed in the company's offices and development centre in Helmond, a few miles east of Eindhoven. Part of the work was also carried out at the Volvo Car Corporation facilities in Göteborg. The model was not discontinued until early 1992 and by then a total of 1.1 million cars had been produced.

The first product to come out of Galaxy in 1986 was a wonderful creation: a front wheel-drive sports coupé called the Volvo 480. This was followed in 1988 by a modern estate coupé, the Volvo 440, and the following year by a saloon variant called the 460. The Volvo 480 was taken out of production in 1995.

From 1981 the plant and other facilities became a State matter as Volvo sold another 25 per cent of its stake.

Sales of cars produced at the Born plant had gone well during all these years and production passed the 100,000 mark annually. This is more than Saab produced in any one year.

Great Britain became by far the biggest market for the Dutch-produced cars, but they became popular also in countries such as Sweden, Holland, Spain and France.

In spite of the large number of cars built during the 1980s, it was not enough to ensure self-financing in the future. The plant had the capacity to produce even more cars.

This matter was solved in 1991 when a third party was brought into the picture, the Japanese Mitsubishi. Volvo, Mitsubishi and the Dutch State split the ownership equally amongst themselves and renamed the company NedCar in January 1992. The intention was for Volvo and Mitsubishi to develop their own middle-class car models based on a common platform. The factory was refurbished and is now an ultra-modern production facility with a capacity of producing 100,000 cars of each make. At present, it takes 17 hours to produce a car at the plant compared with 26 hours for a Volvo 440 just a few years ago.

The task assigned to NedCar is to develop and produce cars, while sales and marketing are carried out in full competition within the respective Volvo and Mitsubishi organizations. In the near future both car manufacturers will also buy up the Dutch State's 33 per cent stake in NedCar.

The Japanese model Mitsubishi Carisma was presented in early 1995, and in September 1995 Volvo introduced the new Dutch Volvo car.

An entirely new era has thereby dawned for the Dutch organization.

RENEWAL OF THE truck range commenced in 1973 – a result of the dedicated efforts of the separate Volvo Truck Division formed in 1969 and headed by Lars Malmros.

The new normal–control N7, N10 and N12 actually comprised the second new postwar generation of trucks from Volvo, after the System 8 models of 1965. Since the latter had retained the appearance of their predecessors and had 'only' been equipped with new chassis components, the new series was to be of crucial importance to Volvo's image during the remainder of the 1970s.

The development of a bonneted series was not an obvious step, but was indicative of the company's aim of dominating the Scandinavian market. Forward–control models predominated in central Europe, as well as in Britain and Ireland, and the bonneted type was used almost exclusively on construction sites, where its robustness and lower overall height, combined with its superior mobility to the forward–control type when unloaded, were important advantages.

The 1973 N series was equipped with the same engines, gearboxes and final drives as the previous generation, but was completely new in other respects. Since the models had been developed exclusively for the heaviest applications, they were built entirely of robust components designed to withstand high stresses and heavy loads while operating under the toughest possible conditions on unpaved roads – or even in the complete absence of roads.

This robustness was mainly due to the new frames. Unlike earlier truck frames, the members were not of uniform thickness, but consisted of channel sections in which the flanges were thicker than the web, affording a high degree of strength and durability.

To withstand tough service, the electrical system

The new normal–control (N–type) truck became a classic which was to be produced for more than fifteen years. Safety was one of its main characteristics. Naturally, the cab was impact–tested to comply with the tough Swedish legislation.

During its production life, the N type underwent major changes, including more ergonomic cab variants and more powerful engines.

was completely redesigned and the brake lines were of glass fibre–reinforced plastic. Initially, the bonnet was also made of glass fibre; however, this was replaced in time by a conventional metal component.

The cab was a redesigned version of the safety cab already used in the N86/N88. This was a controversial choice for the beginning; while some drivers preferred it to the forward–control version, many others felt that it was unnecessarily confined (the N cab was narrower to increase the mobility of the truck and to protect it from damage in tight spaces).

Time was beginning to run out for the bonneted truck in both Scandinavia and central Europe as the proportion of forward–control models increased steadily. Outside Europe, however, in regions such as the Middle East, Africa and South America, both the N series and its successor, the NL, remain highly popular to this day.

The N series was produced in more or less unchanged form from 1973 to 1990. However,

some important modifications were made during that period, the first being the introduction of a new, more spacious cab in 1980.

A sleeper cab had already been introduced in certain non–European markets, in which N series models were used in long–haul as well as construction site applications. In 1986, the original front section, with its twin headlamps, was replaced by a new front featuring single, rectangular headlamps, while the 1965 gearboxes were replaced by a completely new generation of units.

Two different front axle configurations were used. The first of these was the standard arrangement in which the axle was located directly underneath the engine. In the second, which was used only in Australia and North America, the axle was located further forward to increase the legal payload in similar manner to the special G99/G89 models.

The Hällered test track enabled Volvo to test all of its vehicles – cars, trucks and buses – in total secrecy. The model pictured on the track is an articulated bus destined for export to North America.

Volvo 1800ES – just a memory

Fourteen years after the P1800 was presented at the Paris Car Show, the last 1800ES was produced in the autumn of 1973.

In 1964 the P1800 won an award for the most beautiful sports car at the 'Concours d'Elegance'.

The car could also be seen many times in the television series 'The Saint'.

A new variant, the Volvo 1800ES, was introduced in 1971, while production of the original P1800 was discontinued in 1972. So the 1800ES was produced one more year. In all, 39,407 P1800s and 7,530 Volvo 1800ES cars were produced.

That the 1800ES is just a memory is a qualified truth. Many of these classic cars are still on the road and command very high prices.

Hällered

For many years Volvo had a proving ground at Stora Holm a few miles from the Torslanda plant. It soon became far too small and too close to preying eyes on the look-out for secret projects.

Under a veil of secrecy Volvo had started to build an enormous proving ground covering a very wide area in the middle of the forests about 60 km east of Göteborg not far from the town of Borås. The placed was called Hällered.

The new proving ground was opened in early 1973 and its biggest attraction was an oval high-speed track. This track is six kilometres long and has two banked curves in which the cars can be driven at speeds of up to 200 km/h without the driver needing to touch the steering wheel.

The proving ground also had a 1,700 metre long endurance testing track which was partly covered by the worst possible road surfaces to vigorously test the vehicles which were driven along it.

There was also a comfort track with other types of obstacles that can be met on real roads, and also a skid track on which the cars could really spin round.

Another track, which is circular, is called 'Belgian pavé', which is made up of cobblestones. Each stone is at a different level. A particularly torturous track full of holes, pits and bumps is provided for testing heavy vehicles. There are also inclines with some fairly hefty gradients for performing starting and braking tests.

Penta had transferred its production of outboard engines to Electrolux in 1943, not because the latter was short of work, but because all available resources were required for the development and production of the B4B engine for the PV444, and the VDA diesel engine for the B51 bus and LV15 truck.

After an interval from 1966 to 1973, when the units were manufactured by the Nyman company of Uppsala, Volvo resumed the production of Penta and Archimedes engines (which had not previously been owned by Volvo, but had been acquired by Electrolux back in 1941).

This complement to the Volvo Penta was of great benefit to its dealers who, until then, had been unable to offer their customers a 'Volvo' outboard. Now, at a single stroke, they were provided with a complete range of units from 3.9 to 70 hp.

The U22, which was not a relation of the Penta U–22 of the 1930s, but was a direct descendant of the Archimedes BS engine designed in 1912, occupied a special place in the range, of which it remained part until 1979. Thus, the unit was produced in the same basic form for 67 years, making it unique in Swedish engine history.

The production of outboard engines in Uppsala proved to be just an interlude. American and Japanese makers were turning out outboards by the thousand at low prices to secure market shares at

Penta and Archimedes outboards were manufactured side by side at the Nyman plant in Uppsala.

Archimedes was not merely Volvo's 'second' outboard tradename. Dating from 1912, the legendary BS unit (below) was produced until as recently as 1979. Other models, such as the light 4–hp unit pictured at bottom right, were also produced in more recent times.

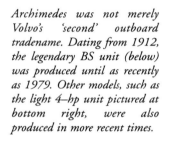

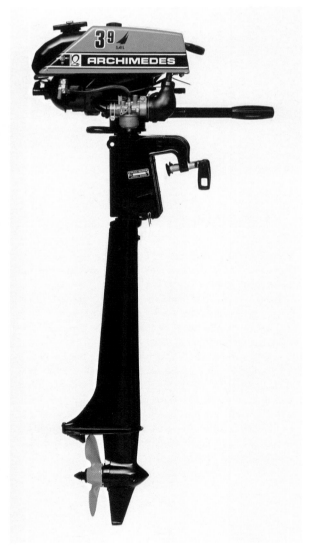

any cost, making it impossible for a Swedish maker of high–quality engines to sell its products at a justifiably higher price.

To produce a better outboard engine, Volvo Penta had built a new P series in small numbers. Nonetheless, despite the elegant design and advanced construction of the new unit, as well as its suitability for more rationalised manufacture, Volvo management took the decision to cease outboard engine production, and what may have been the last Swedish outboard engine was produced in December 1979.

Following a comprehensive reorganisation in 1971–72, when almost the entire top management was replaced, Bolinder–Munktell decided to mark the change by altering both its company and product names. From 1973 on, the company was known as Volvo BM AB and its products as Volvo BM.

Penta's outboards were used in the service of the law as well as in leisure craft.

Car factory planned in the USA

On 13 September 1973, Volvo President Pehr G. Gyllenhammar announced to a well-attended press conference in New York that Volvo would become the first non-American car manufacturer to build a car plant in the USA.

The total investment was estimated to be an enormous 100 million dollars. Construction was to start in 1974 and some preproduction would begin in late 1976. The plant would have a capacity of 100,000 cars a year. It would be situated in Chesapeake on the east coast of America in the state of Virginia.

A plant was built but no car has ever been produced there. The downturn in the economy in the 1970s effectively put a stop to those plans. But the factory was used for a period for producing buses, but even that was short-lived.

Instead, part of the Chesapeake facility has been used for many years for production of Volvo Penta marine petrol engines.

THE PRODUCTION OF cars is more than just a matter of finding buyers for the vehicles; it is also dependent on the production workforce. High–quality cars can be built only by motivated employees who enjoy good health. This was the background to the establishment of Volvo's 'plant of the future' at Kalmar in 1974.

The Kalmar plant was built, not just as an experiment, but specifically to create additional production capacity for the forthcoming 240 and 260 series.

In Kalmar, the traditional assembly line was replaced by a flexible production system in which the assembly workers operated in groups and were largely responsible for their own activities. The cars were conveyed, not along a continuous 'line'

The Kalmar plant represented P. G. Gyllenhammar's vision of safe, satisfying work. The facility represented a departure from conventional mass–production techniques.

Although the 244 was based on the 140, the influence of the VESC was clearly apparent.

moving at a constant speed, but on manually–controlled carriers moving at speeds adapted to the pace of work of the various groups.

Because of the new work organisation, the plant was circular rather than 'linear'.

The 1975 240 and 260 series introduced in autumn 1974 consisted both of new models and successors to the successful 140/160 series of the late 1960s. By Volvo standards, the 140 and 160 had remarkably short lives of only eight and six years respectively (although the 164 was produced for a further year, mainly for the US market).

Externally, the front and rear had been redesigned (the front, in particular, was reminiscent of the 1972 VESC). The 240 also incorporated many of the concept car features, including generous crumple zones instead of the unwieldy bumpers used on the last models of the 140/160.

The most important new features of the 240/260 series were under the bonnet. Although the B20 engine (which had been first used in the PV544 in the original B18 version) was used for a couple of years in the standard 240, it was the B21, with its overhead camshaft and increased swept volume, which attracted most interest when it was introduced. With it, Volvo now had a modern engine capable of meeting the increasingly stricter environmental standards due to come into force during the next couple of decades.

The luxury 260 was equipped with a completely new power source in the form of a 2.7–litre V6

Volvo Kalmarverken

On 30 June 1971, Volvo president P G Gyllenhammar announced that Volvo was going to build a new car factory in Kalmar. It would replace the state-owned Kalmar Verkstad, which was to be closed down.
When running at full capacity, the new factory would be able to produce 30,000 cars and employ about 650 people. The investment costs were estimated at 70 million kronor.
The factory was opened in 1974.
During the 20 years it served the Volvo Group, the Kalmar plant became a symbol of a more 'human' factory. The conveyor belt assembly line had been replaced by work being carried out on manually-controlled trolleys, while carriers running on loop circuits in the floor were used for moving the material around from group to group. The personnel were organised into self-managing groups, each with its own area of responsibility.
It was often Volvo's top of the range models which were produced at the Kalmar plant, and the standard of quality was very high. The employees were proud to work at the Kalmar plant, and the decision taken in 1992 to close down the Kalmar and Uddevalla plants came as a great shock to everyone who worked there. Despite all the protests which were made, the Kalmar plant was closed down in 1994.

developed and built in Douvrin, France, as part of the Peugeot–Renault–Volvo (PRV) project. Available both in a carburettor version and with electronic fuel injection, this was used in the Renault 30, Peugeot 604 and Talbot Tagora, as well as in the Volvo 264.

The standard model was the two–door 242, while the best–selling versions were the 244 and 264 four–door saloons which, initially, were built in DL (carburettor) and GL (injection) versions. One of the most popular versions from the very beginning was the 245 estate which, in time, eventually became even more of a legend than the beloved Duett of the 1950s and 1960s.

The 240 and 260 series were to be Volvo's main revenue earners for the next ten years and helped to sustain the company for a further decade.

In early summer, production of a new series of terrain vehicles was commenced in the old A plant at Lundby (where the P1800 and Duett had previously been assembled). These vehicles were purpose–built for the Swedish Defence Forces, and for public services such as fire brigades and power utilities.

The C300 series was designed and built under the leadership of Måns Hartelius. To ensure

The exclusive 244 and 245 (top and above) were niche models. Another Volvo product was used to demonstrate the load space available in the 245 (below)!

240 – safer than the 140

With the 240 model, Volvo introduced a new expression: handling. It's true that the 144 model had been presented as the 'safest car in the world', but the 240 was now considerably better. Volvo's PR staff demonstrated to motor journalists some years later at the proving ground in Hällered that driveability on difficult road surfaces was much better than with the 140. In fact, they did it so well that a Volvo 144 rolled over right in front of the cameras being held by their colleagues. Fortunately no serious injury was suffered.

The new 240 model had quite a few important new features. In addition to the handling properties, it also had a steering column with several collapsing points, and the petrol tank was located safely in front of the rear axle.

maximum durability and mobility, both the chassis and suspension were designed from scratch. Extra high ground clearance was afforded by the use of drop–gear hub–reduction axles, in which the axis of the wheels was below that of the axle itself, while a differential lock enabled the vehicle to operate even in extremely marshy and slippery terrain. Adequate power and high torque were delivered by the downrated version of the powerful B30 engine.

The body was box–shaped, without a bonnet, creating maximum space within a short overall length while shortening the wheelbase and minimising the turning circle.

Several versions of the C3 series – both two and three–axle – were developed, including open and covered versions, as well as a truck version with a cab and platform. Other prototypes included an amphibian and a four–axle 'Maxi' designed to replace the infantry's bicycle–borne troops.

In 1974, Volvo Penta unveiled its 100S sailboat drive which, although based on the Aquamatic principle, transmitted the power from the inboard engine through the bottom of the craft, reducing the space requirement in small craft. This arrangement enabled the two–stroke outboard engine to be replaced by a more economical, quieter and more reliable inboard unit.

The new drive was introduced together with Penta's last side–valve engine (MB10A), which had actually been designed by Marna of Mandal in Norway (a company which also a supplier of engines to Volvo), and was adapted to use existing components from the Volvo B20 engine and the tractor engines produced in Eskilstuna.

The sailboat drive was also supplied with Honda's little four–stroke engine, with an output of 7.5 or 10 hp (the unit was also available in an outboard version), and with various other small marine diesels.

The C303 terrain vehicle was used for more than military purposes. In 1983, it won the light truck class in the tough Paris to Dakar Rally.

Volvo Fritid

Boats, caravan awnings, skis, skates, ice hockey helmets and life jackets…

In 1974 Volvo acquired a new leg to stand on when Volvo Fritids AB (a sports and recreation company) was formed following several acquisitions of sports and recreation companies in 1973 and 1974.

Some of the companies and trade marks in this corporate constellation were Jofa, Triss and Ryd. Jofa's ice hockey helmet was perhaps the most well-known product as it protected the heads of most of the world's ice hockey players.

It was the aim of the company from the outset to expand internationally.

When it was formed, Volvo Fritids AB had a total workforce of about 750 employees.

The company did not achieve the success everyone hoped it would and was wound up after a few years.

Volvo Penta's popular sailboat drive has been produced in several versions. The picture shows a recent model.

The B55 double-decker became popular both in Britain and in other parts of the world, mainly in southeast Asia.

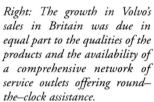

Right: The growth in Volvo's sales in Britain was due in equal part to the qualities of the products and the availability of a comprehensive network of service outlets offering round-the-clock assistance.

Both double-deck buses and trucks are built in the plant at Irvine in Scotland.

Irvine

Volvo trucks and buses had gained a strong foothold on the British market. The man behind the success, Jim McKelvie, wanted to establish Volvo even more strongly in Scotland, and thereby England, by setting up an assembly plant in Irvine outside Glasgow. This plant started up operations in 1974 with local manufacture of the most popular truck, the F86, andt also of locally designed versions and models of Volvo's trucks and buses.

The Volvo B55 became something of a flagship model. This was a unique double-decker bus designed in Scotland. Its design was based on a simple and conservative concept with the engine at the front.

The B55 was well received and several local transport companies, including companies in Glasgow and London, were soon putting the bus into service in city transport systems.

The Irvine plant is now one of Volvo's biggest European assembly plants for heavy-duty vehicles, and is chiefly responsible for production of right-hand drive trucks and buses. One of the models assembled there is the Volvo Olympian, Volvo's double-decker bus.

WHILE 1974 HAD been an important year for Volvo cars, the trucks were the main focus of the company's investment plans in 1975. Until then, Belgium had been the main site of truck production outside Sweden. Now, with the commissioning of a second truck assembly plant at Oostakker, near Ghent (the first plant at Alsemberg was not built by Volvo), Belgium assumed a dominant role in the company's European truckbuilding activities.

This move by Volvo represented a substantial investment in a design and production facility, with adequate space for future expansion.

The Oostakker project was not undertaken merely to increase the company's production capacity or to expand its presence in central Europe; it was also intended to revitalise Volvo's medium–heavy truck range, a class which had always existed in the shadow of the heavier models and which had been introduced originally as far back as 1956 and 1957.

At the time, however, Volvo did not have the financial or organisational resources to undertake the development of a completely new medium–heavy series on its own. As a result, it opted to collaborate with three other medium–sized European truckmakers – DAF, Magirus and Saviem – whose lighter models were also in urgent need of renewal. The main areas of cooperation were the development of a completely new, functional cab and new frames. Other components were manufactured by the individual companies themselves. This included the adaptation of the cabs, which were made in Germany. Only the Volvo cab was strengthened to comply with Swedish impact test legislation.

Initially, Volvo's light F range consisted of models with GVWs from 6.5 to 13 tonnes. The lighter models inherited the Perkins 3.9–litre engine, which had already been used in the

The 245 was Volvo's first true luxury estate car. Although the numbers produced were small, the importance of the model to Volvo's image cannot be underestimated.

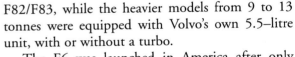

The F4 and F6 achieved greater success in international markets than any previous small Volvo truck.

F82/F83, while the heavier models from 9 to 13 tonnes were equipped with Volvo's own 5.5–litre unit, with or without a turbo.

The F6 was launched in America after only about a year (the USA was, in time, to become the largest single market for the series), contributing significantly to publicising the Volvo name in North America.

The F4 underwent major renewal at the beginning of 1978. Among other changes, the Perkins engine was replaced by the completely new Volvo TD40 unit, which was also used successfully as a marine engine, mainly in medium–sized leisure craft.

An F4/F6 was fitted with a Stirling engine a few years later. However, this unique variant never reached the production stage and was used only as a test vehicle by United Stirling in Malmö.

The new car series was expanded in 1975, making the Volvo range more comprehensive than ever. The introduction of the 265 highlighted the importance of the estate model as part of the range.

The estate had not yet become a status symbol, but was bought as a practical means of transport for large families or by unpretentious middle–class motorists. Anxious to alter the public perception of this practical model, Volvo embarked on a sales campaign which continues to this day.

In the advertising brochures, the Volvo 265 was presented as an exclusive car for successful people

on the move. Now, instead of plainly dressed young families on an excursion to the country, the pictures were of golfers unloading their clubs outside the clubhouse, hunters carrying expensive shotguns, immaculately attired tennis players or fishermen assembling their gear beside a rushing stream.

Volvo cars had always been used as a basis for special models, usually built and sold by independent firms without any assistance from the company. This was now changed; Volvo took more direct control and began to market more expensive specials, most of them custom–built in collaboration with bodybuilders Yngve Nilsson of Laholm.

However, the 264TE (the suffix denoted 'Top Executive') was built, not in Laholm, but by the renowned Italian body stylist, Bertone. The first 'stretch' limousine to be produced by Volvo, the model was essentially a 264GL on a 700 mm longer wheelbase. The 264TE was equipped with every conceivable luxury feature, as well as with two folding seats between the front and rear seats. The 'TE' designation was not new to Volvo, but had already been used on a luxury version (not a stretch model) of the 164 with features including air conditioning. The 164TE was sold only in countries such as Australia and Britain.

Sales of the 264TE received a flying start when the authorities in what was then the German Democratic Republic (otherwise East Germany) purchased about a hundred cars for the use of top

The new facility at Oostakker, near Ghent, was a model plant of the latest type. It is now the largest Volvo truck assembly plant in Europe.

party functionaries, together with a thousand or so 244s with the 264 front to make them resemble the bigger, deluxe models.

No less than three lengthened estate models were produced in 1975, all of them bodyworked by Yngve Nilsson in Laholm.

The 245T (in this case the 'T' stood for 'Transfer') was a lengthened 245 with extra seats between the front and rear seats to make it suitable as a taxi, school transport or shuttle vehicle for air crews.

A custom–built ambulance version of the 265 was produced for Scandinavian health authorities and emergency services. Whereas the Duett had occasionally been used as an ambulance, neither the

The Oostakker plant

When Volvo started producing trucks in Oostakker it signalled a new era.

Trucks (initially only medium duty models) were now assembled in Volvo's own new, ultra-modern plant.

The Oostakker plant also had its own design engineering department responsible for development of medium duty models.

Volvo was no longer a Swedish company with export sales, but a European company with a Swedish base.

Amazon estate nor the 145 had been a success in this application.

The 245 hearse was the third of the 'stretch' estates built in 1975. The longest of the three, its features included a high–capacity cooling system to enable it to be driven in slow funeral processions without suffering from engine overheating.

A somewhat dubious attempt to project Volvo as an exclusive coupé was made in North America. The model in question was either a 242 with the V6 engine from the 264 or a 264 with the two–door body of the 142. Known as the 262, this first example of Volvo's more expensive coupés was created without additional tooling costs. However, the model (which should not be confused with the genuine 262 Coupé) was produced for only a year or so before disappearing without trace.

The marketing experts were slow to appreciate the potential of the expensive two–door coupé, which was launched 'only' in a basic version as the 262DL, with the simpler level of equipment and the less powerful engine.

The saloon and estate versions of the Volvo 66 were two 'new' small Volvos. The cars were slightly modified DAFs which, following a couple of years of design modifications, now had the honour of bearing the Volvo name.

The T500 – the first new Volvo BM tractor for many years – was a medium–sized model which filled the gap between the little 430 Buster and the powerful 650 (the descendant of the Boxer).

The T500 was, first and foremost, an ergonomically designed machine with a completely new, soundproofed cab. As a small manufacturer, Volvo BM had not been in a position to develop its own engine in this size class. As a result, the model was powered by a Perkins engine.

The T500 became relatively popular despite the fact that the standard version was equipped only with two–wheel drive. After a couple of years, the designations were changed to 2200/2204 and 2250/2254, denoting the normally aspirated and turbocharged versions respectively (the '4' in the 2204 and 2254 designations indicated that the model was equipped with four–wheel drive).

By 1975, the quality and performance of the former DAF cars were such that they merited the Volvo name.

The 1975 262 was a powerful six–cylinder, two–door model built for the North American market.

VSG – not a great success

'The most important thing since the PV car warranty in 1954'. That was the verdict on the VSG – Volvo Service Cost Guarantee – when it was introduced in Sweden in 1975.

The VSG supplemented the 5-year PV car warranty, the 1-year new car guarantee without any mileage restrictions, and the 1-year warranty for parts and workshop repairs.

Volvo guaranteed that no visits to the workshop would cost the customer more than 300 kronor plus VAT during three years or up to a mileage of 60,000 kilometres. The VSG was naturally appreciated by those customers who bought Volvo's 1976 car models. But it was also appreciated by Volvo dealers.

It was soon found that the warranty did not yield the expected benefits – parts were replaced unnecessarily and costs rose in quite a disastrous way.

The VSG did not last all that long – it was superseded in 1978 by a 3-year engine failure guarantee – but it remains a monument to Volvo's continuous determination to demonstrate to its customers and the rest of the industry that 'Volvo-owners are slightly better off'.

At the same time, a 3-year workshop damage guarantee was also offered as an alternative to the 5-year guarantee which had been around since 1954.

The extremely wide tractor range from Eskilstuna included the latest addition, the T500 /T2200 (a late T2200 is pictured below).

Tractor assembly plant in Hällby

In 1975, the then Minister for Finance, Gunnar Sträng, and Pehr G. Gyllenhammar opened the new Volvo BM Tractor assembly plant in Hällby, just under four miles from Eskilstuna. At the time it was the biggest investment in the company's 143-year history. With a floor area of almost 65,000 sq. metres it became one of the Volvo Group's biggest single factories.

It was built as an assembly plant with a high degree of flexibility integrated from the outset. The tractor – which has been a main product for 62 years – began to face serious competition from the wheel loader, not as a volume product but as a generator of profits. Therefore, the company took steps to prepare for a future restructuring of the product mix. The Hällby factory was therefore able to switch conveniently to producing products other than tractors.

THE COMPLETELY NEW Volvo 343 was the biggest item of car news in 1976. With it Volvo returned to the size of car represented by its first major success – the PV444 – in 1944.

The model was the first major product from Volvo's Dutch plant (the former DAF works, in which the company now had a controlling interest). The Volvo 343 had actually been on the drawing board as the DAF 77 when Volvo acquired its interest in the Dutch company, a factor which almost certainly influenced P. G. Gyllenhammar's decision in this regard.

The product of Hub van Doorne's genius, DAF cars were ahead of their time.

In the technical sense, the Volvo 343 was a fantastic car whose rather conventional appearance belied its exciting characteristics.

Two the 343's main attributes – its driving simplicity and excellent handling – were familiar from two earlier models, the DAF 46 and the DAF/Volvo 66. The driving characteristics were the product of the unique, infinitely variable, Variomatic transmission, the first (and final) version of which had been used in the Dutch company's first model, the DAF 600, back in 1958.

The superb handling was attributable to the advanced De Dion rear suspension, a design which dates from the early years of the century and had remained unsurpassed ever since.

The extremely uniform front/rear weight distribution was achieved by locating the transmission at the very rear of the car, although the engine was mounted at the front (many of DAF's earlier rear–engined competitors had suffered from handling problems).

Initially, the 340 series was produced only with a Renault 1.4–litre engine which, although adequate for everyday driving, in no way did justice to the car's excellent handling. However, the 343/345 DLS, which was equipped with a Volvo 1.9–litre engine, was introduced in 1980. The option of a Volvo M47R gearbox as an alternative to the Variomatic transmission (which, despite its virtues, had many detractors) became available the previous year. The Volvo gearbox and the rear axle were built as a single assembly to maintain, and even improve, the favourable weight distribution.

The first 343s were available only in a three–door 'semi–estate' version; however, other body options became available in time.

The role of the 340 series in Volvo's history has been greatly underestimated. While the bigger 200 and 700 were the predominant series in several of Volvo's principal markets in North America and Scandinavia, the little Dutch–built cars were playing an important role in the company's expansion in other countries, such as Britain, the Netherlands, Spain and France.

An equally important, but less visible innovation had been introduced in the Swedish–built Volvos exported to North America. This was the catalytic converter (complete with oxygen sensor or Lambdasond), a device designed to produce cleaner exhaust gases than ever before. Cars fitted with the new feature complied easily with the strict emission control standards in force in California, which had led the way in this field for the previous two decades.

Since the catalytic converter (whose only outward indication was a discrete 'Lambda' symbol

The 343 was developed especially with young families in mind.

in one corner of the grille) can be used only with unleaded fuels, it could not be installed on Volvos built for other markets. However, cars sold in markets other than the USA were equipped with converters as an environmental protection measure as unleaded petrol became more widely available. In Sweden, for example, the feature became optional on models from 1987 on.

The 343 and catalytic converter were not the only car innovations announced in 1976. Two other models which were at least equally exciting appeared that year, although these were only test vehicles built to draw public attention to the need for more efficient and environmentally sound forms of transport.

Volvo – with its long tradition of building taxis, from the 1930 TS to the PV831 (which had

Despite its modest size, the 343 was a practical model with both saloon and estate features.

remained in production until 1956) – was one of the automakers invited by the New York Museum of Modern Art to participate in a competition to design the taxi of the future.

Short, wide and high with a spacious interior, the Volvo experimental taxi was designed to make passenger entry and exit as easy as possible, even for the disabled and elderly. The level of safety – both

3 million Volvos built

On 3 February 1976, yet another anniversary was celebrated. The 3 millionth car – a blue Volvo 245 – came off the assembly line at the Torslanda plant.

It took just over 37 years to produce the first million cars, another six years to produce the second million, and another five years to produce the third million.

As with one of the two (!) two millionth cars, the three millionth car was donated to the Red Cross in Geneva.

A car to set the norm in the USA, and an award-winner in England

In 1976, the American National Highway Traffic Safety Administration (NHTSA) carried out a series of various collision tests.

These tests were so successful that Volvo was acclaimed to be the car to set the norm for all future requirements relating to collision safety in the USA.

The NHTSA bought twenty-four 240 cars to perform tests to assist in drawing up the standards. The most difficult test consisted of a head-on collision in which both cars were driven at a speed of 75 km/h.

Evaluation of the impact to which the test dummies had been subjected showed that, in the same situation, human beings would probably have survived the crash. In the same year, Volvo was awarded one of the world's most prestigious road safety prizes, the Don Safety Trophy in Great Britain, for the level of safety offered by the Volvo 240.

trucks were soon to be accompanied by a bus with the introduction of the B609/B6F in 1976.

Although based on the F6 truck (the engine was the same 5.5–litre, 120–hp unit and the transmission the same five–speed ZF box), the new model was modified for use as a 'midi–bus' carrying approximately 30 passengers.

The B6F was in the long tradition of models dating from 1928, when truck chassis were first used as buses.

of the passive and conventional 'active' type – was high, as was the degree of protection (such as a special cashbox) afforded the driver against assault by passengers.

The car was powered by a 2.4–litre diesel engine of the precombustion chamber type. Designed by Ricardo, the four–cylinder unit was a forerunner of the TD30 introduced a few years later for marine applications. Compared with most other types, the exhaust gases from the precombustion chamber engine were cleaner, the low fuel consumption contributing to a reduction in carbon dioxide emissions.

The design competition was never intended to lead to series production. Indeed, economic considerations unfortunately precluded the production of Volvo's or any of the other concept taxis. As a result, the traditional London taxi remains unique of its kind and is likely to continue as such.

A further two concept vehicles were unveiled by Volvo only months after the New York taxi. Extremely small, but functional electric cars for urban use, these were tested under actual traffic conditions in the city of Göteborg. Although the vehicles performed perfectly, they suffered from the same disadvantage as all other electric vehicles – limited battery capacity, resulting in low average speed and restricted operating range.

Now a year in production, the Volvo plant at Oostakker, near Ghent, was turning out a steady flow of medium–heavy trucks on a daily basis. The

The development of its two electric cars indicated Volvo's interest in small, environmental models. This publicity photograph was taken in a studio.

The experimental New York taxi was designed to offer unsurpassed ergonomics and safety. Unfortunately, it never reached the production stage.

Rallycross and Volvo R-Sport

The same year the Volvo Cup for track competition was won for the last time, in 1976, Volvo decided to concentrate on the latest motor sport craze, rallycross.

Thus the Volvo Rallycross Cup was started, backed by the Swedish sales company VolvoBil. The cup soon became a great success both among drivers, race organisers, and the racing public. The cars were cheap to build and all Volvo models were highly competitive. For five years the Rallycross Cup was one of Sweden's most popular car competitions.

These successes led to Gunnar Andersson at the Volvo Competition Service department to take an extra look at the newcomer to the Volvo range, the 343. Under a veil of secrecy, a Volvo 343 was built to take part in the last qualification race before the Swedish Championships in 1977.

There was already a highly qualified driver 'in the house' so to speak. Per-Inge 'PI' Walfridsson, a son of a Volvo dealer in Torsby in the province of Värmland, was already one of the country's leading rally drivers and was keen to try his hand at rallycross racing.

The car came to the competition in an original brown colour and looked more like the ugly duckling. But PI surprised everyone by having the best practice time, and he easily qualified for the final of the Swedish Championship.

After the race, Sweden's leading motor magazine attached a striking title to the car and its success: 'Porsche killer'.

Shortly after that the decisive final of the Swedish Championship was competed for in Tomelilla in the province of Skåne. In front of TV cameras and thousands of enthusiastic onlookers, PI reached the 'A' final where he fought a fantastic battle with another Värmland veteran, Per Eklund, driving a Saab V4. It was not until the final bend that Per-Inge was able to make his move and win the race.

This success meant that Volvo decided to concentrate seriously on the 343 and the European Rallycross Championship.

In 1978, Volvo Competition Service was renamed Volvo R-sport, and the stable was renamed The Volvo R-team. After a couple of years there were four drivers in the team and successes were soon gained. In 1980, PI Walfridsson became European champion, while other Volvo drivers took 3rd, 4th and 5th places. Volvo drivers also won the Nordic championship and several Swedish championship titles.

Thus all the targets had been achieved and it was now time to retreat from the racing tracks, at least for the time being.

Its rallycross activities focused Volvo's attention increasingly on the performance aspects of its cars.

Success for Penta in World Championship

In 1976, Volvo Penta entered in Class OE in the World Championship for outboard engine boats for the first time against the established world elite with engines such as the OMC and Mercury. The debut was made in a race in Italy which consisted of four heats, with some doubtful rules even from the training sessions.

Several drivers drove boats powered by Volvo Penta engines, but Archimedes was also well represented with three second places. Volvo Penta was even more successful, recording two heat victories and several placings on the victory stand.

But it was an Italian driver with a Mercury engine who won overall victory in the World Championship round following a scandalous decision by the judges. But Volvo Penta had arrived and well and truly succeeded in putting the fright up its competitors even in the first race.

The B6 was the first small to medium-sized bus for many years. It was based largely on F6 truck components.

THE INTRODUCTION OF the F10 and F12 in 1977 was the most important truck development in the latter half of the century. The new models were designed as an integrated whole, in which every aspect and function had been considered.

Ergonomics and safety were the key concepts of the '7000' project (as the project was called during the development phase), not merely out of concern for the thousands of truckers who would drive the new models, but also for the hauliers and the owners of the cargoes. The entire F10/F12 range was based on the premise that an alert, wide–awake and well–motivated driver is a safer and more economical driver than a tired and dispirited one.

Most earlier cabs had been limited in width to 230 cm to permit their use in countries (such as Switzerland) where the roads were narrow and maximum vehicle width restrictions were in force. The F10/F12 cab, by contrast, was 250 cm wide (the maximum permissible in most countries) to provide the driver with more room to the side and to give the cab a feeling of spaciousness. The extra width also afforded adequate room for the 12–litre engine (and, later on, for an even bigger unit).

Since the F10/F12 series was designed before the world energy crisis, cab space was assigned higher priority than streamlining or sweeping lines. However, although it was not realised at the time,

The F10/F12 cab set new standards of ergonomics and safety in trucks.

The unprecedented popularity of Volvo's new heavy trucks necessitated the establishment of fully equipped service workshops around the globe, to ensure that no Volvo driver was ever without assistance.

The F12 was perhaps best known for its service in the most demanding of applications, such as timber haulage in Scandinavia or (as pictured below) hauling an Australian road train.

F10/12 the safest truck

Volvo's biggest truck news so far – the Volvo F10/12 introduced in 1977 – was not only a fantastic engineering achievement, it was also a sensation as regards safety features. Here are a few examples:

- A safety cab tested according to the Swedish impact test and Volvo's unique crash barrier test.
- Reinforced cab front section at knee height in front of the driver.
- Doors reinforced by steel beams which transfer the impact forces to the rear of the cab.
- Energy-absorbing dashboard.
- Flame-proof interior fittings.
- Bumper placed low down.
- Smooth cab surfaces without any interfering or sharp parts.
- Doors which remain closed even in a collision.

The ergonomics and production engineering lessons learned in the Kalmar plant were applied in the brand–new busbuilding facility in Borås.

the design of the cab was considered modern right into the 1990s.

Designed to meet Swedish impact test standards, the new cab was the strongest built yet by Volvo. In keeping with the extra width, the windscreen and side windows were larger than in previous types.

The interior climate was an aspect which received particular attention in the course of development. For the first time in a European truck, air conditioning was incorporated as an integral part of the cooling system to cool the interior air under particularly hot conditions. To prevent draughts, the attemperated (or 'conditioned') air was admitted through the normal heating system inlets, while the back window and the side windows to the rear of the doors were omitted in most trucks with sleeper cabs to minimise the loss of heat when the driver was resting or sleeping.

The provision of a separate luggage compartment under the bunk, which was accessible only through a special, lockable, external hatch on the driver's side, was a significant innovation. This feature was of considerable importance to driver comfort on long journeys since the driver's personal effects were no longer strewn about the cab, previously a source of untidiness as well as a security risk.

To suit a range of applications, the F10 and F12 were supplied with a short day cab or a long sleeper cab with one or two berths.

The F10 and F12 were of a modular design, the 'building blocks' of which could be used to create literally thousands of different variants for every application, from regional goods distribution or construction site work to international long–haul service.

The Volvo Bus Division inaugurated its new plant at Viared, near Borås during the year. The separation of bus and truck production was the first step in the process of specialisation which was to lead to the establishment of the autonomous Volvo Bus Corporation and provide the busbuilding operation with a more dedicated focus, a development which continued ever since.

Bus assembly plant in Borås

Volvo announced on 20 March 1974 that it was going to build a bus plant in Borås. The Buses and Public Transport System Division was to move to the new plant, and operations would include assembly and packing of bus chassis, administration, marketing, design engineering and development.

The plant then employed 140 people in Göteborg, but this figure was expected to rise substantially. When running at full capacity the plant would have 240 hourly-paid employees and 150 salaried staff.

The projection and construction time was estimated to be two and a half years.

The plant was opened in 1977.

50th anniversary

Volvo celebrated its 50th anniversary on 14 April 1977 with a whole host of activities. Perhaps the one most appreciated was when all 62,000 employees were presented with a Swiss watch – the biggest single watch order in the world it was claimed.

Volvo celebrated its fiftieth anniversary in 1977. The occasion was marked by the production of two series of jubilee models in a metallic silver finish, with special plates bearing the legend 'Volvo 1927–1977' at the front and rear, as well as on the dashboard (the signature of P. G. Gyllenhammar was added to the latter). Whereas the jubilee model of the 244 was sold all over the world, sales of the more exclusive 264 version were limited to a small number of markets, including North America.

A bigger (but lower–slung) jubilee model was the exclusive 262C coupé, which replaced the simpler 262 sold mainly in North America.

A fairly expensive model, the 262C was built by Bertone in Italy although styled in Sweden. Basically, the car was an ordinary 262 with a steeply sloped windscreen and a much lower roof which, for the first few years, was always covered in vinyl.

The 262 Coupé was built in limited numbers, intended mainly for export to North America. However, it was sold all over the world to customers anxious to buy the most exclusive Volvo ever built (with the exception of the extended 264TE, which also built by Bertone). The 262C and the 264TE were technically identical.

Its distance from Göteborg did not prevent Volvo BM from pursuing its product development activities at a rapid pace. In 1977, the company introduced the 4300, the first of a new generation of wheel loaders which, in time, was to include vehicles of most sizes.

A medium–sized machine, the new model quickly became a best–seller in the Volvo BM range.

Although tractor sales had been satisfactory since the opening of the company's Hällby plant, production volumes were small by international standards and the profitability of the entire agricultural machinery sector raised serious doubts concerning its capacity to support the high costs of product development in the years ahead. To deal with this, a strategic plan incorporating economic guidelines for the next few years was prepared as a basis for the operation's continued survival.

Both of the Volvo Group companies involved in engine production achieved significant progress which was to bring about at least a partial change in direction.

Volvo Flygmotor in Trollhättan was awarded a contract to produce afterburners for the European Ariane launch vehicle, expanding its activities into the space field.

Meanwhile, Volvo Penta commenced production of its MD40/TMD40 engines, the 3.6–litre units developed jointly by Penta and Volvo Truck for marine applications and for the medium–heavy F4 truck.

Rapidly assuming an important position in the Volvo Penta range, the '40' engine demonstrated the feasibility of replacing thirsty V8 petrol engines with economical diesels.

Lambdasond and catalyst

By the 1960s, the environment had become increasingly more in focus. The level of industrialisation, including uncontrolled combustion of fossil oil, had created major problems. Toxic substances were spread uncontrollably into the environment – and who cannot forget the book 'Silent Spring'?

There was greater commitment and eyes were turned more and more towards the car and motoring as they were considered to be a major source of environmental problems. There was considerable debate on exhaust emissions in the USA in the early 1970s and federal laws were introduced. In one state, California, the authorities went even further and created demands which enraged the car industry. One manufacturer protested, 'If we are to comply with these demands by 1977 then we might as well close our operations down'.

But little Volvo in Europe presented the solution to the problem in 1977. A three-way catalyst in combination with an oxygen-sensing control unit, the Lambdasond, was able to clean emissions by more than 90 per cent. Soon all Volvo cars on the US market were fitted with this catalyst.

Volvo was rewarded for this technology with the National Environment Industry Award, and became known as the 'Cleanest Car sold in America' by the California Air Resources Board.

In Europe, though, it took almost ten years for the catalyst to be introduced due to opposition in the car industry combined with the unwillingness on the part of oil companies to produce unleaded petrol.

The LM4300, the first of a completely new generation of wheel loaders, was introduced in 1977.

Proposed merger with Saab

On 6 May 1977, the Boards of Volvo and Saab-Scania proposed that the companies should merge to form a new company to be called Volvo Saab-Scania AB.

Two principal reasons for this proposed merger were the weak economic situation in the 1970s with overcapacity in the industry, and the threatening competition which was foreseen for the 1980s. The cost trend in Sweden had a negative effect on Sweden's level of competitiveness. The two companies were faced with difficulties and saw the chance to reduce the cost base by avoiding duplicate work in the investments.

The products of both companies would continue to be marketed in competition with each other as before, both Volvo and Saab-Scania would retain their existing sales channels and marques.

It was thought that some components could be made similar in type to achieve more effective production and longer series. The aircraft and aerospace operations of the two companies would supplement each other. In all, there were potential savings running into thousands of millions of kronor.

The new company would be headed by Pehr G. Gyllenhammar, with Saab-Scania Chief Curt Mileikowsky as number two.

However, on 29 August 1977, barely two months after the initial announcement that merger talks were under way, the Volvo Board announced that the deal was off. Before that the Saab-Scania Executive Board had adjourned the discussions, which led to Volvo stating that it could no longer await the results of internal discussions at Saab-Scania.

Sporting elegance was the hallmark of the deluxe 262, which replaced the more spartan 'standard' version sold only in North America.

The VHK3500 was the last and best in a long line of road graders from Bolinder–Munktell/Volvo BM. Equipped with all–wheel drive, the model was superior to previous types. Unfortunately, only a small number was produced.

The Vara factory

During 1977, production of engines was started up in a completely new production facility in the town of Vara. It had been built to relieve the plant in Skövde and to serve as a local centre for manufacturing the new six-cylinder 'Garden fence' engine, the MD40/TD40.

This production policy has continued, but nowadays both four and six-cylinder marine versions of the 41/31 engines, which replaced the 40 and 30 engines in the mid-1980s, are also produced at the Vara plant, which is part of Volvo Penta.

OVER THE YEARS, Volvo has successfully produced heavy trucks powered by moderately sized engines, vehicles often used to perform demanding tasks usually carried out by larger models.

The F7 introduced in 1978 superseded one of the most popular Volvo trucks ever, the F86, which had been a best–seller in many markets, mainly in Britain and Ireland, but also in practically every other country in the world, from Sweden to France and from North America to Australia. Indeed, to many observers, the F86 was almost irreplaceable!

Although the F7 did not have the same distinctive appearance as its eminent predecessor, it soon became just as popular.

The F7 was not actually a 100% Volvo product; exactly like the medium–heavy F4/F6 models, it was the product of collaboration between a number of makers in different countries. The cab was related to the 'club' cab used in the model's medium–heavy counterparts, while the side panels

Thanks to its functional qualities and advanced intercooler engine, the F7 became a top–seller in all markets.

The simple but ingenious booster cushion made the seat belt effective even for young children.

Booster cushion for children

For many years, Volvo led the way in developing safety accessories for children travelling in cars. The most well-known of these was the rearward-facing child seat which protected children up to the ages of 6-7 years. But children from the 'child seat age' and upwards to 12 years or so found it difficult to use the belt the right way. It often finished up across their throats and incorrectly fitted over both their stomachs and chests.

Volvo's research engineers therefore designed a special booster for children in this middle age group. The cushion was launched in 1978 and soon became a success, not least because it was also cheap.

The Volvo-Norway agreement

A 'Swedish-Norwegian Volvo Group is to be formed' was the headline when one of the most sensational business deals ever to be proposed in Sweden was announced on 22 May 1978. An agreement in principal had been signed between Volvo and the Norwegian Government which meant Volvo being reorganised to become a joint Swedish-Norwegian company called Volvo (Swedish-Norwegian) AB.

The idea was that Volvo shareholders at the time would become owners of shares in a holding company called Svenska AB Volvo, which in turn would own 60 per cent of the shares in the joint company. Through a newly formed holding company, Norsk Volvo A/S, the Norwegian State would own the remaining 40 per cent. In return, the Norwegian State would put 750 million Swedish kronor venture capital into the new company.

The proposed merger would include energy and industrial interests. A new subsidiary company, Volvo Petroleum AB, would also be formed. This company would have concession rights for drilling in the North Sea.

Part of the deal also meant that Volvo Penta would move its headquarters to Norway. A new range of diesel engines would be developed for production at a new plant in Norway.

Volvo would also set up a combined function for development of materials and components in Norway. Of particular interest was a proposed concentration on car parts made of plastic and aluminium for Volvo cars produced in the 1980s.

The plans also included Volvo developing a new car in Norway and, should the project be successful, the car would also be produced in Norway.

Approval of the proposals was scheduled to be given at an extraordinary general meeting of shareholders on 30 January 1979.

Such a sensational business proposal generated discussion on both sides. Volvo's shareholders were split into two sides and it was found that the opposition of small shareholders was sufficient to get 40 per cent of shareholders to vote against the proposals. A two-thirds majority was required, so four days before the general meeting was to take place the Volvo Board decided to cancel the agreement.

Volvo president Pehr G. Gyllenhammar had staked a lot of prestige in this particular venture and was bitterly disappointed.

and doors were almost identical. The other cab components were modified and widened to provide the driver and his passenger with adequate space despite the cowling over the 7–litre engine.

For the first time, a Volvo truck of this class was equipped with a sleeper cab (a long–awaited feature) with a fixed, single bunk behind the seats.

Technically, the F7 was based on the proven components already used in the F86. Thus, the engine was the same TD70 unit, now available with an intercooler (or charge air cooler).

While turbocharging boosts the engine power by supplying a constant excess of air, enabling more fuel to be injected and burned in the cylinders, it's limitation is that the compressed intake air is hot. As a result, the turbo boost pressure must be limited to ensure reliable running.

In charge cooling (a technique used by Volvo Penta since 1958), an intercooler is used to cool the hot intake air before it enters the cylinders. This enables higher engine power to be achieved at a lower combustion temperature, prolonging engine life and improving reliability.

The remainder of the driveline was basically similar to that used in the last version of the F86, featuring an eight–speed, range–type gearbox and a single–reduction final drive. Since the F7 was designed for delivery and refuse collection duties, it was available with an Allison automatic transmission as an alternative to the Volvo manual gearbox.

The range of variants was almost unlimited. Available in two engine powers, with a day cab or sleeper cab, with two, three or four axles, and as a rigid or a tractor, the F7 was employed as a tough workhorse in many continents.

The F6S, which was built on the heaviest of the F6 chassis (with additional reinforcement), was introduced to bridge the gap between the medium–heavy F6 and the F7. The model was equipped with the more spacious F7 cab which, by virtue of the smaller cowling over the 6–litre engine, accommodated two passengers as well as the driver. However, the F6S was not available in as many variants and was designed mainly as a two–axle vehicle for demanding local and regional goods delivery duties.

The medium–class models were not the only trucks to undergo renewal. A development of the smallest truck in the range, the F4, was exhibited at the Amsterdam Motor Show at the beginning of the year. This was equipped with the six–cylinder TD40 engine (the same as the marine unit introduced by Volvo Penta).

The new F4 was distinguished by the now–familiar diagonal 'stripe' across the grille, the first occasion in modern times that this appeared on a Volvo truck.

Volvo Bus Division also renewed its product range, in which the B59 was replaced by the B10R,

Seen here on the Hällered track, the world's fastest diesel car in 1978 was a Volvo.

The world's fastest diesel

Volvo's diesel engines in the 1970s were six-cylinder units, except in Finland, where a five-cylinder version of just under two litres was used to comply with the legislation there.

Volvo's veteran rally car driver Carl-Magnus Skogh got the idea of trying to break the world record over a flying kilometre using a car powered by this particular engine.

He built a Volvo 343 with a plastic body and removed all other unnecessary parts. This reduced the weight by 200 kg. The car drove on four 'special spares', the light spare wheel with which it was permitted to drive only at 80 km/h. Skogh fitted a turbocharger to the engine which gave the 900 kg light car a power rating of 140 hp. The gearbox, placed behind the rear axle, was taken from a Formula 1 car.

On a wet and windy autumn morning in 1978 it was time to try to beat the current world record of 205 km/h, which was set in the American salt desert.

Carl-Magnus Skogh was allowed to borrow the main runway at Landvetter Airport for half an hour after the second plane had taken off for Stockholm and before the first plane was due to take off for Copenhagen.

Despite the terrible conditions he broke the record and recorded an average speed of 209.18 km/h. He had already driven the car at 230 km/h in perfect conditions at the Hällered proving ground. The car, a Volvo XD-1, can now be seen at Volvo's museum in Arendal not far from the Torslanda plant.

with major chassis modifications to improve the safety and manoeuvrability of the model. Like its predecessor, the B10R was a city bus with a rear–mounted, horizontally installed engine, and was available in low–emission and low–noise versions.

The FL6 was a successful synthesis of the medium–heavy F6 and the efficient F7.

In 1978, the totally revamped Volvo BM range of wheel loaders was completed with the addition of the powerful L4600 and the compact L4200.

VSCC taught the USA traffic safety

Volvo succeeded well on the back of its good safety reputation ever since the Volvo 240 was acclaimed to be the car to set the norm for traffic safety in the USA. In 1978, Volvo presented a new safety car in the USA, the Volvo Concept Safety Car, VSCC.

The VSCC resembled a normal 244 but was easily recognisable by its wide reflecting side markings and special lamps under the front bumper. The car had a total of 25 extra safety features on the equipment list. To be seen or to enable the driver to see better it had also been fitted with a pulsating brake light, a speed-adapted horn, a warning lamp in the door, a signal for low tyre inflation pressure, an anti-skid warner, and electrically heated wing mirrors. It also featured puncture-proof tyres, airbags, child seat, and head restraint on all seats.

A number of the parts were already standard features in Sweden but the opportunity now presented itself to demonstrate day notice lights and child protection features to a wider American public.

The VSCC was also fitted, of course, with a catalyst, the Lambdasond.

At the same time, the NHTSA in the USA presented its own safety car. This was a rebuilt Chevrolet Impala, with a transverse, turbocharged Volvo B21 engine. The car was called the 'Large Research Safety Vehicle'. The NHTSA chose an engine from Volvo because the Swedish company was not only a pioneer in the field of safety, but also in the field of the environment.

The two bus developments of 1978 were contrasting.
Above:
The rear–engined B10R.
Right:
The conventional front–engined B6FA.

THE GLOBETROTTER CAB was introduced 'only' as an alternative to the short day cab or the long sleeper cab in the F12. It was really intended as an option for hard–up east European hauliers whose drivers – who usually lacked sufficient hard currency to stay in west European hotels – required the extra space for overnight accommodation.

However, when the F12 Globetrotter appeared, it was immediately hailed as 'the Rolls–Royce of trucks'.

The F12 Globetrotter cab was more spacious than any previous type and was soon regarded as the most comfortable ever built, contributing significantly to Volvo's growing reputation as a truckmaker during the 1980s.

The Globetrotter was not of an especially remarkable design. It consisted basically of a standard, long sleeper cab with an elevated roof, with provision for installing comfort amenities such as a sink unit, water tank, cooking stove and cashbox.

The production of heavy vehicles – starting with buses and continuing with trucks the following year – commenced in Brazil in 1979. This event signified Volvo's return to one of its first major export markets, which it been forced to abandon in the early 1960s, when the Brazilian government of the day ordered that all vehicle components, as well as their assembly, should be of local origin.

Built between 1976 and 1980, the new Volvo plant was located at Curitiba in the state of Paraña. Progress was impressive from the very beginning and, today, Volvo commands almost one–third of the Brazilian truck market. Furthermore, since Scania is also a dominant force in Brazil, the preponderance of Swedish trucks is almost total.

The Dutch–built range of cars was augmented in 1979 with the introduction of a five–door version of the 300 series. The new estate was much sought–after in most of the countries of central Europe, where small family cars traditionally had at least four, and preferably five doors.

For the first time in the history of DAF/Volvo, a conventional manual gearbox was available as an alternative to the Variomatic transmission. The new unit soon became popular; car owners are conservative by nature and modern automatic transmissions are often derided despite their limited similarity to the big, inefficient units of earlier days.

Until 1979, Volvo had never produced a diesel–engined car, which was perhaps one of the main reasons for its surprisingly poor representation at taxi ranks. Thus, the appearance of a diesel version of the Volvo 244/245, which achieved rapid popularity as a taxi, came as a major surprise. Because of the limited numbers produced, the engine was not designed by Volvo itself, but was bought from Volkswagen. The D24 diesel was a six–cylinder type (in contrast to the four or five–

In 1979, Volvo Flygmotor joined the European Ariane space project as supplier of one of the most important rocket components, the combustion chamber.

cylinder units used by Volvo's main competitors), although a five–cylinder version (D20) was sold in countries where cars under two litres were preferred for tax reasons.

Volvo won its first 'Truck of the Year' award in 1979.

Truck of the Year 1979

Volvo first won the Truck of the Year Award in 1979 with its F7 model, which soon became a top-selling truck in the Volvo range.

Renault takes a shareholding stake in Volvo

The major problems facing the car operations in the late 1970s became apparent when Volvo and Renault agreed on 19 December 1979 that Renault would acquire 10 per cent of the shares in the Volvo Car Corporation as from 1 January 1980. In return Volvo would receive 330 million Swedish kronor. Volvo was given priority for 10 per cent of the financing company Renault Acceptance BV, but this was never used.

From being a company whose operations are carried out on behalf of another company under a special 'commission' agreement, Volvo Cars was re-formed as an independent subsidiary company.

Renault was given the opportunity of increasing its shareholding to 15 and 20 per cent respectively by converting convertible loans. The first stage in the increase to 15 per cent was taken advantage of in 1981, but Volvo bought back the first shares in 1983 and the remaining 9.4 per cent the following year.

Two variations on the 340 theme were announced in 1979 – the series-produced 345 estate and the 'Tundra', a design concept by Bertone of Italy (only one example of the latter was built).

Safety-type steering wheel and seat belt

Two other safety features were presented at the same time as the Globetrotter which decisively increased the level of passive safety in Volvo trucks. Both innovations were a direct result of the surveys carried out by Volvo's unique Truck and Car Accident Investigation Teams, and work of this kind had already influenced the design of the F10 and F12 trucks in 1977.

Alongside the impact-tested cabs, the seat belt is the most important single feature to increase the level of safety developed during the past fifty years. But although the seat belt had been available for trucks, there were practically no drivers who used it even though it had a proven safety effect.

The reason was that the suspension driver's seat in a truck renders a fixed belt unusable. At the same time, a conventional inertia reel belt has to be tensioned by the movements of the seats and after a while makes the suspension driver's seat become a fixed driver seat. Volvo's design engineers succeeded in solving the problem in 1979 by introducing an inertia reel belt which, with the help of electronic signals, could distinguish between normal vibrations emanating from the road surface and seat and the enormous stresses encountered during a collision.

Unfortunately, the use of seat belts has not increased among truck drivers during the past decades, partly on account of Volvo's sophisticated solution not being available in other truck makes, but chiefly because of the unwillingness of drivers to use a seat belt.

The Volvo Truck Corporation and many trade press journalists have applied pressure to generate opinion in favour of the use of seat belts even by professional drivers. But we are still a long way from seeing general use.

The design of the steering wheel is of significant importance to how serious injuries a driver can suffer in a collision. Traditionally, the truck steering wheel has been solid and very big, to provide sufficient support and a lever-type force to drive a heavy truck without the need for power steering. Times have changed and now all trucks have a good power steering system.

At the same time as the electronic seat belt was launched by Volvo, a collapsible steering wheel was also introduced. This type of steering wheel protects the driver in a collision and alleviates or eliminates injuries in above all the stomach area.

Volvo Bus Division undertook series production of its B10M high–volume model to replace the B58 (except in Brazil, where the latter is still part of the range). Although the B10M boasted many improvements compared with its predecessor, it did not represent a significant advance, being a developed rather than a new model.

Flexibility was a key concept of the B10M. While the conventional two–axle and three–axle articulated versions of its predecessor were retained the series was soon augmented by a long, three–axle, high–capacity chassis and a double–decker version with an extremely high passenger capacity. Charge cooling (using the engine coolant rather than a separate Intercooler) was introduced in the mid–1980s, boosting the engine output to 340 hp and enabling the model – despite it's somewhat smaller engine – to compete effectively as a tourist coach. In this respect, the excellent

With features including a collapsible steering wheel, reel– type seat belts and a spacious new cab, the ergonomics and comfort of the new Volvo F12 Globetrotter were unsurpassed.

The fourth generation B10M mid–engined bus became a huge success. Today, in refined form, it remains one of VBC's best–sellers.

weight distribution afforded by the mid–engine configuration was another contributory factor.

Volvo Truck Division met internal competition from Volvo BM when the latter introduced its 5350 articulated dumper. With a well–tuned suspension and a top speed of over 50 km/h, the new model offered a real alternative to the conventional site truck over short distances and in applications where high mobility was the most important consideration.

In other respects, the 5350 dumper was a conventional vehicle with cab accommodation for the driver only. The model was finished in Volvo BM's traditional yellow.

Wide-angle mirror

One of the new features presented with the 1980 model was a small but very valuable safety feature: the wide-angle rear view mirror. The mirror has a large inner section which gives a small reduction and then a continuously increasing curvature. This curvature gives the driver a 45-degree field of vision to the rear as opposed to just 22-degree with a standard mirror. In principle, the Volvo driver can see the car in the adjoining lane in the wing mirror right up until he can see it in the corner of his eye.

Volvo's Back Ailment Research Award

In cooperation with the well-known researcher and doctor, professor Alf Nachemson, Volvo instituted an international 'Back Ailment Research Award' in 1979 for the best medicine research results in the field of back ailments. The award was in two categories: for the best clinical contributions, and for the best contributions within basic general scientific research. The prize money amounted to 9,000 US dollars.

The award board, led by professor Nachemson, annually receives suggestions from different countries. In 1995 there were 42 suggestions from 16 countries.

The award is a long-term part of Volvo's efforts to achieve higher levels of safety and comfort, chiefly through the development of the seats in the vehicles.

Limited production of the B58 bus (left) commenced in the new plant in Curitiba, Brazil in 1979.

The DR5350 combined the superb mobility and robustness of the articulated dumper with a top speed of over 50 km/h.

Restructuring of Volvo BM

With a follow up of the L77 Strategy Plan, which was put forward in 1977, it was shown that a winding up of the whole of the forestry and agricultural equipment production operations was the only way the company could remain in business, and that all available resources should be transferred to the construction equipment sector.

This signalled the start of one of the biggest restructuring programmes in Swedish industry.

The following measures were adopted in 1979-80:
- A joint venture was set up with Valmet Oy in Finland to create a joint Nordic range of tractors, and in the long term to transfer all tractor operations to the Finnish company.
- The foresty equipment business was sold to Valmet in Finland.
- The combine harvester business was sold to Överums Bruk AB, which was part of the Electrolux Group.
- The manufacture of mobile cranes was transferred to A/S Moelvens Brug in Norway.
- Co-operation with Lundberg-Hymas AB was wound down over a transitional period.
- The road grader business had already been wound down.
- The tracked vehicle business was transferred to Hägglund & Söner AB.

Concentration on three types of products was started up immediately. These were: wheel loaders, articulated dumpers, and earthmoving machines.

IT IS THE DREAM of every automaker to mass-produce just one model which is popular with all customers and is approved in all countries. Sadly, this utopian concept is nothing more than a dream – the reality is quite different.

In some, less bureaucratic countries, legislation is confined to what is absolutely necessary. By contrast, other countries (whether from choice or necessity) insist on special vehicles which demand a great deal of development work, are expensive to produce and buy, and are often much less efficient than would otherwise be the case.

Switzerland, with its special natural conditions and its unique system of government based on largely autonomous cantons, is a perfect example of a country which has imposed individual regulations on truck traffic. As a result of its special traffic legislation, Switzerland itself was, for many years, home to a number of small, domestic truckmakers producing unique designs and manufacturing products of recognised quality.

In 1980, Volvo introduced what was perhaps its most distinctive truck yet, the CH230, which was developed specifically for Swiss conditions. Created from elements of other models, the model was – despite its uniqueness – designed to be economical to produce and relatively inexpensive to operate.

Essentially, the CH230 was built on an F12 chassis fitted with an F7 cab and equipped with lighter axles than other heavy Volvo trucks.

The legislation in force in Switzerland at the time required that the cab should not be wider than 230 cm (to permit vehicles to pass on narrow alpine roads). The GCW was limited to 28 tonnes (to afford adequate climbing speed on gradients and to ensure safe braking on downhill runs), while a high horsepower per tonne ratio was also a requirement.

The result was a narrow truck with a powerful engine, which was built in many versions ranging from two–axle to four–axle, and even trailer types.

It is interesting to note that Volvo's approach was different to that of many other truckmakers, who opted for a standard cab width of only 230 cm. Most of Volvo's heavy trucks were (and are) equipped with 250 cm cabs and special versions are built for individual markets despite the additional development costs involved. Thanks to this, 99% of the world's hauliers and drivers are spared the compromises which must be made for the 1% in countries with special regulations.

The second truck development announced by Volvo in 1980 was the introduction of a longer day cab in its established N series models, providing drivers with an improved standard of comfort. The N7/N10/N12 Mk.2 models remained best–sellers for many years, particularly in countries outside Europe, where buyers attached a higher priority to simplicity and ruggedness than to sophisticated design and complexity.

The Volvo Concept Car (or VCC) appeared in 1980. This was not a production model but a conceptual design used to evaluate public taste and reaction to the new 760, which was to be introduced just two years later.

The VCC was built as an estate version of the 760 to demonstrate Volvo's standing as a maker of safe, comfortable models of this type. Although the estate was a chosen option prior to the launch of the 765/745, it was later abandoned in favour of the bigger and more spacious version introduced at the beginning of 1985.

The CH230 represented the optimum compromise between an 'ordinary' Volvo truck and a version designed to comply with special road traffic legislation, as in Switzerland.

Volvo Chalmerists

The Chalmers Institute of Technology in Göteborg celebrated its 150th anniversary in 1980. On this occasion Volvo instituted a scholarship for 50,000 kronor to be presented every year to the Chalmers engineer(s) who produced the best undergraduate thesis on subjects relating to the automotive industry.

With this scholarship Volvo wanted to improve its contacts with technical universities and encourage future engineers to concentrate on the automotive industry.

Volvo Concept Car

"The Volvo of the '80s" is what the VCC – Volvo Concept Car – was called when it was presented in the spring of 1980.

The VCC was one way in which Volvo could test in advance reactions to the next car model, the Volvo 760, which was to be presented less than two years later. The car was an estate model, a very realistic car showing how Volvo saw the future in terms of the environment, safety and energy.

New materials were tested in the VCC to save weight and fuel, including aluminium in large body sections. Following exhaustive wind tunnel tests among other things in Volvo's climate unit, the body was given a favourable shape with a speed-variable spoiler as a prominent feature. The engine was fitted with an 'economy turbo' and electronic combustion control. The gearbox was an automatic unit with four gear stages and electrically disconnecting overdrive for low fuel consumption.

The VCC demonstrated much of what the Volvo Car Corporation had in its pipeline for the 1980s.

At the same time as the VCC, Volvo exhibited another concept car, the Volvo 244 Diesel Turbo Special. This particular model was based more on 'an inclination to play'. The normal diesel engine had been fitted with a large turbocharger and a slightly reduced intercooler of the type used in trucks. This increased the power rating from 82 to 177 hp, which in turn gave this diesel a real sports car performance rating – but with the same fuel consumption as the standard car.

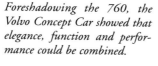

Foreshadowing the 760, the Volvo Concept Car showed that elegance, function and performance could be combined.

Truck plant in Brazil

On 4 December 1980, the Brazilian president João Figuereido and Volvo president Pehr G. Gyllenhammar opened Volvo's new bus and truck assembly plant in Curitiba in southern Brazil.

At the time of the official opening the plant was already producing B58 bus chassis and N10 trucks. The plant then had 650 employees and a capacity for producing 7,000 heavy-duty vehicles a year.

The investment costs amounted to 560 million kronor.

Volvo acquires Beijer Invest

On 15 November 1980, the Boards of Volvo and Beijer Invest decided that the companies would merge to form "a new forceful combination" of industrial, energy, and food operations.

The proposed merger meant that AB Volvo would be re-formed as an investment company to be called Investment AB Volvo Beijer.

Pehr G. Gyllenhammar would be Managing Director and Chief Executive Officer, and Anders Wall the full-time Chairman of the Board.

The headquarters of the new company would be chiefly located in Gothenburg, and also in Stockholm where the Chairman of the Board would have his office.

This time the proposed merger went through and Volvo suddenly became a much bigger company with several strong business legs to stand on. Just a few years after the merger, Volvo was able to report a turnover exceeding 100 thousand million kronor.

A NEW ERA dawned for Volvo in 1981 when the company acquired the truck operations of the White Motor Corporation in the USA. Now established as one of Europe's leading truckmakers, Volvo thereby proclaimed its intention of expanding substantially worldwide.

The company which Volvo took over was by no means prosperous and Volvo itself did not have a particularly happy experience of selling vehicles in the USA. Although White boasted the longest and most interesting history of all US truckmakers, it had undermined its own financial stability by borrowing heavily for investment purposes at the start of the recession and, at the time of its acquisition by Volvo, the company was in receivership under the US statute known as Chapter 11.

Volvo had attempted to market trucks in North America on three occasions – in the late 1950s and the mid–1970s, both times on its own, and at the end of the 1970s, in collaboration with the American truckmaker, Freightliner. None of these efforts was successful and the situation became acute when Volvo's fiercest competitor, Mercedes–Benz, bought Freightliner, leaving the company without a North American importer or dealer network.

However, out of disaster came triumph. The takeover of White represented Volvo's only remaining option of retaining a presence in North America – and it proved to be a fortunate one. White was acquired for the bargain price of SKr75 million and Volvo invested the same amount in consolidation of the organisation and dealer network, and in improving the quality of the product range.

By the end of 1981, White's market share had fallen to about 4%. However, this was quickly doubled and was stabilised at three times the figure within a further couple of years.

With the purchase of White, Volvo now had four marques in its truck stable.

The company had already marketed its F6, F7 and F10 models in collaboration with Freightliner. This activity was now continued by the newly established Volvo White Truck Corporation, which was headed by Thage Berggren (formerly head of Volvo in Belgium). The Volvo products provided an ideal complement to the White range which, until then, had lacked a medium–heavy Class 7 model.

Based on advanced component standardisation, White's own trucks consisted mainly of heavy models for regional and long–haul transport.

The White products were modern (the trucks had been introduced as brand new models between 1975 and 1980, and were produced in plants built in the 1970s). Despite this, some of the teething troubles had not yet been overcome and the dealer network was shaky.

However, White had produced a winner in the form of its Integral Sleeper model, which had been introduced in 1980. Although not especially revolutionary in the European context (consisting, as it did, of a normal–width, bonneted truck with a sleeper cab), the model was new to American drivers accustomed to narrow models with a separate sleeping compartment behind the cab.

Almost immediately, the Integral Sleeper became the best–selling model in the White range, providing the main reason for the fantastic success enjoyed by the new company during the first half of the decade.

Autocar was another well–known make with a long history. The name stood for extremely robust trucks of relatively simple design built for construction site, oilfield and tough transport applications.

Western Star was the fourth and last marque marketed by the new Volvo White Truck Corporation. Long–haul models which were basically similar to their White counterparts, the Western Star models were handcrafted, lavishly outfitted, and equipped with extra large and powerful engines. Built especially for fastidious customers on the US west coast, they were frequently finished in imaginative and elegant designs.

The production of bus bodies in Säffle is now an integral part of VBC's operations. The plant has now been producing 'System 2000' bodies for a number of years.

Increased environmental demands

Emissions from Volvo's facilities became the subject of increasing discussion around 1980. The smell which spread from the paint shop at the Torslanda plant towards the residential area of Biskopsgården caused many people to question whether or not it was healthy.

In September 1981, the Concession Board for Environmental Protection assembled and placed new demands on Volvo. Demands had been placed by the Environment Conservation Board stating that emissions of solvents (hydrocarbons) must be reduced from 3,900 tonnes a year to 3,400 tonnes. New and effective purification methods were installed quickly, and new solvent-free materials were developed, and when all paints eventually became water-based, emissions could be reduced quite considerably.

At present the highest permitted figure is 400 tonnes a year.

In December 1981, an environmental cooperation programme was set up between the British Petroleum refinery close to the Torslanda plant and the Volvo factory. As the factory was able to take care of waste heat from the refinery through a pipeline running across Torslanda Road, Volvo was able to save more than 15,000 cubic metres of oil annually – which is more than half the energy requirement of the Torslanda plant.

Volvo acquires Höglunds

In October 1981, Volvo acquired all shares in the bodybuilding firm AB H Höglunds & Co in Säffle. This enabled the Volvo Bus Corporation to offer complete omnibuses, and Volvo assumed full responsibility for both the chassis and the body.

The company was a pioneer in Sweden in the late 1940s when it produced stainless bodies made of aluminium. The company produces mainly inter-city coaches and city buses.

Volvo's acquisition of White GMC's truck operation was followed by a comprehensive re-organisation programme directed by VTC President Sten Langenius. After a couple of years, this yielded major success in the form of a growth in sales.

Volvo's North American truck range was completed with the combination of the Volvo and White products.

THE INTRODUCTION OF the 760GLE signified the end of a long search by Volvo for a successor to the 240/260 series, and for its own distinct identity as a carmaker.

Until 1982, the company had concentrated on the development and production of small and medium–sized family cars, supplemented by more expensive versions of the same models. The appearance of the 760GLE and the simultaneous retention of the 240 series as a high–volume model was an indication of the company's shift towards comfortable medium–class cars offering high performance, generous equipment levels and inherent status.

The 760GLE cost almost SKr100,000, in return for which the buyer received every conceivable luxury as standard equipment – automatic transmission, air conditioning, a sunroof, aluminium wheels, electric window winders and central locking.

In technical terms, the new model was a natural successor to the 264GLE. Then, as now, the conventional configuration of front–mounted engine and rear–wheel drive was the obvious choice for a top–of–the–range model. The six–cylinder engine was the same V6 PRV unit used earlier in the 264 (and in the 265 Estate, which was to remain part of the range for a couple of years more).

The rear suspension was a further–developed design based on a beam–type rear axle, a type which offered more or less the same standard of comfort as independent suspension but which, by maintaining a constant track width under all conditions, afforded the best possible behaviour on slippery surfaces.

The styling of the 760GLE was highly distinctive. At a time when rounded lines were the fashion in the industry, the Volvo design team under Jan Wilsgaard went against the tide by creating a typical 'razor–edge' exterior, a style distinguished by its flat surfaces and sharp angles, in which the more or less horizontal and vertical main lines were joined by diagonal elements.

The distinctive Volvo identity meant that the aerodynamics and drag were not as highly optimised as in many of the car's competitors with their sweeping lines. Although limiting the top speed to some extent, this factor became less important as it became increasingly difficult to drive without restriction on good roads in almost every country except Germany.

A success from the outset, the 760GLE gave Volvo cars a more exclusive image which was later reinforced in several other models.

Synonymous with trucks with special characteristics, built for the toughest of site work or as exclusive long–haul vehicles, the Autocar name has always had a special connotation in the USA.

In the truck sector, the Autocar AT64F was the equivalent of the 760GLE car, which also belonged

to an exclusive class and was built specifically to satisfy high customer demands in North America. In this case, however, the model was a heavy truck for commercial applications.

Autocar trucks had not been projected as commercials during the decade immediately preceding Volvo's takeover of White. However, the new model was intended as an exclusive, tandem–drive semitrailer tractor for single–truck operators who were unenthusiastic about the Integral Sleeper with its integral, but small cab. The model never sold in large numbers, although it retained the loyalty of conservative buyers, especially on the US west coast.

Mechanically, the ATF64 was of conventional design, although usually equipped with an extra powerful engine.

By now, Volvo had almost completed its reorganisation of Volvo BM in Eskilstuna. As Swedish agriculture was modernised, and farming

The Volvo 760 (the picture shows a late 1980s model) was a comfortable, well–equipped car.

The safe Volvo 760

The Volvo 760 was no exception to the rule when it comes to Volvo promising safe new features. One example was that the platform was designed in such a way under the rear seat that it would not be possible for a belted passenger to slide under and out of the belt in the event of a collision. Another effective but simple safety feature was a red warning lamp in the rear edge of the doors.

In 1984, ABS brakes were presented for some models, as was also an electronic anti-spin system.

Performance-linked bonus for employees

In December 1982, Volvo allocated a performance-linked bonus to its employees. During the ensuing years, Volvo generated high profits, which led to contributions being made to the Volvo Result Foundation for many years. The foundation administrated the money by dealing in shares amongst other things.

After five years, the bonus for the first year was distributed. Almost all Volvo employees had accepted the bonus and were well pleased by this extra money in the wallet each year.

Formation of subsidiary companies

On 5 April 1982, it was decided that several organisational units within AB Volvo would be reformed as subsidiary companies as from 1 January 1983 (some of them six months later, however).

The Volvo Car Corporation had already become a subsidiary company in 1980. It was now the turn of Volvo Trucks, Volvo Buses, Volvo Components, Volvo Bil (the Swedish market company), Volvo Penta, and Volvo Data to become limited companies. The so-called K/S unit Transport was also formed as a company with Autocarrier System as a fully-fledged subsidiary.

Autocar AT64F.

The Volvo Turbo Cup attracted wide interest, especially on Swedish television.

An early 760.

Volvo Turbo Cup

P I Walfridsson had hardly returned home to Torsby with the European Championship trophy for rallycross racing before Volvo decided to withdraw its factory support for the discipline. But the following year saw the next concentration – but not to the same degree.

This concerned a new cup which was competed for on the track: the 'Volvo Turbo Cup'.

The entire Swedish 'racing elite' were on the starting line in this even economy class for Volvo 240 cars. The cup proved to be just as tough as any of the Volvo cups which were competed for on the track in the 1970s.

declined and became more large–scale in nature, the company had concentrated its development resources on becoming a world leader in the earthmoving plant industry, with special emphasis on articulated dumpers and loaders. However, rather than abandon its farming customers, Volvo collaborated with Valmet of Finland in the development of a new generation of 'Nordic tractors' which were styled by the Volvo Design Centre in Göteborg. Undertaken jointly by the two companies, the aim of the project was to meet the requirements of farmers in Scandinavia, as well as in other parts of the world.

Introduced in 1982, the first versions of the new tractors were basic three and four–cylinder models, all with turbo engines.

Although the new tractors were normally equipped with fully integrated four–wheel drive, rear wheel–drive versions were also available. High tractive effort was afforded by the extremely favourable weight distribution achieved by locating

Above and bottom right: Volvo BM Valmet tractors were produced both in agricultural (red) and industrial (yellow) versions.

Below left: The Kockum trucks included in the Volvo range since 1982 are extremely large models. Marketed for a time under the Volvo BM name, these are now known as Euclid trucks and form part of the VCE range.

the fuel tank in a low position at the mid–point of the vehicle, between the engine and the all–synchromesh gearbox.

The ergonomics were enhanced by the low noise level and the completely flat cab floor.

The new range was marketed under the trademark of 'Volvo BM Valmet', although it was understood from the outset that the Volvo name was only to be used during a transitional period until 1986, after which Volvo BM was to devote itself exclusively to the development, production and marketing of earthmoving machines.

Volvo BM celebrated its 150th anniversary in 1982. Further expansion of the Volvo BM product range took place in the midst of the celebrations, when the southern Swedish firm of Kockum Landsverk was incorporated in the company. Kockum was well–known for its rigid tipper trucks which, with their extremely high payload and capacity, were designed to operate exclusively on large construction sites and were never driven on the road. Bearing designations from 425 to 565 (the last two last indicated the payload in US tons, or short tons, a unit equal to 2,000 lb), the Kockum models provided an ideal complement to the articulated dumper range, a field in which Volvo BM was now a world leader.

Kockum also produced articulated dumpers; however, these were soon discontinued as an unnecessary duplication of the Volvo BM models.

In 1982, Volvo Penta unveiled its greatest advance since 1959, in the form of the new Duoprop I/O drive. Although based on the same principle as the Aquamatic, the Duoprop configuration featured twin propellers to increase the efficiency and reduce the power losses. Since the propellers were contra–rotating, the propulsive force was generated without interference from lateral forces.

The Tuve plant gave VTC the production capacity which it required in Scandinavia. In the picture above, the chassis are seen moving, not along a conventional assembly line, but on battery–powered guided carriers. The engines were conveyed on air–suspended carriers (right), affording maximum flexibility of operation.

A double–deck version of the B10M bus was launched in 1992.

Volvo Trucks in Tuve

On 15 April 1982, after two years of construction, the Volvo Truck Corporation opened its new assembly plant in Tuve, five kilometres from the Torslanda and Lundby plants.

Experiences gained from the Kalmar plant had been put to good use in Tuve, and the 275 employees worked in groups of four to eight. There were no conventional types of assembly line in the plant, as the work was performed completely on battery-powered carriers which were handled by the line operators.

The approach to quality ran right through all parts of the factory and in all stages of the assembly process.

THE WHOLEHEARTEDNESS OF Volvo's involvement in White was demonstrated by the fact that Sten Langenius, then president of Volvo Truck Corporation (VTC), took leave from his post to evaluate and plan the course of Volvo's North American truck operations.

Positive results emerged with surprising speed from the company's acquisition of White two years earlier. With its reputation as an major international truckmaker, Volvo regained the confidence of those customers who, not long before, had forsaken the ailing White company.

While Volvo was investing money and confidence in the North American dealer and service network, it was also planning a strategic product development programme, the first part of which was introduced in the early summer of 1983.

To show that White was now part of Volvo, all of the White trucks – in common with Volvo's other products – now bore the famous diagonal stripe across the grille.

The bonneted trucks had undergone the greatest changes. The 'Road Boss' name was now replaced by the more descriptive title 'Conventional' (the Road Boss Integral Sleeper was now known simply as the Integral Sleeper), while the exterior of all normal–control White models had been redesigned to reduce the drag.

Volvo's European models also underwent comprehensive restyling in 1983. The best–selling F10 and F12 were equipped with more spacious cabs of rounder shape. However, the modifications made to these two trucks (in effect, the 1984 models) were much more far–reaching, to the extent that they were completely new in many respects. Apart from the further developed cabs, the trucks were available with a completely new range of chassis, with new frames and a wider choice of suspensions. The engine range had also been renewed. The F10 was now also available with an intercooler unit (as the F12 had been since autumn 1979).

Most of the developments on the car front concerned the smaller models. The most exciting of these was the LCP (Light Component Project),

Although the LCP was conceived basically as an urban car and had a low fuel consumption, it boasted high performance (demonstrated here on the Hällered track).

Too few children protected

In April 1983, the Traffic Accident Research Department at the Volvo Truck Corporation presented a survey of 11,562 serious accidents occurring between 1974 and 1982. This showed that, in spite of all the propaganda, only 20 per cent of the 1,989 children included in the survey sat on a child seat, on a child cushion, or wore a seat belt. The researchers made a special study of those children who sat on a child safety cushion with a seat belt and found that none of these children suffered injuries more serious than a few bumps and bruises.

A survey on chemical products

In 1983, Volvo's Occupational Hygiene Group was set up and organised under the Central Company Health Care Unit. Two years later, the group was organised under the Technological Development Unit.

The group was given the task of surveying, assessing the risks of, and marking all the approximately 900 chemical products used within the Volvo Group.

In 1991, the work carried out by the group resulted in an internationally acknowledged data base called 'Motiv'. This data base now contains detailed information on more than 4,000 chemical products. Motiv is accessible to everyone throughout the Volvo Group, and there is both a Swedish and an English version. Since the data base was started, the number of new chemical products used by Volvo has been halved and many unsuitable products have been deleted.

The next stage came in 1992 in the form of a unique measuring system to calculate the total environmental impact of Volvo products. This system is called Environmental Priority Strategy, EPS, and was created in cooperation with the Institute of Water and Air Conservation Research in Sweden, as well as the Swedish Industrial Association.

The EPS system provides Volvo's design engineers and decision-makers with facts to make it possible to include the environmental aspect even when choosing system solutions and design materials.

The overall environmental impact of the product, from basic idea to destruction, is included and emotionally supported arguments are replaced by a higher degree of knowledge.

which was Volvo's first front–wheel drive model. The LCP was built only as a concept car for test purposes and was not intended for production or sale.

The second development also concerned a small car, the Dutch–built 340/360, which was now offered in a saloon version, with a conventional boot instead of the hatchback–style tailgate characteristic of the three and five–door models.

Italia 99 was an exciting luxury tourist coach built on a B10M chassis and styled by the noted italian designer, Giugiaro. Built initially in Italy only for Italian customers, the model was later produced by Berkhof, the Belgian bodybuilders, for the international market.

The Italia 99 project was an indication of Volvo's determination to gain a foothold in the huge Italian market.

A smaller, but similar model, the Italia 66, based on the front–engined B6FA chassis, was produced later. However, this model never attracted the same interest as the elegant, full–scale Italia 99.

The LCP was a small, but roomy car, with space for four people. The estate configuration made it versatile.

LCP – with the sights on the next century

The Volvo LCP, Light Component Project, was presented in June 1983. Since then it has fascinated everyone who has seen any of the two cars which were exhibited.

The LCP was a study for the future, particularly with regard to new, light materials and new fuels. The objective was to analyse the total energy requirement of a car, from materials manufacture, via production and use, to recycling.

For four years the project, headed by the legendary Rolf Mellde, worked with the aim of finding low-weight materials without renouncing economy, safety or quality. The aim was to achieve materials that could be put into practical use within a 10-15 year period. Aluminium, magnesium, carbon fibre, and oil-based high-strength materials were used to a major extent – engine cylinder blocks and wheels, for example, were cast in magnesium. The entire car weighed just 700 kg and had a good performance rating. It could accelerate from 0 to 100 km/h in less than 11 seconds and the top speed was 180 km/h. The air drag coefficient was less than 0.30 and the frontal area less than 1.8 m2. This was necessary when the requirement placed on fuel consumption in all types of driving would be 0.36 litres per 10 kilometres.

The project was based on the fact that the family of the future would be smaller than the family in 1983. The LCP was therefore a small car, a two-seater with space for luggage, or a four-seater without luggage space. The two additional passengers would then sit with their backs to the direction of travel.

The project studied various engine and gearbox options – conventional piston engines of the Otto and diesel type, gas turbines, electric motors, and various types of hybrids. It was found that the best solution that could be achieved in a reasonable space of time was a direct-injection, turbocharged diesel engine. The engines in the LCP are three-cylinder units with cylinder dispacements of 1.3 and 1.4 litres respectively. One engine has a power rating of 53 hp and the other 89 hp.

The transmission units which were tested were a variable automatic gearbox and five-speed manual gearbox.

One of the engines was adapted to run on various types of fuels. It was most appreciated when the car ran on rape oil. The emissions smelt of French frieds.

The project also included an unprejudiced analysis of possible future production methods and production set-ups, and also how suppliers can be integrated into the new systems.

No elephants in the back, thank you!

The four Nordic countries proclaimed 1983 as 'Traffic Safety Year'. Even if the number of deaths resulting from road accidents had been reduced quite considerably, traffic causes quite a lot of suffering. Volvo's contribution to the Nordic Road Safety Year '83 included providing information about its many years of research in creating safer cars and safer traffic. The film 'Children in cars', which described how a child should – and should not – be transported in a car, was shown for the first time in public in schools and at various seminars.

In the province of Kopparberg, successful trials were started up with aerial reconnaisance of elks along the main roads. Volvo took part in these trials through its insurance company Volvia. Once the elks were sighted, warning signs were put up very quickly.

In conjunction with NTF, the National Association for the Promotion of Traffic Safety, Volvo conducted an intensive campaign during the year on the theme 'No elephants in the back, thank you'. This dealt with the issue of getting everyone travelling in cars to use a seat belt.

The 1983 White trucks became 'genuine' Volvos with the addition of the diagonal stripe across the grille. The Integral Sleeper and High Cabover were two of the new models.

Right: In 1983, Volvo and NTF conducted a safety campaign under the theme 'No elephants in the back, thank you!'.

Italia 99.

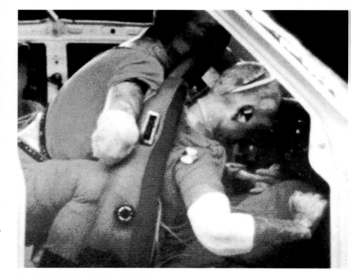

Gas-powered company cars

In the early 1980s, Volvo devoted a lot of effort to introducing LPG (Liquified Petrol Gas) as a fuel to an increasingly greater extent. Many company cars were fitted with LPG drive as an alternative to petrol, and in 1983 the company car department used large advertisements to target employers with a challenge to buy these 'economical and environmentally-safe' used gas-powered company cars.

Despite Volvo's unyielding efforts to get this environmentally-safe fuel off the ground, the authorities did not provide the necessary backing or subsidies. The powers to be obviously did not want to have an environmentally-safe alternative to petrol. LPG soon disappeared and was later replaced by natural gas.

Håkan Frisinger

When the Volvo PV 444 was presented in 1944, Håkan Frisinger from Skövde was just 16 years old. That particular year was the third year in succession he worked during his summer vacation at the Volvo Penta-verken, which delivered engines to Sweden's new car. There the young Frisinger learned to turn, grind, mill, make tools, renovate engines, and how to run errands.

On 13 August 1943, he had been presented with a certificate after leaving his job "at his own request". In the certificate it was stated that Håkan Frisinger's main tasks consisted of "polishing valves and taking turns at the grinding machine". The last hourly rate was quoted at "28 öre" and he was credited with having "good conduct" and "good technical skill".

He graduated as an engineer from the Chalmers Institute of Technology in Göteborg and at the age of 23 was employed by the Volvo Skövdeverken in 1952, first as a materials handlings manager, and then as a workshop engineer.

Håkan Frisinger made a brief sortie to Bahco in Enköping as workshop manager for the period 1959-1960. He then returned to the Skövdeverken as assistant to the plant general manager. In 1963 he was appointed Chief Engineer and Head of the Production Engineering department.

In the same year as Volvo presented its new 144 model, 1966, Frisinger moved to Göteborg to take up a position as Head of Product and Production Coordination. In 1969, he was appointed Head of the new Product Planning Division at Volvo Cars. In 1971 Frisinger became General Manager of the Volvo Köping plant.

In 1973, he enrolled on a higher management training course at the Harvard Business School in America, and moved back to Göteborg in 1975. This time as Volvo's Car Production Chief and a member of the Volvo Executive Management.

Volvo's car operations suffered a severe crisis, and in 1977 Håkan Frisinger was appointed to head the Industrial Division at the Volvo Car Corporation. In 1978 he became Executive Vice President of AB Volvo and Managing Director of the newly formed Volvo Car Corporation. Here he headed the important project which later became the Volvo 760.

From 1983 up until his retirement in 1987, Håkan Frisinger was Managing Director of AB Volvo. During these years he signalled the start of Volvo Car's project (P10) which later became the successful 850 GLT.

Håkan Frisinger's more than fifty years' experience of all types of components for cars, and in particular engines and gearboxes, his wide experience of product and production development, plus the fact that he was successful in heading a car company in times of economic upswing and downswing, made him a natural authority on the new Volvo Board which shareholders voted in on 19 January 1994.

Håkan Frisinger.

A new front–engined bus was introduced in 1983 as a successor to the classic BB57.

Below: A Volvo C303 terrain vehicle won its class in the 1983 Paris to Dakar Rally.

Below: The 1983 F10/F12 models were largely revamped.

FOLLOWING THE INTRODUCTION of the Italia 99 in Italy the previous year, Volvo was now anxious to develop a total bus concept. More than just another model, this was to be 'the mother of all tourist coaches'.

The mid–engine configuration was the obvious choice. The new model was intended not only to meet the need for passenger comfort and safety, but also to afford unsurpassed driving performance. Since perfect weight distribution was a prerequisite, the engine location was slightly different compared with the B10M.

Volvo's 10–litre engine was actually a little small for the power requirements of central European tourist coach operators. However, the output was increased to 340 hp by adding an intercooler, making the unit ideal for fast autobahn driving or operation in alpine regions.

A long wheelbase (6.3 or 7 metres) was specified for comfort, affording superb handling and ride comfort, although sacrificing a little of the mobility otherwise offered by a shorter wheelbase.

To enable a large number of passengers to be transported even in the two–axle version, it was decided to build the new model from strong, light and maintenance–free materials, such as stainless steel and aluminium.

To ensure the necessary production capacity and quality, Volvo concluded a joint venture agreement with a Swiss busbuilding firm, which acted as a supplier.

Since safety was the main priority throughout the project, the design incorporated a system of roof members which served as anti–roll protection in the event of an accident.

The C10M was a technical triumph and a commercial disaster. Although acclaimed for its handling and voted 'Coach of the Year' by an international jury, it attracted almost no buyers.

The model was too advanced (and too expensive) at a time when operators were more concerned with maximum passenger capacity and luxury rather than with safety. Since only about 70 of the vehicles were built, the project was an

White Integral Tall Sleeper.

expensive lesson for the young Volvo Bus Corporation (VBC).

However, the C10M was used extensively as a test vehicle for future models. In time, the weight distribution of the standard B10M chassis was improved on the basis of results obtained from the C10M, while the experience gained from the body design was to prove invaluable during VBC's rapid expansion in the late 1980s, when it became a market leader in most of the developed nations.

Volvo's collaboration with Valmet of Finland was ongoing. In 1984, Volvo Valmet introduced the 905, a more powerful tractor than the first two models in the 'Nordic tractor' range which emerged from the 1982 joint venture agreement. The 905 was equipped with a powerful, straight–six diesel engine of the same family (i.e with the same cylinder dimensions) as the 505/605 and 705/805. Since turbocharging was still a relatively new feature in agricultural machines at the time, the 905 was not equipped with a turbo to avoid 'frightening off' conservative buyers.

The 905, which was a fairly long machine, was always supplied with four–wheel drive, making it ideal for large and medium–sized farms.

A new articulated excavator loader, the 6300, was launched on the Swedish market. In terms of size, the model was in the heaviest class.

Although Volvo introduced no new European truck models in 1984, it did unveil its new F10 Eurotrotter cab, a short sleeper unit in which the fixed bunk was located above the driver's seat. This configuration made the cargo space as long as with a short day cab, at the expense of a higher cab, a small increase in weight and marginally inferior aerodynamics.

Unlike the plastic Top Sleepers of its competitors, the Eurotrotter cab was built entirely of steel and complied easily with the strict Swedish impact test regulations.

The Eurotrotter combined the sleeping comfort of the long cab with the maximised payload of the short cab.

Productivity bonus

In 1984, Volvo's salaried employees were offered a new incentive and a way of putting pressure on their managers – a productivity bonus system, PBS.

The criteria to be met for this system varied from company to company, but included factors such as the number of units sold, profit levels, quality targets achieved – and also the number of personal development discussions held.

PBS gave salaried employees a couple of hundred kronor extra in their pockets now and then, which was obviously appreciated by most people – even though some critical voices were raised when the system was first introduced.

The new White Integral Tall Sleeper was introduced in North America. Essentially, this was a normal–control model with full standing room in the cab, a feature made possible by an elevated roof, which also served as a spoiler.

The performance of the horizontal turbo engine was boosted significantly by the addition of an intercooler.

Prestige car racing in Europe

In early 1984, Volvo presented a new technical feature which many people thought was a joke: water injection. In addition to the fuel, a well-dimensioned amount of water was injected into the combustion chambers on turbocharged engines. With the help of advanced electronics, the fuel-air-water delivery could be regulated. The effect would be less knocking, but above all a higher power rating.

Water injection was 'the secret' when Volvo started to compete in the same year in one of Europe's most prestigious racing series, the European Touring Car Championship (ETC) for Group A cars.
The competitions comprised long distance races with two drivers taking it in turns to drive the car during the race.

Here, the Volvo 240 Turbo was matched against classic racing marques such as BMW, Jaguar and Rover. The competitors were not particularly frightened of the new upstart, but already in the first race Volvo gained respect by leading the race for 100 of the 150 laps.

Through its competition department, Volvo Motorsport, Volvo designed and classified competition equipment but did not compete under its own auspices. The racing teams competed with support from own sponsors. There were several Swedish teams from the beginning. One professional team was backed by Volvo dealers in Europe. Several highly qualified drivers drove the Volvo cars in the ETC, including Thomas Lindström, Anders Olofsson, Eje Elgh, Gianfranco Brancatelli and Ulf Granberg.

The cars had power ratings of about 330 hp and achieve top speeds of at least 260 km/h.

The first year was a stimulus and the efforts were broadened during 1985. After 13 rounds, the desirable European Championship title went to the driving pair Lindström/Brancatelli.

The Volvo BM 6300 was the most advanced excavator–loader yet built by the company. The model has survived in modified form as the present–day EL70.

C10M buses were sold e g in the Taiwanese capital, Taipei.

1985 WAS A YEAR of contrasting product developments, from exclusive sports cars to efficient trucks and rugged tractors.

The first development of the year was the appearance of the new 700 series estate, which was designed to uphold the tradition of the Duett 445/210, Amazon 220 and 145/245/265 commercial traveller models. However, eager Swedish buyers were obliged to wait; the model was launched first in North America and it was to be autumn before it appeared in Europe – an indication of the high importance attached by Volvo to the transatlantic market.

Since Volvo had already displayed an estate version of the 700 (the VCC) in 1980, the appearance of the new, versatile and practical model occasioned little surprise.

The styling was conservative, featuring straight, angular lines rather than the fashionable rounded and sporty shapes of its competitors. The design of the model was dictated largely by functional considerations, the straight sides and rear providing the maximum interior space for carrying goods – even bulky items like fridges and armchairs, which could not possibly be accommodated in a combi coupé or a hatchback with a sloping tailgate.

Since the new 700 Estate was a relatively luxurious model, the 200 Estate was retained in the product range for the benefit of economy–minded customers and professional buyers. Basically, the functional differences between the new model and its predecessor were minor. The main improvements were enhanced ride comfort, handling and load management (the rear seat could be folded down to enable long items to be transported, together with three or even four occupants).

Launched and marketed initially in North America, the 760 and 740 estates were the most sought–after 700 series models.

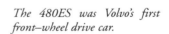

The 480ES was Volvo's first front–wheel drive car.

Technically identical to the saloon, the estate versions offered a between the luxury 760 and the medium–class 740, and between a powerful V6 and a four–in–line engine.

In early summer, Volvo unveiled its most luxurious car ever, in the form of the 780 sports coupé. Although this was essentially a 700 model variant, there was little resemblance between the 'ordinary' versions and the exclusive new two–door model.

The 780 was styled, not in Göteborg, but by Bertone, the Italian designer who had earlier built the deluxe 264TE limousine. With its pure, classic lines, the model was tasteful and elegant rather than fashionably trendy.

With one exception, the 780 was technically similar to the 760GLE; as the top–of–the–range model, it was available with a turbocharged 2.5–litre variant of the PRV six–cylinder engine (the unit used in the fastest version of Renault's exclusive Alpine 310 sports car). However, this version never actually entered series production.

Most 780s came equipped with the ordinary B280 engine, the D24 diesel (with a turbo and intercooler) or the B230 four–cylinder turbo.

The 780 was a high–priced, luxury car with every luxury as standard equipment, including leather upholstery, a sunroof, cruise control and air conditioning.

The model was actually not a true sports car. With the exception of the few examples produced with the four–cylinder B204GT engine (a 200–hp, 16–valve unit with a turbo and intercooler) towards the end of the production period, it was particularly fast.

Yet another exclusive two–door coupé was unveiled in 1985. This was the Dutch–built 480S which, although displayed to the motoring press

and exhibited at shows, did not become available to buyers for another year.

The first front–wheel drive Volvo, the 480ES was styled in the Netherlands in consultation with the design office in Göteborg, and was the first of a completely new generation of medium–class models which were later augmented by four and five–door versions.

The 480ES was actually developed for the US market, where Volvo dealers wanted a sports car to stimulate sales of the rest of the range. In the event, the dollar exchange rate militated against Volvo and the 480ES was never sold in North America.

The 480 was built on the same technical principles as the forthcoming 800 series, using a transversely–mounted, four–cylinder Renault engine.

Produced until autumn 1995 (when the production capacity was required for the new 640), the 480ES was a small, but expensive car with excellent driving characteristics. Like the 780, it was built in relatively small numbers.

By the mid–1980s, Volvo was a large, internationally recognised maker of heavy, long–haul trucks. In the smaller classes, in which the marque was predominant only in a number of specific markets, mainly Scandinavia, Britain and Ireland, its position was somewhat more tenuous.

With a GVW of 11 to 16 tonnes, the FL6 was Volvo's new trump card in the small truck sector. The series was of an entirely new design which Volvo – despite the huge development costs involved – had opted to undertake completely on its own, without partners who might have exploited the company's reputation to market similar models.

Volvo 780.

The Uddevalla Plant

Plans were announced in 1985 to build a car assembly plant on the former shipyard site in Uddevalla.

This signalled the start of very extensive surveys, and also an intense debate on subjects such as the environmental impact the plant and, not least, the transportation between Uddevalla and Göteborg would have.

The financing of the plant also came in for some serious discussion. Volvo received a substantial regional development grant from the Swedish government, even though the company was enjoying exceptionally good success at this time.

Volvo was made to feel welcome in Uddevalla, especially as the town had been hit very hard by the winding down of the shipyard operations. Many of those who had been made redundant from the shipyards jumped at the chance to build cars instead of ships.

The factory was built under a veil of secrecy. The Volvo Car Corporation wanted to have both the assembly plant and the production set up completed before the press and other people were given the opportunity to behold the miracle that had been achieved.

Production was performed entirely in self-supervising groups in which many operators gradually became 'whole car builders'.

This meant they could assemble a car in its entirety. Each employee was given a lot of responsibility for his or her part of the work in the factory. The level of job satisfaction was high and after the initial teething problems the level of quality was also very high.

The new plant was visited by many people. Researchers from near and far studied pretty well all there was to study.

This model assembly plant pointed the way to the future for the entire car industry – at least that is what they thought. Instead, the 1990s heralded a very severe period of recession which hit Volvo very hard indeed. Sales fell dramatically, profits were turned to losses, and tough cost-cutting programmes were the order of the day. One of the things the company needed to do was to cut capacity. Two assembly plants were to be closed: Kalmar and Uddevalla.

The people who worked at the Uddevalla plant just could not understand it, neither could the personnel at Kalmar. 'They are, after all, Volvo's two best assembly plants - so why us?'

Nothing helped, and in the spring of 1993 the Uddevalla plant was closed.

But as everyone knows, the economic situation and success can change very quickly. It took two years from when the Uddevalla plant was closed to when the Volvo Board decided to open it once again. This time the plan was for the Volvo Car Corporation to cooperate with the English company TWR to start developing and producing 'niche' cars – coupé and convertible versions of the Volvo 850. The plant was renamed Auto Nova, and the first cars are expected to be produced at the turn of the year 1996-97.

The FL6 was developed primarily to provide drivers with comfort and hauliers with an economical vehicle.

The ergonomics were far superior to those of earlier models. Maximum importance had been attached to locating the cab at a low level for the safety and well–being of the innumerable delivery drivers required to climb in and out of their vehicles anything up to 200 times daily. The spacious cab accommodated the driver and a single passenger (although a folding seat was provided for a second).

The rear axle in all variants was equipped with air suspension to cushion the cargo, and to facilitate loading and unloading (the system enabled the chassis height to be adjusted to different loading pier levels).

The FL6 was a jack of all trades. Versions included delivery and light, long–haul trucks, as well as all–wheel–drive terrain vehicles.

The Volvo 240 Turbo achieved major success in the European Production Car Championship.

All of the engines used were turbos, to limit the fuel consumption and exhaust emission levels, while the heavier models were also available with intercooler units.

The brakes were of a heavy–duty type for maximum safety. The heavier models in the series were equipped with basically the same air braking system as Volvo's heavy trucks, while the lighter versions were fitted (for the first time on a Volvo truck) with disc brakes at the front.

With their rugged construction, the new medium–sized trucks were suitable for light construction site work and long–haul transport of light cargoes, as well as for delivery duties. For this reason, it was equipped with a folding bunk as a sleeping berth, while a longer cab with a fixed bunk behind the seats was introduced a couple of years later. The low engine cowling made it easy to move from one side of the cab to the other.

Initially, the FL6 was produced only in Oostakker, Belgium, where the model had been developed.

The FL6 was not the only model in the new, low–built FL range, to which the FL7 and FL10 were added to bridge the gap between Volvo's medium–heavy and heavy trucks. Although built to carry the same payload as the heaviest models, the low cab facilitated entry and exit, and increased the mobility of the vehicles in tight spaces.

The FL7 and FL10 were developed in Sweden separately from the FL6. Basically, the models were built from the same chassis components as the F10 and F12, with the cab mounted in a lower position. With their 7 and 10–litre engines, the models were suitable for local and regional goods distribution, as well as for single–driver long–haul work, with GCWs of up to 38 tonnes (the legal limit for truck and semitrailer rigs in most EC countries at the time).

In terms of ergonomics, the cabs in the FL7 and FL10 were far superior to those in any previous model. The floor was extra low and the fully–sprung unit was mounted on coil springs, while the large windows afforded excellent visibility and the efficient soundproofing ensured a low noise level.

To ensure maximum cargo protection and driver comfort, as well as fast, simple goods handling, the models were available with air suspension all round. This enabled a trailer to be coupled and uncoupled

Nils Bohlin.

New technology was introduced in the Umeå cab plant to produce the FL cabs. Robots took over some of the more complicated and physically demanding operations, while almost–rustproof hot–galvanised steel was used in most of the cab.

1985 – Another award for Bohlin

When the West German Patents Board celebrated its 100th anniversary in 1985 it selected eight patents which, over the years, had had a particularly significant impact on mankind.

Among the patents selected, special mention can be made of one dated 1886 relating to a 'gas engine-powered vehicle' by Carl Friedrich Benz, Thomas Alva Edisons 'phonograph' from 1878, Rudolf Diesel's combustion engine – you know which one – from 1892, and a patented dated 1959; but Volvo research engineer Nils Bohlin. This was, of course, for the three-point seat belt.

One wonders if Nils Bohlin knows how many awards have been bestowed on this invention assigned to more important though, how many lives it has saved.

whereas the 5.5–litre, six–cylinder unit used in the 2015 was also equipped with an intercooler.

This largest of the tractor range remained in production until 1987, although the Volvo BM logo disappeared from the bonnet during the last year and the Volvo workforce found themselves assembling Volvo tractors under the Valmet name.

After almost three–quarters of a century, the tractor story was finally at an end.

in an instant, while the the platform or other body could be swapped quickly and easily without the need for ancillary equipment.

Production of the FL7/FL10 was commenced almost simultaneously in both Göteborg and Irvine, Scotland.

Awarded the distinction of 'Truck of the Year', the FL6 and FL7/FL10 contributed decisively to the stronger position which Volvo also achieved in the light and medium truck sectors.

Volvo BM was now an earthmoving plant manufacturer and its involvement in agriculture was drawing to a close. The final stage of the 1985 'Nordic tractor' project was reached in 1985 with the introduction of the smallest models in the series, the 305 and 405 which, although smaller than the earlier 05 series models, were identical in design and function. Both of the new additions were equipped with a slightly smaller 2.7–litre engine, with a turbocharger as standard. Although both were normally equipped with four–wheel drive, two–wheel drive versions were also available.

Both the 305 and 405 were built in Finland, Volvo's main contribution to their development being in the area of styling.

Although the company's tractor history should have ended at this point, development of the biggest 'Nordic tractor' model had been delayed for a variety of reasons and tractor production actually continued until 1987. The 2005 and 2015, which were technically similar to the present Volvo BM T2654, were introduced in 1985. The main difference between the new tractors – which owed their new appearance entirely to the smaller 305 to 905 models – was in the powerplant; the engine in the 'basic' 2005 was a straightforward turbo,

Public transport at the World Exhibition in Japan was provided by a fleet of Volvo B10M articulated buses. The vehicles attracted worldwide interest.

The White Xpeditor Low Entry was built mainly for refuse collection duties. The model featured an extremely low step and a steering wheel on each side!

The VME venture

As part of the ambition to become one of the leading players on the world construction' equipment market, the international group VME was formed in 1985. (The initials VME stood for 'Volvo Michigan Euclid', the three most important trade marks in the joint product range.)

The new company was owned jointly by the Swedish Volvo and the American Clark Equipment Company, and for various reasons it was registered in Holland. There was no joint headquarters to start with, but a new VME head office was built a few years later in Brussels in Belgium.

VME soon became a successful enterprise, and up until 1995 (when Volvo acquired the whole of VME) it took over new companies in the industry, expanded its range of products, and continuously refined and broadened the product ranges of both Volvo and Clark Michigan.

The Volvo BM Valmet range was completed in 1985 with the addition of the little 305 (above) and the big 2005/2105 models (right).

Below: The versatile FL7/FL10 models are equally suitable for public authority service and long–haul or delivery applications.

Action against pointless legislation

In the autumn of 1985, the Swedish parliament voted to introduce legislation governing the use of seat belts in the rear seat – but it was to apply only to passengers over the age of 15.

Volvo felt this was wrong. Children, irrespective of age, should naturally be covered by this legislation.

"*Since the legislation does not cover children's lives, we voice our protest*", said an angry Roger Holtback.

As a protest against the proposed legislation Holtback and his team donated 10,000 seat cushions to be used in all school transport vehicles.

THE LAUNCH OF the low–built FL truck range was completed in 1986.

As the last element in the European range, the FL4 was exhibited at the Amsterdam show in February. In appearance, the model was identical to the lightest (11 tonne) version of the FL6; however, it was designed exclusively for suburban delivery applications.

As the replacement for the F4, the FL4 was equipped with the same Volvo 3.6–litre engine. However, the earlier TD40A precombustion chamber diesel had been superseded by the TD41A which, although of comparable performance, was a more economical, direct–injection unit.

With its rugged construction and six–cylinder, in–line diesel engine, the FL4 was heavier than its competitors in the same weight class. Rather than a high payload, the model offered reliability and outstanding ergonomics, driver comfort and safety.

In the course of time, however, it became clear that buyers of this class of vehicle were unwilling to pay for the model's extra ruggedness, while the 3.6–litre engine was somewhat too small to haul a trailer. For these reasons, production was discontinued only a couple of years later, after a mere 2,000 or so examples had been built.

With a GVW of 8,600 kg (a tonne heavier than the FL4), the FL608 possessed the power necessary to deliver satisfactory performance, even when hauling a trailer, and was duly introduced as the FL4's replacement.

The North American version of the FL6, which was still produced in Belgium, but had been refined

The new A20 dumper was actually a highly modified version of the classic 860/861.

A revised wheel loader range was unveiled at the end of 1986. The L90 (below) superseded the L4400.

in a number of respects to suit the transatlantic market, also appeared in 1986.

Since 'FL' is the accepted abbreviation for Freightliner, the Mercedes–Benz marque in the USA, the North American versions of the FL series were assigned the designation 'FE'.

Two versions – the FE6 and the FE7 – were produced. The FE6 was largely similar to the European FL6, whereas the FE7 was introduced as a substitute for the FL7 which, at the time, was considered too advanced for the US market.

The FE7 was essentially a combination of the FL6 chassis and FL7 driveline (consisting of a 7–litre engine and R52 gearbox). After a couple of years, the gearbox was replaced by the R1000, a unit built partly of aluminium.

In appearance, the FE7 was recognisable by the higher cab position required to provide room for the bigger 7–litre engine. Because of this, the grille was also higher than before.

The FL6 cab was used for many purposes. Another model to which it was fitted was the FS10, which superseded the CH230 and was built especially for narrow Swiss roads.

Consisting of the low–built FL10 chassis and the cab from the medium–heavy FL6, the FS10 provided Swiss customers with a unique, special truck for all heavy applications, from delivery duties (twin–axle version) to long–haul and site work (four–axle, tandem drive version).

Volvo BM was integrated increasingly in the VME joint venture company. Several major additions to the product range were announced towards the end of 1986, the most important of which was a powerful articulated dumper, the A35, with a load capacity of 35 short tons and a 12–litre engine capable of transporting this impressive load across tough terrain at a high average speed.

Consisting of Volvo's own design of automatic gearbox with a torque converter, the PT1660 transmission (the name 'Powertronic' was also used later) was one of the new features of the A35.

The popular 861 dumper, now of a more modern appearance, was introduced under the designation A20 at the same time as the A35. The

Truck of the Year 1986

In 1986, Volvo became the first truck manufacturer to win the Truck of the Year award a third time. This time it was for the FL range. The citation quoted the good ergonomic features, the high level of safety and earnings capacity, and the low operating costs.

intermediate 5350 model remained almost unchanged, although it was now known as the A25 (all model designations indicated the load capacity in short tons).

The entire wheel loader range had also undergone component improvements and had been assigned new designations: L10 (formerly 4600), L120 (4500), L90 (4400), L70 (4300) and L50 (4200B).

Volvo Penta introduced Volvo's first series–produced four–valve engine in its Aquamatic 171 drive (although a limited series of the rallycross version of the B21 unit had been produced in 1980).

The new engine was a bored–out version of the B23, with a unique top cover housing the double overhead camshafts which operated the sixteen valves. The unit was a carburettor type and was not fitted with balance shafts.

This unique engine was manufactured in limited numbers, mainly for light speedboats. However, since its advanced design made it expensive to produce, it was replaced, after a few years, by engines developed in collaboration with the company's partner, Outboard Motor Corporation (OMC), and manufactured outside the Volvo Group.

Refaat el–Sayed and Pehr G. Gyllenhammar.

Refaat el-Sayed

In January 1986, Volvo and Pehr G. Gyllenhammar were a hair's breadth from entering into what would have been a really bad business deal.

In its ambition to strengthen its interests in the field of biotechnology, Volvo and the 'dynamic managing director of Fermenta, the rising star in Swedish business, Refaat el-Sayed' agreed to try and put together a rather complicated but major business deal.

In brief, Fermenta would become the majority shareholder in the pharmaceuticals companies Leo, Pharmacia, and Gambo by the acquisition of Sonesson, while Volvo would own 20 per cent of the new and enlarged Fermenta. Provendor, Volvo's large food group, was also to be included in the deal. 'Volvo identifies Fermenta in a new way and provides the company with new financial muscle', commented Pehr G. Gyllenhammar in an interview.

Before the deal could get off the ground the environment debater Björn Gilberg revealed that el-Sayed did not have the education qualifications he claimed to have. The doctor's hat he was supposed to have qualified for proved to be a bluff.

In the meantime, Volvo had scrutinised Fermenta and its managing director thoroughly.

The trust shown in Fermenta disappeared as fast as the false hat was disclosed.

The last model in the FL series, the 7.5–tonne FL4, was introduced at the 1989 Amsterdam Motor Show.

The GM venture

Towards the end of 1986, it was announced that Volvo had acquired the assets of General Motor's heavy duty truck operations. This was made possible by the formation of a joint company in which Volvo would be the majority shareholder and have management responsibility. The new company commenced operations on a small scale in 1987 under the name Volvo GM Heavy Truck Corporation.

Full-scale operations were started up at the turn of the year 1987-88 when production of the entire GM heavy truck range (except the Brigadier model) was discontinued.

With this strategic alliance with GM, Volvo achieved a broader customer base, a wider dealer network in the USA, and a stronger presence on the Canadian market.

Production of a new, aerodynamic White truck was initiated at the New River Valley plant in Virginia, USA, in mid–1987.

SINCE FIVE TO SIX years is the normal lead time required to develop a new vehicle, whether a car or a bus, it came as no surprise when the company's US subsidiary, Volvo White Truck Corporation (which Volvo had acquired in 1981), unveiled a series of radically modified trucks in spring 1987.

The new Aero series was based on the earlier bonneted models, with modified styling (in the form of much rounder bonnets) to achieve a substantial reduction in the drag coefficient. The front axle was located further back to improve the axle weight, improve the level of comfort and reduce the turning circle. The front headlamps (taken directly from the 240 car) were classic Volvo components which harmonised perfectly with the streamlined front end.

The new Extended Sleeper – an extremely long and spacious cab by European standards – was introduced at the same time as the Aero series. Like its European equivalents, the Extended Sleeper provided accommodation for the driver and a passenger. However, unlike European sleeper cabs (in which two bunks are installed one above the other), it was equipped with a double bed occupying the full width of the cab. In addition, generous space was provided for facilities such as a clothes locker, TV/video and microwave oven.

The feeling of spaciousness in the Extended Sleeper cab was accentuated by the fact that the engine was in front. Thus, the cab floor was completely flat, making it easy to reach the sleeping section (an integral part of the cab) from either seat.

Yet another new American truck was launched in the autumn, in the shape of a completely new Autocar model. This was not a long–haul truck, but was intended as a tough construction site vehicle, a heavy tractor or a large refuse collection vehicle.

During the development phase, the new Autocar truck had been known by the codename 'OP' (for 'Optimum Payload'), the main priority being to minimise the service weight and maximise the payload despite the model's extremely high strength and overload capacity. As one result of this aim, the model was also available (for the first time in many years) with an aluminium cab.

The introduction of the new Autocar model was accompanied by the announcement of the new WHITEGMC name, which was to be used from

Gunnar L. Johansson.

White's Aero model was introduced in autumn 1987 under the WHITEGMC badge.

The WHITEGMC Autocar is a rugged model built for the toughest applications.

Gunnar L. Johansson

Gunnar Leonard Johansson was born in 1928 in Nyfors in Eskilstuna. It was natural for him to get some job experience at the major industry in that town, Bolinder–Munktell. Before that, however, he graduated from his 'studenten' sixth-form college studies in 1948 and took a temporary job at B–M in 1952 whilst studying at the Royal Institute of Technology in Stockholm, from where he graduated in 1955.

His career at Volvo began that same year at the Köpings Mekaniska Verkstad (which was renamed the Volvo Köpingverken in 1958). He became manager of the methods department in 1958. In 1962 he moved to Göteborg as production engineering manager.

Gunnar L. Johansson's career at Volvo developed with several appointments during the 1960s. He was managing director of Volvo–Data from 1969 to 1971. He was made a member of the Volvo Group executive management in 1972 where his brief was to have overall responsibility for organisational structures, business administration development, ADP operations, personnel development, as well as research and development.

In 1978 he moved to Trollhättan to become managing director of Volvo Flygmotor. Eight years later he was called back to head office in Göteborg, this time to take up an appointment as senior executive vice president of AB Volvo, and on 20 May 1987 he was appointed President, a position he held until his retirement on 25 April 1990.

Before taking up his position as President of AB Volvo, Gunnar L. Johansson described his role as head of Volvo Flygmotor as 'Swedish champion in international cooperation'.

With that qualification and also his wide and varied experience from various types of appointments, not least in the field of administration management techniques alongside all other engineering positions, he was well suited for the heavy responsibility he was entrusted with at head office.

Gunnar L. Johansson is also known for being an experienced negotiator, a facet he displayed in his position as vice chairman of the Swedish Metal Trades Employer's Association. His personal record also includes many important directorships.

New Year 1988 on, coinciding with the start of series production.

As a significant indication of Volvo's ambitions in North America, the normal–control WHITEGMC models were now available with an all–Volvo driveline, consisting of a Volvo engine, gearbox and final drive. In addition, the rear axle could – at the customer's request – be mounted in Volvo's own suspension (usually a B–ride or T–ride bogie with tandem drive).

In Europe, Volvo unveiled its most powerful truck to date, the F16 with a new, six–cylinder, in–line engine, a 16–litre unit with four valves per cylinder, developing a massive 470 hp. Although based on the existing F12, the components of the new model were reinforced to accommodate the enormous forces generated by the powerful new engine.

The F16 was developed primarily for demanding applications in countries where high train weights were the norm. Typical examples included timber haulage in Scandinavia and long–haul transport of train weights ranging from 52 to 115 tonnes in Sweden and Australia. The raw

power of the engine made the gearbox almost superfluous on long journeys, permitting high average speeds, even at a constant top speed. With its high–camshaft design, the engine had a higher braking effect than small truck diesels, a crucial advantage in severely undulating country.

The front of the F16 was of an improved streamlined shape, a design change which was made to the F10 and F12 models at the same time.

VME introduced the L30, the smallest of its range of wheel loaders with a bucket capacity of one cubic yard, which was produced at its plant in Penedeiras, Brazil.

The F16 (bottom right) was the major truck event of 1987. Meanwhile, the F12 Globetrotter continued to be a top seller.

Volvo Penta introduced complete power packs for industrial use.

Below left: With the L30, Volvo BM again offered a small, versatile wheel loader.

Activities at the new car plant Uddevalla commenced in earnest in 1987.

The B7 bus was designed for service under tough conditions, in developing countries or in mountainous areas.

THE PRINCIPAL VOLVO car development in 1988 originated in the Netherlands, where the medium–class 440 – a modern, front wheel drive, family version of the 480 – was introduced to supersede both the 340 and the 240 series.

The 440 was a practical five–door model with a fold–down rear seat for maximum flexibility.

Since the 440 was technically identical to the 480ES/480 Turbo, it boasted the same superb handling as the earlier DAF models (and the 340 series). The performance (especially that of the turbo model) was excellent for a practical family car.

The 440 became a best–seller in many countries, including Britain, the Netherlands, Spain and France; however, it failed to inherit the mantle of the almost–venerated 240.

The very first product launch of the year was actually of much earlier origin. The deal between Volvo and General Motors in 1986 (when Volvo took over GM's heavy truck operation) was to be followed by the introduction of a new, light, Class 8 model in autumn 1988. Although development of this model had already been in progress at Volvo White for a considerable time, a stopgap solution was needed for about a year to fill the gap in the range. This was provided by retaining one of the existing GMC/Chevrolet models (the other GM trucks having been discontinued under the terms of the agreement).

The model in question (the GMC Brigadier) was renamed the WHITEGMC Brigadier and was marketed in two versions known as the J8000 and J9500.

In autumn 1988, the Brigadier was replaced by the WHITEGMC WG which, although based on the same components as the rest of the range, was shorter in front and was built for regional, short–distance transport and medium–heavy site applications.

Since the WG was not designed for long–haul use at high speeds, function and production technology took precedence over aerodynamics as development goals. Consequently, the model had a functional rather than a 'fast' look.

The 440 provided Volvo with an up–to–date, front–wheel drive, family car as a complement to the larger, rear–wheel drive 240, 740 and 760.

White trucks became known as WHITEGMC in 1988.

Volvo's Environmental Award

At the annual general meeting of Volvo in May 1988, shareholders approved a proposal put forward by the board of directors to institue an environmental award. The purpose was to promote research and development in the field of the environment by drawing public attention to people who had made a significant contribution to the understanding of, and the conservation of, the earth's environment.

Volvo allocated 20 million kronor to the Volvo Environmental Award, which carried an annual prize of one and a half million kronor.

The WG achieved rapid popularity and, together with the established Integral Sleeper model, has formed the basis of the Volvo GM Heavy Truck Corporation range since then.

The transport of new cars from the production plant was one important application of both the Brigadier and the WG. In this role, the WG was later superseded by the WHITEGMC Autohauler, a model designed especially for the purpose and built largely from WG components.

The plant which Volvo opened in former docks area of Uddevalla in 1988 represented a departure (at least for a time) from the 'old' method of building cars. The work organisation in the completely new facility, in which assembly was carried out by groups rather than on a conventional assembly line, was designed to give the workforce greater responsibility.

The new facility did not replace any of Volvo's existing plants, but was more in the nature of an experiment in new production techniques. Neither was it equipped with a full range of facilities; for example, since there was no paint shop, finished bodies were transported by road from Torslanda (using a fleet of FL10s equipped with Volvo's new 'CityFilter', a device which practically eliminated harmful exhaust gas constituents).

Early in the year, Volvo Car Corporation unveiled its first 16–valve engine at the Geneva Motor Show, a stage which the company was now using more and more to launch its executive models. Produced in both saloon and estate versions, the 740GLT 16V was powered by an engine related to that used in Volvo Penta's Aquamatic 171 drive, in the original 2.3–litre size. This unit was equipped with electronic fuel injection instead of a carburettor and with twin

Curt Göransson
European Champion

Volvo's trucks assumed a 'sporty' image when the Swedish timber haulier Curt Göransson became European Champion in Truck Racing driving his Volvo N12.

Göransson was among the top European drivers for many years and became well-known for winning his races more often than not, for treating the crowd to some spectacular driving, and for his sportsmanship. Truck Racing to 'Curtan' (as he was affectionately called) was just a hobby to indulge in during the summer months. Once the competitions were over for the season he returned to his home in Färila in the province of Hälsingland in the north of Sweden and transported timber from the large Swedish forests.

Curt Göransson and his Volvo N12 left the competition in their wake during the 1988 truck racing season.

The Brigadier – actually a renamed GMC model – was added to the Volvo American range in 1988. The 'fuzzy' picture is a typical 1980s publicity shot.

balance shafts to compensate for the vibrations often inherent in four–cylinder engines of this capacity.

As a family car, the 740GLT 16V was designed for comfort rather than performance.

To Volvo Bus Corporation, March 1988 signalled the start of a period of expansion which has continued unabated since then. This commenced with the announcement that the company had taken over the busbuilding division of Leyland in Britain which, since the collapse of the Leyland Group, has been run successfully by the former management.

Volvo thus acquired the most famous bus marque in the world. Leyland was renowned especially for its double–decker models, the jewel in the crown being the Olympian, which was destined to outlive the other models in the range at that time.

The other famous Leyland model was the Tiger, the last in a long series of Leylands with pancake engines (in fact, the Leyland equivalent of the time had provided the inspiration for Volvo's very first mid–engined model in the late 1940s). However, the British company's success with this type of model had declined over the years, to the extent that by the time of the Volvo takeover, it had long since abandoned the production of its own engines and was using units built by independent suppliers.

Smaller buses had become increasingly popular as the British bus market expanded. The Leyland entry in this class was the Swift, a relatively simple model with a vertically–installed midships engine. Although this configuration naturally raised the floor level, it also afforded a high degree of flexibility, making the Swift popular not only as a midi–bus, but also as a special–purpose model, such as a mobile library.

The fourth and last member of the Leyland bus family was the modern Lynx city bus, which was powered by a horizontal, rear–mounted engine (and was not dissimilar to the Volvo B10R in its

Above and below: Leyland Lynx.

Above: Leyland Tiger.

Right: Leyland Olympian.

Below: Leyland Swift.

basic design). Although built essentially in finished (bodied) form, the model was, in time, supplied as a bare chassis to those operators anxious to exercise more influence over the finished product.

With its purchase of Leyland, Volvo acquired not only the marque and a range of four models, but also two plants, one for chassis production and the other for bodybuilding. These facilities were now used to produce some of Volvo's own bus chassis, mainly the B10M.

Built at VME's plant in Landskrona, the Euclid R32 truck received its premiere at the Intermat Show, the major American earthmoving plant exhibition.

THE 400 SERIES was of crucial importance to Volvo in many countries where compacts built for rationalised city traffic systems are preferred to large cars. For this reason, it was natural that Volvo Car BV in the Netherlands should opt to complement the 480 sports car and the 440 hatchback with a four–door saloon designed to appeal to buyers with a preference for classic models of this type.

The 460 was an elegant medium–class model distinguished by its chrome grille, which gave a much more expensive impression than the black grille on the 440 –an impression reinforced by the model's GLE tag (which it shared with the 760). The deluxe version of the 440, on the other hand, was known as the GLT, a sportier designation appropriate to the stubbier, more aggressive combi coupé.

Like other 400 series models, the 460 was also available with an automatic transmission – not, however, a development of the Variomatic drive, but a conventional, multi–speed unit with an hydraulic torque converter (the Variomatic was not suitable for use in a front–wheel drive car).

By now, Volvo was recognised as a maker of safe and exclusive cars, but was not particularly noted for fast or sporty models. There were at least four reasons for this: aerodynamics which were far from perfect (function and space were higher priorities), high weight (due to the high level of passive safety), fairly generous dimensions (Volvo built spacious family cars rather than special models for the single man) and reliable rather than powerful engines.

An exciting engine, the B204GT, which was sold in only a few countries, was introduced in the 700 in 1989. Developing 200–hp, this was basically

Although the Volvo 460 was traditional rather than revolutionary, it was equipped with much of the latest technology and was the precursor of the bigger 850.

In the late 1980s, the 760 Executive was the choice of owners who wanted both a Volvo and a high standard of luxury.

the 16–valve unit used in the 740GLT (the 2–litre version sold in Italy, France and Finland), with a turbo and intercooler. The end product was the fastest car ever built by Volvo.

The 700 with the B204GT was equipped with the same multilink rear suspension as the 1988 760.

Although the model came with an extremely high price tag, those who drove it testified that it was 'worth every penny'. However, this did not include Swedish motorists; since the car was not equipped with a catalytic converter, it could not be certified for sale on the home market.

The reason for using the 2–litre rather than the 2.3–litre engine was simple; the torque which it developed was exactly what the gearbox could transmit with a satisfactory margin of safety (the higher torque of the bigger engine may well have caused failure of the gearbox internals).

Whereas Volvo was selling increasing numbers of forward–control (or 'cab–over–engine') trucks in

Europe, the normal–control (bonneted) type was predominant in Brazil, a market which was growing steadily in importance. However, the company's bonneted models were now showing their age and were clearly in need of renewal.

The resultant products, the NL10 and NL12, were introduced in 1989. For the first year, these were reserved for the Brazilian market and were built exclusively in Curitiba in the state of Paraña (from 1990 on, the models were also produced in Sweden and Australia).

The NL models were based on the F10 and F12. Inspired by the WHITEGMC Aero, the front

The Volvo 460 – an attractive car pictured in an attractive setting.

Pehr G. Gyllenhammar welcomes his successor, Christer Zetterberg, to Volvo's HQ in autumn 1989.

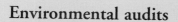

Environmental audits

To demonstrate still further that environmental issues were being taken seriously, Volvo employed an environmental auditor in 1989.

His task was to audit all of the Volvo Group's global plants and facilities on a long-term basis with regard to their effect on the environment.

Continuous attacks on Volvo during the 1980s and the company's ongoing battle to contribute to a better environment had taught the company that it needed to take the initiative in the efforts towards achieving a better environment, and preferably be one step ahead of the legislation put forward by authorities.

section had been modified to reduce the drag and modernise the appearance, while the cab was also raised to improve the insulation against engine heat and noise.

In addition, since the cab was now supported on coil springs, the new trucks offered a much higher standard of driver comfort than the N types.

The NL models enabled Volvo to maintain and increase its competitiveness in South America. In Europe, on the other hand, the trend towards forward–control trucks for all applications was maintained. As a result, Volvo no longer markets bonneted trucks in most European countries (although the type may, in certain cases, be supplied to special order).

The B10C ('10' stood for '10–litre' and 'C' for 'Coach') was one of the least known buses built by Volvo over the years – hardly surprising since only five of the vehicles were built and sold.

The model was unique in that it was a tourist coach with a rear–mounted engine and appeared several years before Volvo Bus Corporation launched the B12 and B10B, the company's first 'genuine' rear–engined tourist models.

Developed by the Volvo design office in Australia and produced only in a three–axle version, the B10C was a functional and elegant model finished with a locally built tourist coach body. However, although it performed satisfactorily, development and production were discontinued after only a few of the vehicles had been built, due to the forthcoming introduction of VBC's new, rear–engined B12 with its powerful 12–litre engine. In this situation, it would have been economic madness to build both the Australian model and the new, worldwide standard model which, apart from its more powerful engine, was produced in volume from standard components.

Although the B10C was no more than a footnote in Volvo's bus history, it did stimulate the development of powerful, modern, rear–engined chassis for luxury tourist coaches of the largest and fastest type.

Equipped with the RM12 (the most powerful aero engine built by Volvo to date), the JAS39 Gripen, Sweden's new interceptor/strike/reconnaissance aircraft, flew for the first time in 1989. Built by Volvo Flygmotor, the RM12 powerplant was developed from a commercial aircraft engine (to reduce the development costs to a reasonable level) and was equipped with an afterburner manufactured in Trollhättan.

In 1989. Volvo became the first European truckmaker to market its products in Japan on a regular basis.

The modern WG replaced the Brigadier in the American range at the beginning of the year.

Equipped with a Volvo RM12 powerplant, the JAS39 Gripen flew for the first time in 1989.

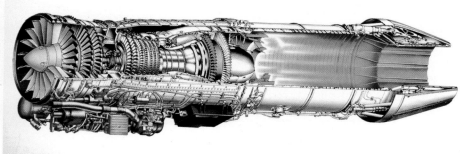

Left: The rear–engined B10C bus was produced in Australia in small numbers, foreshadowing the introduction of the series–built B12 and B10B a couple of years later.

Below right: The streamlined NL series superseded the ageing N type in Brazil in 1989.

Below: Volvo invested heavily in providing truck and bus owners with 24–hour service in all countries.

IN PRODUCT TERMS, 1990 was characterised by refinement rather than renewal. This applied equally to cars and trucks.

The 960 was one of the most sought–after new cars in Volvo's history. After the luxury 264/260 and 760 models – which never quite outclassed the competition – Volvo now had a medium–class executive car which, in every respect, was more than a match for any comparable model on the market.

Not completely new, the 960 was based on the experience gained from the 760. However, the latter's two greatest disadvantages – the V6 engine and the model's boxy lines – had been magically overcome by Volvo's ingenious engineers and stylists.

The basic styling was derived from 700 series, with completely modified front and rear sections (although the basic shape of the now–classical front had been retained). The new lines were rounder, making the model more attractive and more comparable with its most recent competitors, while marginally reducing the drag coefficient.

Developing 204 hp, the new B6304F engine ('B' standing for 'Bensin' or 'petrol', '6' for six cylinders, '30' for 3.0 litres, '4' for 'four–valve' and 'F' for a fuel–injected unit with a catalytic converter) was the most powerful car engine ever built by Volvo. The unit was produced in a completely new petrol engine plant in Skövde, which was opened in 1990 to manufacture light–alloy engines only.

To obtain the highest possible performance from what was a modestly sized engine for a luxury car, the 3.0–litre unit was equipped with double overhead camshafts operating four valves per cylinder. The unit was combined with an automatic transmission in all cases.

The 960 is a big, relatively heavy model with a top speed somewhat over 200 km/h.

The standard 940 variant was introduced at the same time as the 960. Identical in appearance (with the exception of the exterior trim and badges), this was equipped with the same 2.3–litre engine as the 740 and with a beam–type rear axle instead of the multilink rear suspension used in the 960.

The 960 and 940 saloons were accompanied by estate versions, which were of the same appearance as the 760 and 740 (except in front) and were built from the same components as the corresponding saloons (however, like the 760 Estate, the 960 Estate had a beam–type rear axle).

One of the most beautiful Volvos ever was exhibited at the Geneva Motor Show early in the year. This was the 480 convertible which, although based on the 480ES, had been transformed into an open sports car. Despite the considerable interest which it attracted, the model never reached the series production stage, largely due to production engineering problems.

Top: The 960 was the most luxurious series–built model yet built by Volvo.

Second from top: The 960 Executive is produced in limited numbers for discriminating customers.

Above and right: Conceived for customers anxious to buy a Volvo sports car, the 480 convertible never progressed beyond the design study stage.

Christer Zetterberg

In November 1989, Pehr G. Gyllenhammar took everyone by surprise by presenting his successor as managing director and chief executive officer of AB Volvo. His name was Christer Zetterberg, relatively unknown to most people, even though he was at the time managing director and CEO of the state-owned PK-Banken.

Christer Zetterberg was 48 years old and had made a career in the Swedish forestry industry before becoming a bank executive.

He took up his appointment as Managing director on 25 April 1990, and became CEO on 15 October that same year. He was presented with a thankless task at Volvo as the company had just begun to experience serious economic problems at the start of the recession which was to prove to be just as bad as the depression years in the 1930s.

Christer Zetterberg initiated a large-scale cost-cutting programme, and this was continued by Sören Gyll when he succeeded Zetterberg in May 1992 after the latter had been in the hot seat for just two years.

Volvo President P. G. Gyllenhammar and Raymond H. Lévy, his counterpart at Renault, were the men behind the proposed merger.

Christer Zetterberg.

Volvo produced an extremely wide range of special models. The pictures below show an elegant 960 limousine and two hearses based on the 960 and 940.

The alliance with Renault

An announcement which amounted to the biggest news ever in Swedish industry was made at a press conference in Amsterdam on 23 February 1990. This was that Volvo had entered into an alliance with the French state-owned automotive manufacturer Renault.

At first the news was received positively. Volvo's shares rose substantially on the stock exchange, but later fell about 20 per cent in just a few weeks.

The two companies had formed a 'Joint General Policy Committee' with the two respective company chiefs, Pehr G. Gyllenhammar and Raymond H. Lévy, heading the management team.

In the ensuing years the cooperation was intensfied point by point. One joint group after another was formed.

Estimates showed that Volvo would 'save' up to 25 thousand million kronor before the turn of the century as a result of the alliance.

Initially there was little or no opposition to the alliance, or it may have been that not enough scope was offered for an open debate on the subject. But nothing seemed to impede development towards a merger.

In September 1993 it was announced that the two companies would merge subject to approval by the respective boards and shareholders. During the years of the alliance Renault had achieved relatively good success, while Volvo had faced serious problems resulting in extensive cost-cutting programmes and major losses. It was easy to get the impression that the way was open for the big company Renault to swallow the smaller Volvo.

A serious and at times heated debate was generated in the autumn of 1993, and it was Volvo's engineers in particular who expressed doubts about the proposed merger. They did not think it would be beneficial to Volvo. Over a period of several years they had seen that it was not always easy to overcome the cultural differences that existed.

The shareholders also started to voice their protests. The debate columns in newspapers were full of letters stating arguments for and against the merger. Two former Volvo directors, Lars Malmros and Håkan Frisinger, both of them with integrity and credibility, involved themselves in the debate on the side of those who were not in favour of the proposed merger.

Suddenly, nothing appeared to be easy or self-evident any more when the Volvo Board assembled for a decisive meeting on 2 December 1993. Sören Gyll came to the meeting to present a letter signed by a majority of Volvo's top managers expressing their opposition to the proposed merger.

The Board realised that with this level of opposition it would be impossible to implement the merger, so Volvo withdrew. The Board, led by Pehr G. Gyllenhammar, resigned with immediate effect.

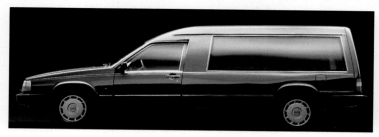

Since taking over White a decade before, Volvo had made continuous safety, ergonomic and comfort improvements to the White and White GMC trucks, while maintaining the simplicity and American characteristics of the models. Three major new trucks were introduced during 1990.

Perhaps the most important of these was also the least obvious. The earlier, Belgian–built FE6/FE7 series was replaced by the brand new FE model which, because of the unchanged cab, was almost identical in appearance to its predecessors.

Now built in the USA, the Volvo FE was of an equally simple and intelligent design, the proven WG chassis being equipped with the Swedish–built FL6/FS7 cab to create a relatively light and extremely powerful Class 7 truck (the second largest class in the USA).

As an economical engine option for the often price–sensitive American market, the FE was available with a 6.6–litre Caterpillar 3116 engine in outputs from 185 to 215 hp. Volvo's own 7–litre unit was available for more demanding applications.

In appearance, the trucks with the two different engines were distinguishable from each other by the slightly higher cab (similar to that used in the earlier FE7 and the new European FS7) in the Volvo–engined version.

Initially, the FE was produced only as the FE42, a two–axle (four–wheel) version with a single driving axle (or two driving wheels). This was followed shortly by the FE64, which was a three–axle model with two driving axles.

Limited numbers of the FE6/FE7 were built with the same short sleeper cab used in Europe. However, a new, longer sleeper cab with sufficiently generous interior space to satisfy the most exacting demands, was introduced before long. Built in Umeå, Sweden, this unit actually consists of a standard FL6/FS7 sleeper cab extended to double the sleeping accommodation.

The traditional WHITEGMC trucks also underwent further refinement in 1990.

Full standing room was provided in the top–of–the–range Aero Integral Sleeper (a North American equivalent of the Globetrotter) by utilising the exterior space normally occupied by a roof–mounted spoiler as interior space for the occupants. With this modification, the model was renamed the Aero Integral Sleeper ES.

The forward–control High Cabover model had previously lacked the enormous space available in the most exclusive version of the bonneted model. Now, the forward–control model also became available with the spacious cab with the wide double bed.

A High Cabover with a 'setback axle' (i.e. with the front axle located further towards the rear) offering enhanced comfort, improved axle weight

and a smaller turning circle, was introduced at the same time.

Production and marketing of the L90 wheel loader in Brazil commenced in 1990.

Boije Ovebrink began to make a name on the truck racing scene in his FL10 in 1990. Since then, he has climbed steadily up the rankings.

VME's product range became even more comprehensive when the company took over Åkerman.

The world's first middle seat belt

Volvo presented its new 960 car model in the summer of 1990. One of the most startling safety features of this car was the introduction of the world's first inertia reel belt in the middle of the rear passenger seat. And that was not all: the seat belt was combined with a child safety cushion integrated into the middle armrest. A simple hand operation could change the armrest into a very safe place for a child to sit – protected by the reel belt.

The advanced 24–valve engine used in the 960 is manufactured in a new extension to the Skövde plant, where a limited number of 16–valve units was produced during the development phase.

The most modern engine factory

The first engine variant to be built in the new East Factory at the Skövde plant was the in-line aluminium six-cylinder engine for the Volvo 960 model. This was in 1990.

But the factory was not officially opened until 1991 when the new 850 model was introduced on the market. This was part of the 16 thousand million kronor investment in developing and producing the Volvo 850.

The factory is a veritable marvel as regards a modern working environment and equipment. All production is performed in what is known as 'dock assembly' on small carriers running on circuits in the factory floor. Line operators are assisted by advanced computer equipment showing each assembly operation and tool.

The work is performed in modules by independent groups of between ten and twelve operators.

1990 – The first operating loss in 61 years

When the 1990 annual accounts for Volvo were published they showed a minus operating result for the first time since 1929.

Every year from 1930 onwards Volvo had provided its shareholders with a surplus. The share dividend was unchanged or increased every year, up until the serious economic crisis hit the company in the early 1990s.

During the crisis years times were really depressing. Issue after issue of the house journal 'Volvo Nu' carried reports of declining sales, falling exchange rates, enforced early retirements, and redundancies.

There was a gloomy atmosphere throughout the company. And perhaps it was symptomatic when the Torslanda plant employed a priest on a full-time basis.

Zettelmeyer and Åkerman

VME, the international corporation which at this point in time represented Volvo's interest in the field of construction equipment, made two important company acquisitions in 1990 and 1991. Both companies supplemented their own products with new product types on markets where Volvo up until that point did not have a strong position in those parts of the construction equipment sector.

Åkerman was all that remained of what was once a large number of Swedish manufacturers of large earth-moving equipment. With a wide product range and a good quality reputation, a valuable broadening of the product range was achieved when a decisive share of the Åkerman company in Eslöv was acquired in 1990. Volvo's own manufacture of earth-moving machines was limited to the powerful tractor excavator the 6300. With Åkerman in the range there was now access to a full range of earth-moving equipment which could swing through 360 degrees, both as a tractor version and a wheeled version.

Zettelmeyer was and still is a German company of good repute manufacturing wheel loaders, and VME acquired this company in 1991. Zettelmeyer has a strong position in Germany, where VME did not have a strong base in the wheel loader sector. Zettelmeyer produces both small and large wheel loaders. The smaller Zettelmeyer models in particular soon became a valuable addition to Volvo's own wheel loader range, where there had not been any really small wheel loaders since the LM422 in the 1960s.

In 1990, Volvo acquired control of Steyr Bus, the well–known Austrian busbuilder.

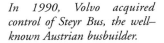

The 850 was Volvo's first big, front–wheel drive car.

THE INTRODUCTION OF the front–wheel drive 850GLT in 1991 was something of a revolution in the history of Volvo Car Corporation. This Volvo was not only equipped with the very latest technology; it was one of the most enjoyable cars in the world to drive!

Although front–wheel drive was perhaps the most interesting new feature of the 850GLT (which had been developed in record time), it was certainly not the most important. Equally significant was the new 'delta–link' rear suspension which, as regards handling, made the car more than a match for other family and executive models, and superior to many low–slung sports cars.

The engine was a 960 unit with five cylinders instead of six, a swept volume of 2.5 litres and an output of 170 hp. For the second time in its history, Volvo adopted a double overhead camshaft configuration and four valves per cylinder in a light, aluminium unit.

A wide range of engine options was soon available. A 2–litre version of the DOHC 20 was available in certain markets from the start, while a 225–hp 2.3–litre turbo, as well as 2 and 2.5–litre, five–cylinder units with double overhead camshafts but only two valves per cylinder, were also introduced in time.

The FE42 was built from chassis components developed for North America and was equipped with the safe, ergonomic FL cab from Umeå.

The first woman on the Volvo Board

Volvo has never had many women in prominent positions. Therefore it was something of a sensation when Volvo announced in 1991 that a woman had been appointed to the Board. This was the Baroness Lydia Dunn from Hongkong.

Although the 850GLT was the fastest and sportiest Volvo ever built, the safety aspects had not been neglected. In fact, the basic development philosophy had been to design a car offering unsurpassed active and passive safety.

In terms of size, the 850 was not remarkable for a Volvo. On the contrary, its introduction meant that the range now included no less than three model series of the same class. Apart from the 850, these were the classic 940/960 and the ageing 240 which, especially in the estate version, was as popular with many buyers as the PV445 Duett had been almost forty years before.

1991 was also an eventful year in trucks. Volvo Truck Corporation introduced a new model, the FS7, in which the light chassis and cab of the FL6 were combined with the power of the bigger 7–litre engine. The chassis was reinforced to enable this class of vehicle to carry a high payload.

The first FS7 engine developed 230 hp, while a 260–hp unit was added shortly afterwards when Volvo decided to introduce an 'environmental' engine designed to meet the tougher emission control standards due to come into force a couple of years later. The company's aim was to promote a cleaner environment and to encourage buyers to specify low–emission engines to a greater extent than before.

The 'new' Volvo NE – which, in fact, was simply the WHITEGMC WG with a Volvo badge – appeared in the autumn. However, this was an important symbolic step which paved the way for the change in name of all the company's North American models from WHITEGMC to Volvo.

The year was also an exciting one for Volvo Bus Corporation. For the first time since 1950–51, the company introduced all–round models with rear–mounted engines, mainly for use as tourist coaches in the biggest and smallest classes.

The B12 was the first Volvo bus with a 12–litre engine, initially with an output of 365–395 hp (the latest B12 models are powered by units up to

The Munktell Museum

In November 1991, the Munktell Museum was opened in the centre of Eskilstuna. This was to be the home of a collection of historical VCE machines. The museum has a floor area of 1,100 sq. metres and consists of two sections: an auditorium where the focus is on the company's history, and an exhibition hall. The latter is divided into the main product groups Tractors, Engines, and Construction equipment. A large number of 'maiden' works have been created within VCE and its predecessor companies. These products are on show and/or described in the museum, which houses some fifty exhibition models. The museum has attracted a lot of interest and there is a constant stream of visitors.

The Munktell Museum in Eskilstuna was inaugurated in autumn 1991.

SIPS (not to be confused with simple crash reinforcement in the doors) distributes the collision forces throughout the car. The picture on right shows the relatively minor damage caused by a heavy side collision.

The NE was the first US–developed truck to be sold under the Volvo name.

Volvo stays in the lead with SIPS

The Volvo 850 GLT not only represented an enormous shift in the Volvo Car Corporation's technological ideology, it also brought huge advances in the field of safety. SIPS (Side Impact Protection System) consolidated Volvo's lead in the safety stakes.

While competitors boasted of beams in doors, Volvo had created a system which offered a 25 per cent reduction in personal injury from side impacts.

SIPS is a combination of a robust structure, impact-absorbing interior surfaces, and impact-absorbing elements embedded inside the doors. The force of a car crushing into the SIPS system from the side is absorbed by the car and dissipated throughout the structure, so interior penetration is far less. It therefore takes longer for passengers to be struck by the force of the impact, and this force also strikes the passengers at a lower speed, thanks to SIPS.

The Volvo occupants' vital 'longer period of grace' is a mere ten milliseconds long – a hundredth of a second. But an immensely short period is in many cases sufficient to spell the difference between life and death, between a severe personal injury and a couple of bruises, or between a light injury and no injury at all. With 21 per cent of all vehicle accidents involving side collisions, they are the second-most common type of road accidents after head-on collisions. And if we look at the statistics for fatal accidents, this proportion is even higher, at 26 per cent. So a 25 per cent reduction in personal injury from side impacts means that SIPS prevents an awful lot of agony all round.

Environmental award to atmospheric researcher

Volvo's 1991 Environmental Award was granted to professor Paul Crutzen of the Max Planck Institute of Chemistry in Mainz, Germany. He received the award for his work on identifying and explaining critical properties in the atmosphere's chemical behaviour.

The Volvo B6 was a highly modern medium–class bus.

420hp).With the vertical engine mounted longitudinally at the rear, the model provided a powerful and exclusive alternative to the mid–engined type (which Volvo had consistently championed) in those markets in which the rear–engined bus is king. New European legislation permitting higher axle weights was one of the main reasons for the introduction of the B12, since it enabled two–axle, rear–engined models to be used without contravening the law.

The B6 'midi–bus', initially with a 6–litre, 180–hp (later 210 hp) engine, was introduced in the autumn. This rear–engined model replaced the ageing front–engined B6 of the late 1970s.

However, VBC was also developing other products. Early in 1991, it launched a new Mk.IV version of the world's best–selling bus, the B10M, with improvements such as better weight distribution and a more efficient radiator location.

At the end of the year, the engineers at VBC's bodybuilding plant at Säffle unveiled a new generation of bus bodies ('Säffle System 2000') in which the body frame is constructed from a number of aluminium sections. Different combinations of these can be used to create urban and interurban buses of various types and sizes.

In Eskilstuna, VME introduced a number of new earthmoving machines in what was an eventful year for that company. The new L150 wheel loader was the first of a new generation of vehicles in which a completely new chassis and an ergonomically designed cab, as well as a further developed lifting unit and more efficient engines, were the most important innovations. Although normally equipped with a steering wheel, the L150 can also be provided with a joystick for control purposes.

The articulated A30 dumper, with a 30–tonne capacity and a 10–litre engine, was introduced simultaneously in the USA, filling the gap between

the 7–litre A25 and the 12–litre A35. The A30 is basically similar to the A35, but smaller in size.

The Powertronic gearbox used in both the A30 and A35 dumpers was also offered as an option in several heavy Volvo trucks, notably the FL10 (for construction site work) and F12 (as an emergency fire–tender, mainly in airports). The Powertronic is a fully automatic, five or six–speed gearbox with an hydraulic torque converter and hydraulic retarder, which provides the driver with three driving modes, Performance, Economy and Engine Braking.

Since conventional automatic transmissions are unnecessarily complex and expensive for 'normal' transport applications, the unique Geartronic self–changing gearbox was introduced as an alternative. The Geartronic is a mechanical, all–synchromesh Volvo gearbox with an automatic, microprocessor–controlled gearchanging unit. The unit, which changes gear automatically, exactly like a highly skilled driver, not only offers the highest possible standard of driving comfort, but also affords optimum fuel economy and minimum environmental impact, even on long journeys.

Emission control standards for trucks and buses are rapidly becoming stricter. In 1991, Volvo introduced a new generation of diesel engines, many equipped with electronic fuel injection systems, to minimise exhaust emissions while maintaining the same or even a lower fuel consumption. Notable among the new units was the TD163E, with which Volvo broke the 500–hp barrier for the first time.

The most significant engine advance of 1991 was the Volvo Penta KAD42, the first diesel engine in the world to be equipped with both an exhaust–driven turbocharger and a direct–driven, compressor-type supercharger, combining the power of a big V8 with the economy of a diesel. This arrangement combines the efficiency of the turbo in continuous operation with the direct action of the compressor when throttle is applied, even at very low engine revs.

The new System 2000 bodies from Säffle were equally suitable for small long–distance buses and long, highly efficient, articulated city buses. Pictured here is a B10M Mk.IV in Göteborg.

The advantages of the configuration are not confined to high performance; since fuel combustion takes place at the same efficiency at both low and high engine speeds, the environmental benefits are equally important.

The Zettelmeyer models again provided Volvo with a complete range of small wheel loaders.

The fast and powerful B12 bus was popular in many countries, even across the Atlantic. The model in the picture is Brazilian.

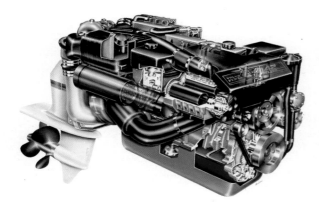

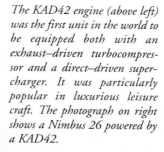

The KAD42 engine (above left) was the first unit in the world to be equipped both with an exhaust–driven turbocompressor and a direct–driven supercharger. It was particularly popular in luxurious leisure craft. The photograph on right shows a Nimbus 26 powered by a KAD42.

Left: New machines introduced in the early 1990s included the L150 wheel loader and the A30 articulated dumper.

Arna of Norway was one of the first companies to bodywork the new B10B.

IN MANY RESPECTS, 1992 was a transition year in which no new products emerged from most of the Volvo Group companies. Volvo's entire energies were concentrated on two important issues: expansion of its cooperation with Renault and implementation of the intensive rationalisation programme which was to cut the workforce, lower costs, improve efficiency and reduce the production volumes required to guarantee and maximise profits, even in times of recession with declining output.

However, one company – Volvo Bus Corporation – was in the throes of renewal. Although two entirely new products and a new generation of bodies had been introduced the previous year, VBC exhibited its new, rear–engined B10B at the Geneva Motor Show early in the year.

The B10B brought an end to Volvo's total concentration on mid–engined buses. Unlike earlier models of its type, it was a genuine

all–rounder which was equally suitable as a city or intercity bus, and as a luxury tourist coach.

The B10B was, at one and the same time, a new model and a natural product of the comprehensive rationalisation programme implemented under VBC President Larserik Nilsson. The model was built largely from existing components from the B10M Mk.IV and the B12, shortening the development time while limiting the development costs to an acceptable level, and facilitating parts production and stock control.

In terms of performance, the B10B was comparable to the B10M, with its horizontal 10–litre engine developing up to 340 hp and a wide choice of transmissions, including Volvo's manual gearbox and automatic transmissions supplied by a number of independent makers.

Although not greeted by immediate acclaim, the B10B did become popular. While the model did not meet the demand for a low–entry bus designed to facilitate disabled and elderly passengers, it represented the first step in this direction.

The next development appeared the following year in the form of the B10B LE (Low–Entry) model, the front section of which was modified to accommodate a low–level entrance. Despite its fairly basic design, the new variant was custom–built as an ergonomic urban and interurban model.

The B10B LE was shown with several different bodies and was projected mainly as an interurban bus (the B12, with engine ratings up to 395 hp, had

Volvo's Environmental Award 1992

Volvo's 1992 Environmental Award, which carried a prize of one and half million Swedish kronor, was shared by an Englishman, doctor Norman Myers, and an American, professor Peter H. Raven.

They were reward for their efforts in creating international awareness of the importance of the biological diversity of the environment of our plant Earth.

Doctor Myers was one of the first to raise the alarm about the threat to the global environment caused by the devastation of the tropical rain forests. Professor Raven is a botanist and specialises in the problems of biological diversity and in the evolution of plants.

Gas–powered 'environmental' buses became a feature of Göteborg traffic in 1992. The vehicles were powered by a horizontal 10–litre engine converted to burn natural gas.

been available as a tourist coach for the previous six months). One of the very first demonstration models was equipped with the last Säffle body of the 'old' type (although the Säffle 2000 generation had been introduced the month before, there had not been time to fit the new chassis with it). Meanwhile, the other bodybuilder in the Volvo Group, Steyr Bus of Austria, also unveiled a B10B with a body of its own design.

In 1992, Volvo Bus Corporation delivered the first of its gas–powered test buses to the City of Göteborg. These were diesel–engined vehicles converted to burn gas by United Turbine of Malmö, a subsidiary of Volvo Flygmotor.

The gas buses are totally 'green', with negligible emissions of most exhaust gas constituents.

Series–built gas–powered buses have since been delivered to customers both in Sweden and abroad.

VME introduced its L180 wheel loader in 1992.

Sören Gyll.

Strategic joint venture for Volvo Penta

In the summer of 1992, Volvo Penta entered into a joint venture with OMC (Outboard Marine Corporation) in the USA. This led to the formation of a joint company, Volvo Penta Marine products, L.P. in Lexington, Tennessee. The company was owned to 60 per cent by Volvo Penta, and to 40 per cent by OMC. I/O drives for petrol engines are developed and produced at the company's factories. Up until January 1995, a joint single propeller drive was manufactured under the respective product names (Volvo Penta SX and OMC Cobra). Then the joint venture was expanded and the petrol engine drive was marketed and sold through the world's biggest service network under one name: Volvo Penta SX Cobra.

In September 1992, just after the start of the OMC joint venture, Volvo Penta and the English marine engine manufacturer Perkins announced that they had entered into a major joint venture. This was to develop, manufacture, and sell small, compact diesel engines for marine applications, and in particular for sailing boats and also small motor boats.

The engines, which are manufactured in Perkins' factories, are marketed to boat builders all over the world under the Volvo Penta trade mark.

Sören Gyll

Sören Gyll was born in 1940 and began his business career at Rank Xerox, but was later recruited in 1977 as head of the steel and forestry conglomerate Uddeholm.

In 1984, he took on the responsibility of head of the State-owned Statsföretag, many parts of which ran at a loss. He re-named the company Procordia, turned it into a profitable major company, and started the procedure towards privatisation. The fact that he succeeded in this 'impossible' task qualified him to take on the top job at Volvo. On 13 May 1992, Sören Gyll was appointed managing director and CEO of AB Volvo in succession to Christer Zetterberg. Despite the hard work put in by Zetterberg in cutting costs, Volvo found itself in a deep economic crisis.

The most important task facing Sören Gyll was to lift the company from this depression. He put into action a comprehensive programme called 'Volvo 95'. With an holistic approach, shortened lead times, and increased turnover of capital, the company would be able to recover from the crisis. Extensive cost-cutting programmes continued. During the first three years of the 1990s, Volvo cut its workforce by almost 20,000.

The tough rationalisation programmes concerned everyone in the entire organisation. The turning point came in late 1993.

The product programme for 1993-94, with the highly acclaimed 850 series from the Volvo Car Corporation, and the recently introduced FH series from the Volvo Truck Corporation, was ensured of success once there was an upswing on the market. In just a couple of years the operating figures turned from red to black, and record results.

The other major task which Sören Gyll had to apply himself to when he took over as managing director and CEO was to assist Pehr G. Gyllenhammar in the work in the alliance leading up to the proposed merger with Renault.

During the turbulent autumn months in 1993, however, many of Volvo's top managers voiced their opposition to the merger.

Sören Gyll informed the Volvo Board of this opposition at its meeting on 2 December, the meeting which saw the resignation of the Board and Gyllenhammar's hasty retreat from Volvo.

After the break up with Renault, Volvo's owners decided that the company should return to its core business operation – that of an out and out transport equipment industry enterprise. Volvo sold off its food and pharmaceutical industries bit by bit. Instead VME was brought back into the Volvo fold from Clark Equipment Corporation. The Volvo Bus Corporation was made a separate business area in the Volvo Group, and expanded considerably through acquisitions.

Sören Gyll has led the company through the extensive programme of changes since 1992 with vigour, unyieldingness, and with long-term development of the strength factors outlined in the strategic policy.

The Environmental Concept Car

The Volvo Environmental Concept Car (ECC) was presented in September 1992. The car caused something of a sensation in as much as the concept combined future environmental demands with Volvo's own demands on a family car – quality, safety, comfort, and performance. The Volvo ECC was a very realistic answer to the increasing number of environmental requirements, with California as the 'locomotive'

The Volvo ECC is not only a stylish car, it also provides sufficient space for a family of four. Its body is made of aluminium and is fully recyclable. The materials used in the car have been developed and produced to give the least possible effect on the environment. When the time comes to scrap the car, all constituent parts are to be taken care of in a way that has the least possible effect on the environment.

The time in-between should also mean that the vehicle yields the least possible pollution of the environment. The ECC car has two drive systems – parallel hybrid operation. It has an electric motor for when operating in cities and built-up areas, and a gas turbine when operating on highways and when charging the batteries.

Electric power operation gives zero exhaust emissions (even if the generation of electricity can often cause pollution of the environment) and the car runs quietly for the benefit of people living in city and metropolitan areas. The performance rating and the range of the electric motor do not, however, correspond to car buyers' demands. For that reason the car is offered with an alternative 'heat motor', a gas turbine. This High Speed Generation (HSG) motor has been developed by United Turbine, a subsidiary of Volvo Aero Corporation. The motor operates at high revs. By developing a generator for these high revs it has been possible to make the entire power unit both efficient and compact.

When operating on highways with the gas turbine, the batteries are charged effectively before the next time the car is to be used in city areas. The gas turbine is also designed to run on several different types of fuel, especially bio-fuels, and this keeps fuel consumption and emissions to a minimum.

The biggest threat to the earth's environment is the uncontrolled emissions of carbon dioxides (CO_2) into the atmosphere. Combustion of fossil fuels are a major source of these emissions. Government authorities around the world are becoming increasingly more environmentally conscious and are placing tougher demands on car manufacturers. With the ECC, Volvo has demonstrated that the company is on the right road. But the ECC is not enough. The work has only just begun, even if Volvo's first environment policy was put into print in the early 1970s.

Volvo does not only have an environmental responsibility, however. It also has a responsibility towards its customers all over the world. The demands they make on comfort, on a car that is rational and useful in all situations, on active and passive safety, and on performance must be met.

Volvo ECC.

In 1992, several small to medium–sized Volvo BM wheel loaders were equipped with the same ergonomic cab already used on the L150.

Quarrel over the break-down of the Volvo-Procordia venture

In a surprise announcement in January 1992, Pehr G. Gyllenhammar informed the industrial world that a new giant business deal was being planned. Volvo and Procordia (in which Volvo had a 40 per cent ownership) would merge as a result of Procordia buying up the whole of Volvo (!). The new enterprise would be called Volvo and Pehr G. Gyllenhammar would be the chairman, Procordia chief Sören Gyll would be managing director, and Christer Zetterberg would be deputy managing director with responsibility for the transport equipment operations.

The market was taken by total surprise by this proposal, but the 'Privatisation Commission' were unanimous in their opposition to the venture. There then followed a public quarrel between Pehr G. Gyllenhammar and Swedish prime minister Carl Bildt. As one trade union boss put it, nothing more than a 'baby thumb' ever came of this venture either. Volvo increased its shareholding to 45 per cent, and the Swedish State retained 40 per cent.

But Sören Gyll was appointed managing director and CEO of AB Volvo in succession to Christer Zetterberg. The following year, in June 1993, a deal was concluded between the State and Volvo involving Procordia. The company was split into two parts: one for food, called BCP, and one for pharmaceuticals, called Procordia. Volvo became the full owner of BCP and had a 25 per cent ownership of Procordia.

Volvo displayed all of its high–tech expertise as part of the Swedish pavilion at Expo 92 in Seville.

World exhibition in Seville

Volvo was one of the seven main Swedish sponsors of the 1992 World exhibition in Seville in Spain. The exhibition was an enormous success and Volvo, as did also all Swedish exhibitors, attracted a lot of attention and received positive reports.

Left: Two views of Bokenäs taken in 1948 (left) and 1992 (below).

Bokenäs

Throughout its history, Volvo has always offered its employees the use of various recreation centres, either directly or through another organisation such as the Staff Union. 'Bokenäs', a leisure and recreation centre previously owned by Svenska Flygmotor/Volvo Flygmotor, was opened in 1992. It comprises cottages which can be hired by Volvo employees at a cost price.

In its new guise, Bokenäs was something of a pioneer as regards concern for the environment. It was built entirely in such a way as not to have any negative effect on the local surroundings, despite the modern facilities.

Volvo FH12

PRODUCT DEVELOPMENTS WERE not the main focus of Volvo's attention in 1993. Rather, it was the forthcoming merger with Renault which dominated the headlines.

As events transpired, the marriage never took place and the episode was to lead to the resignation of P. G. Gyllenhammar as chairman of the board of Volvo (he had already relinquished the post of company president three years earlier). Although the reasons for the breakdown were complex, it is interesting to note the similarities to the failure of Volvo's proposed Norwegian venture in 1978–79, when the question of the company's valuation proved the decisive factor. Just as the value of Volvo had been increasing on the previous occasion, the company was also making handsome profits in 1994. Under the circumstances, it was hardly surprising that the shareholders proved reluctant to surrender their valuable holdings and, effectively, to hand over control of a Swedish company to the French government.

Nevertheless, 1993 was an interesting year in product terms. The eagerly awaited 850 estate appeared in January. Technically identical to the saloon, it was an immediate hit despite its basic price of over SKr210,000. As a safety–enhancement feature, the designers opted for a vertical rear–light cluster on each side. Easily visible from behind, this arrangement was a logical development of the high–level brake light introduced by Volvo some time before to reduce the risk of collision from the rear.

The buyer of the new estate had a choice of two engine types – powerful and more powerful. The 'standard' option was the same five–cylinder, 20–valve, DOHC unit introduced in a 170–hp version in the 850GLT in 1991, while the top–of–the–range 225–hp turbo/intercooler unit was available to the more sports–minded owner. The model had a top speed of 200 km/h (850GLT automatic) or 240 km/h (850 Turbo with manual gearbox).

However, the 850 estate is more than just a performance car; it is also a practical everyday model. The luggage compartment is almost as spacious as in the 900 estates. In addition, both the luggage blind and safety net are now an integral part of the basic design and are retracted when not in use.

Cars did not monopolise the news in 1993. The major event of the year (in several respects) was the launch of the new FH series of trucks. Although the heirs of the F88 (from 1965) and the F12 (1977),

Volvo FH – the safest trucks so far

True to its usual custom, Volvo presented a new generation of trucks in 1993 with a whole host of new technological features. But important advances had also been made in the field of safety. These included:

- A safety cab offering the same level of safety as in the F trucks, but with a 30 per cent lighter cab shell.
- A three-point seat belt in combination with an occupant movement limiter feature.
- Specially designed pedals to minimise the risk of injury.

The centenary of the Swedish combustion engine in 1993

J & CG Bolinders in Stockholm (one of the predecessors to VCE) manufactured the first combustion engine in Sweden in series in 1893. It was a single-cylinder, four-stroke paraffin (kerosene) engine with horizontal cylinders. It was designed by an engineer called Weyland. This means that the Volvo Group is Sweden's (and one of the world's) oldest engine manufacturer. Engines have been produced continuously since 1893 in the companies that have been called (in chronological order) Bolinders, Bolinder-Munktell, Volvo BM, VME Industries, and Volvo Construction Equipment.

Volvo 850 estate.

the new models were of completely new design, the product of a seven–year development programme costing SKr6 billion.

The FH was acclaimed for its aerodynamic styling, although this was not the main reason for its unique success in the marketplace. Its popularity was due more to its consistently high standard of driver comfort and safety, combined with its reduced environmental impact (thanks to its cleaner engines), higher payload (a product of the lower kerb weight) and lower fuel consumption, all of which generated sales well in excess of production.

Perhaps the most exciting aspect of the FH series was the new D12A engine (in ratings from 340 to 420 hp) – the first Volvo truck engine of the overhead–camshaft type. This, combined with an innovative design of engine brake, yielded a dramatic increase in engine braking power, greatly improving the standard of safety compared with the F12.

The engines in both the FH12 and FH16 feature four–valve technology. The electronic fuel–injection system is supplied by a common, centrally located fuel pump in the FH16 and by six smaller, individual pumps (one per cylinder) in the FH12.

FH buyers were offered an extremely wide choice of variants from the outset, from the

Freon-free car rewarded in the USA

The American Environment Conservation Board's 1993 Special Ozone Protection Award was won by Volvo for its solution for taking care of environmentally hazardous freons, CFCs, in the best possible way in used cars.

two–axle FH12, equipped with a 340–hp engine and a short cab, to the four–axle FH16, with a 520–hp powerplant and a Globetrotter cab.

The FH quickly became the highest–selling semitrailer tractor in Europe, contributing significantly to the growth in the company's share of the European heavy truck market from 12 to 16% within about a year. In the same period, Volvo increased its share of the world truck market to 12%.

In June 1993, Volvo Penta introduced the largest group of marine products in its history. The company's joint ventures with OMC and Perkins produced two new drives, a completely new engine series and various other new engines.

The major item of news was the 'Compact Collection', which consisted of seven compact diesels with outputs from 10 to 76 hp.

The 2000 series consisted of four engines, two and three–cylinder units ranging from 10 to 38 hp.

The three largest engines – all four–cylinder units from 50 to 76 hp – were known collectively as the 22 series.

From the outset, the five smallest units were awarded certification under the Lake Constance (Bodensee) emission control regulations – the toughest in force anywhere in the world.

A completely new range of marine diesels, consisting of four and five–cylinder engines, as well as V6 and V8 types, with shaft outputs from 120 to 390 hp, was also launched.

The turbo engine used in the fastest versions of the 850 delivered speeds in excess of 200 km/h.

Both the DPX drive for extreme high-speed craft and the single-propeller SX drive were developed from Volvo Aquamatic technology, featuring spiral bevel gears, a cone clutch and a forward/reverse gearshift unit in the upper angle gearbox.

VME introduced several new products – the Zettelmeyer ZL702 and 802 loaders, the Volvo BM L50B loader, the Euclid R60 truck, the EL70 excavator loader and the modified A25C articulated dumper.

Volvo BM EL70.

Built originally on the B10M chassis, the attractive Italia 99 bus appeared in a new, more powerful version based on the B12 chassis in 1993.

With its powerful 7.4–hp Volvo Penta engine and Duoprop drive, the high–performance B28 speedboat (unveiled in 1995) achieved speeds approaching 100 knots. The unit is shown below.

The last Volvo 240

The last Volvo 240 car came off the assembly line on 5 May 1993. It was a green estate and it was 19 years after the first car in the series was produced. More than 2.8 million cars of this model had been produced.

This meant that 500 employees of the '240 company' were without a job, but instead of being made redundant they were relocated to another project on a temporary basis to be subsequently re-employed the following year when the Volvo 850 was about to be produced at the Torslanda plant. The '240 company' went out of operation in true style. During the last weeks before the closure everyone in the company wore T'shirts carrying the text 'The last 240 – the best'.

In its final years, the '240 company' was headed by Anna Nilsson-Ehle, the only woman ever to hold the position of product company general manager at the Volvo Car Corporation.

The following year, another woman, Lena Olving, was appointed General plant manager of VTM, the assembly facility at the Torslanda plant.

While the bus played a major role in public transport before the car achieved really widespread popularity, its importance declined as 'ordinary' people became car owners. Today, the bus is once again in the spotlight as attention focuses on means of reducing pollution and freeing our towns and cities from the car (especially now that the tram – sadly – has been so widely abandoned). In this new situation, the demands on the bus are very different.

Volvo introduced its most dedicated city bus to date, the B10L, in spring 1994. Unlike earlier Volvo buses, most of which were designed for a variety of applications, the case B10L is purpose–built for public transport in large conurbations. The model features a low floor designed to facilitate fast, comfortable, safe and ergonomic boarding and disembarking, particularly for the disabled and elderly, as well as parents with prams.

Volvo B10M with Aabenraa body.
Volvo B12 with Drömmöller body.

Although based on the experience gained from earlier rear–engined city buses, such as the B59 (1971), B10R (1978) and B10B (1992), the B10L incorporates a number of features necessitated by the low floor and the absence of a step inside the vehicle (even at the rear). The low front entrance level is achieved by the use of independent front suspension, while the horizontal engine (a 10–litre unit available only in a version complying with the 1996 EU emission standards) is installed asymmetrically at the left rear of the vehicle to provide space for a rear door.

Progressed was maintained at Volvo Bus Corporation in 1994. Until then, VBC had specialised mainly in bus chassis, bodyworking city buses only in limited numbers in its plants in Vienna and Säffle. Now, the company took over two reputable bodybuilding firms, Aabenraa of Denmark, which was mainly a producer of intercity buses, and Drögmöller of Germany, which specialised in luxury tourist coaches –acquisitions which provided Volvo with an expertise which it had previously lacked.

In early summer, Volvo published pictures of the modified 960 which, with its softer lines, a 2.5–litre, 170–hp, six–cylinder engine (still with

Volvo B10L.

Truck of the Year 1994

Volvo won the 1994 Truck of the Year award. This means that Volvo is the first manufacturer to win the award four times.

Euclid-Hitachi

VME and Hitachi Construction Machinery Co. Ltd. signed a joint venture agreement concerning rigid trucks, and in 1994 formed the jointly-owned company Euclid-Hitachi Heavy Equipment Inc.

Volvo Penta joint venture in the USA

The American diesel engine manufacturer Detroit Diesel Corporation (DDC) and Volvo Penta signed a joint venture agreement in early 1994. Via DDC's 36 well-established and reputable distributor companies, with more than 400 dealer outlets, Volvo Penta gained access to the whole of the NAFTA (USA, Canada, Mexico) area. This agreement broadened Volvo Penta's global base.

DDC was supplied with Volvo Penta engines, and this enhanced DDC's level of competitiveness. DDC also became the sole importer of Volvo Penta's smallest engine range, Compact Collection, and also of the largest diesel engines.

It also meant that all international boat-builders who used Volvo Penta products in their boats that were exported to North America were now offered improved diesel engine service facilities.

The cleanest paintshop in the world

After several years of construction and teething troubles, the new paintshop at the Torslanda plant was officially opened in the spring of 1994. Once it was in operation it proved to be a veritable marvel of modern painting technology. No other car plant in the world could boast such a high level of cleanness – emissions of solvents were as low as about 1.4 kg per car body. In Germany, a country well-known for having the toughest demands in the world, three times as high levels of emissions are permitted.

The plant also has very high demands on the working environment, while the demands on efficiency and quality are also high.

At least one and a half million cubic metres of air flow through the spray booths every hour. This air is concentrated by several energy-saving techniques and is then burnt in what are known as 'sand trays', a technique invented by a research engineer in Göteborg, Björn Heed, and which was tested at the Torslanda plant in the early 1980s.

General ventilation is concentrated in zeolite rotors. The air from automatically-operated booths is recirculated, while the air from the manually-operated booths is treated in electric filters and carbon rotors. All paints are now water-based.

Emissions from the new paint shop at Torslanda are the lowest in the industry.

In 1994, Volvo demonstrated a driver's airbag for trucks. From 1995 on, the feature will be available as an option in certain models.

Airbag in trucks too

In March 1994, Volvo invited a large number of journalists to its cab assembly plant in Umeå. There they could witness the world's first collision test with a truck fitted with an airbag on the driver side.

Following an analysis of 94 accidents, Volvo was able to demonstrate that the airbag would have had a very substantial injury-preventive effect in those accidents.

double overhead camshafts and four valves per cylinder) and a manual gearbox, offered an alternative to the 3–litre automatic and. Retailing at a considerably lower price, the car attracted a growing number of buyers. In addition, both the saloon and estate versions were now equipped with a modified version of the earlier rear suspension, which had been heavy, complicated and expensive.

Neither was the 850 neglected when the 1995 models were unveiled in August 1994. In this case, the new features were of a more advanced nature, the most notable being the provision of side airbags (or SIPSbags) to protect the driver and front seat passenger from chest injuries. Of slightly lesser interest was the introduction of the 850S 2.0, a 'popular' version of the car with a 2–litre, five–cylinder, 10–valve engine developing 126 hp. At the other end of the scale was the second new version of the model, known as the T5–R, which was built in small numbers for discriminating customers willing to pay for every imaginable luxury and even higher performance than the 'ordinary' 850 Turbo. Equipped with a more powerful 240–hp engine and with stiffer suspension, this was Volvo's highest–performance car ever. The T5–R was produced both as a saloon and an estate, and was available in a number of different finishes.

Interest in this special version was high, especially when Volvo – in cooperation with the British racing team, TWR (Tom Walkinshaw Racing) – resumed its activities on the track with the 850 estate, in the five–cylinder, 2–litre version developed (among others) for the Italian and Finnish markets.

Although Volvo's close relationship with Renault had ceased with the collapse of the merger negotiations, collaboration continued in some areas. In autumn, it was announced that the Renault Laguna was to be equipped with the new

The 'new' 960 introduced in mid–1994 gained a fresh lease of life from technical improvements and a more competitive price.

20–valve engine from Skövde (basically the same unit as the four–cylinder version used in the 850GLT).

Volvo and Renault supplied all of the transport requirements at the Winter Olympics in Lillehammer.

Volvo at the Winter Olympics in Lillehammer

As early as in August 1990, Volvo signed a contract with the organisers of the XVIth Winter Olympics in Lillehammer, which were held in February 1994.

The 'entrance ticket' cost Volvo SKr50 million – and the company had to pay a further 150 million kronor for the right to exhibit and demonstrate its operations and products during the Games.

The Winter Olympics proved to be a phenomenal success from an organisational and competition point of view, and it was also a triumph for Norway, the like of which has never been seen before.

It was a triumph for Volvo, too. The whole of the Lillehammer area was studded with white Volvo and Renault vehicles; cars, trucks, buses, and other transport vehicles. No-one could fail to notice the strong Volvo presence there. It was also marked by a large Volvo globe and other distinct activities. Thousands of Volvo customers were given the opportunity of seeing the Games at first hand.

Sales rose – in Norway, at least.

A new strategy

When the final separation from Renault became a fact on 2 December 1993, a new strategy was needed for the company.

The new strategy in the form of an 8-point programme was presented by Sören Gyll at the Volvo AGM on 20 April 1994. A year later, it was presented in writing in the publication 'Volvo's Strategic Development'.

The main points of the strategy mean that Volvo shall concentrate on the vehicle and transport equipment industry. Gone are the days of dealing with various products in the food and pharmaceutical industries which characterised Volvo's business operations in the 1980s.

Furthermore, Volvo shall attempt to attain full control over its core business, substantially improve the balance sheet figures, and concentrate strongly on development and making the on-going operations more effective.

From a Group standpoint, the new strategy policy means a concentration on the vehicle and transport equipment industry to achieve increased growth and competitiveness. This implies having control over the core business within the framework of a global Volvo network. The strategy is to maintain a sound balance sheet for balanced growth and to increase the level of dividends in pace with growth in operating result and solvency.

Advantage is taken of the Volvo name – one of the world's most widely-known and respected trademarks – with the help of among other things the strong products.

Volvo's core values – quality, safety, and concern for the environment – offer a potential that is far greater than the present-day production volume. The trade mark shall be powerfully maintained and developed.

The Volvo Group's strategy is based on risks and opportunities being well-balanced to allow the necessary prerequisites to be created for technological and commercial development.

Leadership and the development of employee skills and expertise are areas in Volvo has high ambitions. The ability and capacity to take advantage of and develop employees is decisive to the company's future business success.

The strategy also incorporates a policy for each subsidiary company, where Volvo Construction Equipment (the former VME) is also included as a business area alongside the Volvo Car Corporation, Volvo Truck Corporation, Volvo Bus Corporation, Volvo Penta, and Volvo Aero.

As early as 1992 when he took up the position of chief executive officer, Sören Gyll put into action a programme of change for the entire Volvo Group: 'Volvo 95'. This programme has proceeded at a fast pace ever since. No Volvo Group employee has been left unaffected in the years since 1992.

Many of the points taken up in the Volvo 95 programme are recognisable in the new Group strategy.

Perceptions of Volvo began to change when the 850 estate began to appear in the British Touring Car Championship.

The SIPSbag is designed to reduce injuries in side collisions.

The SIPS airbag

In the first three years of its life, the Volvo 850 won no less than 35 awards and prizes in all corners of the earth. Many of them were awarded for the car's extremely high level of safety.

Yet another world feature was presented in the 1995 models of the Volvo 850: a side impact protection airbag – the SIPS airbag.

According to calculations made by research engineers, the SIPS airbag provides 25 per cent better protection in the often highly dangerous side collisions than a car which is not fitted with such an airbag. Here, comparisons are made with one of the truly safest cars in the world, the Volvo 850 *without* SIPS airbag, but with the car's integrated system for protection against side impacts, SIPS.

The first Volvo bus sold in the People's Republic of China was delivered in 1994.

Bus assembly plant in China

In December 1994, a joint venture project involving local interests was started up to manufacture complete Volvo buses in China.

The prototype of Volvo's first–ever, series–built, front–wheel drive car was unveiled at the Geneva Motor Show at the beginning of 1995.

The model in question was the four–wheel drive version of the 850 estate which, however, had not been designed as an off–road vehicle per se, but as a four–wheel drive car offering a higher level of active safety on difficult road surfaces and improved mobility under winter conditions.

'You get out what you put in' is a popular saying, the truth of which was demonstrated in spring 1995, when the 850 (a refined version of the four–door saloon rather than the estate) began to record a series of victories in the British Touring Car Championship, having made its debut the year before.

It was driver Richard Rydell, in particular, who demonstrated that the 850 – now fully developed – was a winner in the right hands. However, the margin between success and failure was small; the experience of other competitors in the championship showed that a combination of a good car, a top–class driver and, perhaps, a modicum of luck, was needed to take the coveted chequered flag.

TWR (Tom Walkinshaw Racing) entered the limelight early in the year, when it was announced that the company was to build cars in the disused Volvo plant at Uddevalla, a decision which was welcomed not only in the locality, but also by those who had been involved in the design of a facility once described as 'the car plant of the future'. Under the new arrangement, TWR will be mainly responsible for the production operation, with Volvo as a minority partner.

The production of exclusive 850s, mainly the convertible and coupé versions, will commence at the reopened plant in 1996 (while the possibility that TWR may build other Volvo models, and even other makes, in Uddevalla has not been excluded).

The major car event in 1995 was the unveiling of the new medium-class Volvo at the Paris Motor Show in September. The previous June, Volvo had published sketches by Chief Designer Peter Horbury, to prepare customers for the softer styling of the new medium–class model, whose lines are strongly reminiscent of the Volvo ECC (Environmental Concept Car).

The new car will be built in the Netherlands alongside the 440 and 460 series, in parallel with the Mitsubishi Carisma which, although of the same basic design, is completely different in appearance.

From the technical aspect, the new Volvo is smaller to the 850 concept in many respects. The model is powered by a four–cylinder, 16–valve aluminium engine produced in Skövde and basically identical to the Volvo unit used in the

Volvo's new medium–class model will be a vital weapon in the company's drive to expand its European car sales.

Renault Laguna. Other engines, including a Renault diesel, will be introduced later.

New features in the Swedish–built range were few. The executive 960 was fitted with side airbags (SIPSbags) as standard equipment, while a diesel version of the 850 was introduced in response to requests from many customers.

The engine used in the latter case was not the Renault diesel, but an Audi/Volkswagen direct–injection unit developing 140 hp and offering excellent performance combined with extremely low fuel consumption and high mileage between refuelling.

Volvo Truck Corporation started 1995 with the launch of its new FL12, a model based on the FL10 but equipped with the high–tech D12A engine (as used in the FH12), creating an efficient, low–built truck with the capacity to perform demanding long–haul duties, hauling train weights up to the 60–tonne maximum permissible in Sweden.

Watched by millions of TV viewers, Richard Rydell drove his 850 to a series of victories in the British Touring Car Championship.

Below: The S4 is built in the Netherlands in a plant owned jointly by Volvo and Mitsubishi.

Also new to the FL range was the FL10, a low–emission model burning natural gas. Several of these vehicles have been delivered to customers in Göteborg for field testing under actual traffic conditions, monitored closely by Volvo engineers. Built by United Turbine, the Volvo Aero Corporation subsidiary in Malmö, the truck engines are further developed versions of the units used in the gas–driven buses already supplied to operators in Göteborg and Norway.

Other significant developments also took place at VTC in 1995. With effect from mid–year, White GMC products in the USA were renamed Volvo, marking the start of an aggressive marketing campaign and signifying the company's intention of building the American models with the same components and characteristics as their European cousins. However, the change in name was the only step taken at that stage, no new models being introduced during the year.

The B6LE, a new version of the B6 midi–bus, was introduced at the Paris show. Although based on the B6, the entry and exit doors in the new model are located at a lower level to expedite and facilitate passenger movements, especially for the elderly and disabled.

The Globetrotter XL is an even more comfortable FH series truck developed for demanding drivers and for extreme long–haul applications.

Seat belts became standard in all Volvo trucks in 1995.

The most radical development in the bus sector was the B10L Articulated city bus, a three–axle version of the low–entry B10L chassis in which the front and rear sections were connected by an articulated joint at the mid–point. The extremely low floor afforded by this configuration enabled passengers to step straight onto rather than up into the bus.

The B10L Articulated is of the 'pusher' type, in which the engine – for the first time – is installed in the trailer section. As in the standard B10L, the engine is mounted horizontally at one side, to provide space for a door at the extreme rear.

Developments at VBC were not confined to products. In spring, the company announced its acquisition of Canadian busbuilders Prevost, a move which gave it a renewed foothold on the North American continent. Volvo negotiated the deal in partnership with Plaxton, the British bodybuilders, which purchased half of the Prevost shares. Prevost builds luxury tourist coaches and is also known for its special models, such as racing car transporters.

VBC reached another major milestone in 1995, when it became an autonomous business area rather than a subsidiary of Volvo Truck Corporation. As

Left: Prevost of Canada was taken over by Volvo in partnership with Plaxton, the British busbuilder with whom the company has enjoyed a long and fruitful collaboration.

Right: The articulated version of the low–floor B10L combines high passenger capacity with advanced passenger ergonomics.

part of this reorganisation, the president of VBC became a member of Volvo Group management.

The importance of 1995 as a year of major change was underlined when the earthmoving plant company, VME (which had previously been owned jointly by Volvo and Clark Equipment of the USA) became a wholly–owned Volvo subsidiary. This was marked by a change in name to Volvo Construction Equipment (VCE), signalling the start of an expansion drive by the company, with the stated aim of making further acquisitions in the field and capturing market shares from its competitors.

VCE marked this new phase in its history by launching several major new products at the Bauma 95 exhibition in Munich in the spring, including two new machines.

The first of these was the Volvo L330C, a new wheel loader introduced to replace the Michigan L320. The model is powered by Volvo's 16–litre engine, the first time the unit has been used in an earthmoving machine. It was announced at the

The Environmental Concept Truck and the Environmental Bus are two of the vehicles used by Volvo to test the environmental qualities of the commercial vehicles of the future. Both are powered by hybrid drives developed jointly by VTC, VBC and VAC (the developer of the gas turbine).

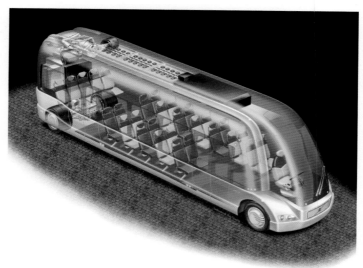

Left: Volvo delivered four ethanol–powered trucks to the City of Göteborg in 1995. Compared with conventional diesels, the level of harmful exhaust emissions from these models is lower.

Ethanol-powered trucks

Several players on the market, including the Volvo Truck Corporation, Bilspedition (a forwarding company), and several Swedish local authorities started up a project in 1995 called 'Transport–Environment–Future', the aim of which is to test ethanol-powered trucks operating in built-up areas.

The four trial trucks have been developed by Volvo on the initiative of the Swedish forwarding company Bilspedition.

Two of the trucks are used as refuse disposal vehicles in public service, and two as normal distribution trucks in city traffic in Växjö.

The people responsible for the project hope that the respective authorities will level out the present-day difference in costs between various fuels by introducing tax relief. As ethanol is much better than diesel from an environmental point of view, and can also be produced by resources that can be recycled in Sweden, there is much to support the use of this type of fuel in the future.

same time that all Volvo wheel loaders would henceforth be marketed worldwide under the Volvo name (until then, they were sold in the USA as Michigans).

The new A40 dumper was the second major Volvo development unveiled at Bauma 95. With its 40 short ton capacity, this huge machine is the largest of its type made by Volvo. Basically similar to the slightly smaller A30 and A35, the model is powered by a 12–litre Volvo engine (not, however, the D12A, but the TD123 unit also used in the L180 and A35).

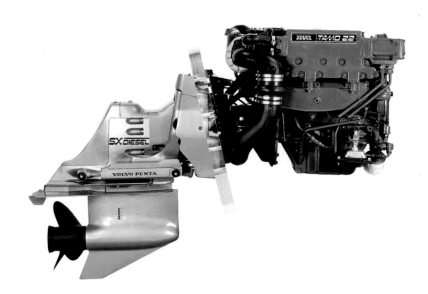

'Wanted: The perfect boat for the perfect engine.'

At the boat shows held in early 1995, Volvo Penta exhibited an important new feature – the 22 SX drive assembly. A diesel engine in the power range 59-130 hp combined with the company's famous Aquamatic drive had not previously been offered on the market.

The size of boat – both leisure and all-round commercial boats – requiring corresponding power ratings represented the fastest growing boat segment in the world.

But there were no suitable boats (read customers) to exhibit the new feature with. It was decided instead to enlist the help of the biggest magazine in the trade, IBI (International Boating Industry). In this, a design competition was announced, the first prize being the first series-produced 22 SX unit.

The two major developments from Penta in 1995 were the 7–litre marine diesel with electronic fuel injection (below) and the compact 22SX drive (above).

Volvo Construction Equipment

After ten years as a half-owned Volvo company, VME once again became a wholly-owned company when Volvo acquired Clark Equipment's shareholding in VME for the sum of 4.2 billion Swedish kronor. This is Volvo's biggest-ever acquisition in the vehicle industry. The total value of VME would therefore amount to 8.4 billion kronor, which can be compared with the 13.7 million kronor Volvo paid to Handelsbanken in 1950 for the acquisition of Bolinder-Munktell.

When VME became a wholly-owned Volvo company once again, the name of the company was changed to Volvo Construction Equipment Corporation as a group name. The constituent companies were assigned names with association to the company's operations; these included Volvo Wheel Loaders, Volvo Excavators, Volvo Articulated Haulers, etc. The Volvo BM and Åkerman and Zettelmeyer product names were retained for the time being.

With an annual turnover (1994) of SKr12 billion, Volvo Construction Equipment is the third biggest business unit in Volvo.

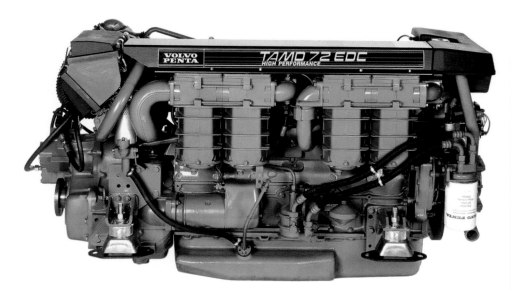

A museum, at last!

Over a period of several decades, Volvo had single-mindedly amassed a collection of historical Volvo cars. These were stored in various aircraft hangers and other concealed locations. As many other enthusiasts had done before him, the present curator of the museum, Heinz Linninger, strove to create a museum to house and exhibit all Volvo's old car 'treasures'.

A very significant step was taken when Volvo purchased the former shipyard buildings at Arendal, just a couple of miles from the Torslanda plant. Here it was possible to place a large number of cars in a suitable premises.

In 1995 it was finally decided to convert the premises at Arendal into a proper Volvo museum. Now the cars were joined by trucks, buses, Penta and aircraft engines, as well as racing cars and samples of Volvo's safety and environmental efforts.

The Volvo museum was officially opened on 30 May 1995 to the immense delight of all nostalgic people with an interest in Volvo's history.

The Volvo Museum was inaugurated in summer 1995. Its exhibits include cars (below) and trucks (above), as well as products from other Volvo companies.

Right: In early 1995, Volvo introduced a satellite navigation system which will help drivers to minimise transport distances and times.

VCE unveiled several new products, including the Åkerman EC450 excavator and the Volvo BM L330C wheel loader, in 1995.

TABLES
TABELLER
TABELLEN
TABLEAUX

Cars designed in Sweden:

Vehicles / Véhicule / Fahrzeuge / Voertuigen / Fordon	Years / Année / Jahre / Jaren / Årtal	Number / Quantité / Anzahl / Nummer / Antal	Wheelbase / Empattement / Radstand / Wielbasis / Hjulbas	Engine type/power (hp) / Moteur/puissance (cv) / Motortyp/Leistung (ps) / Motortype/vermogen (pk) / Motortyp/effekt (hk)
ÖV4			285cm	DA/28
Prot.	1926	9		
ÖV4	1927–29	205		
ÖV4 TV	1927–29	70		
ÖV4 ch.	1927–29	27		
PV4			285cm	DA/28
Prot.	1926	1		
PV4	1927–29	443		
Special	1928–29	251		
PV65				DB–EB–EC/55–75
PV650	1929–34	206	295–355cm	
PV650 Cabr.	1930–33	26	295cm	
PV651	1929–30	601	295cm	
PV652	1930–33	1.549	295cm	
PV653	33–35	230	295cm	
PV654	33–35	361	295cm	
PV655	33–35	62	355cm	
PV656	35–36	16	295cm	
PV657	35–36	55	355cm	
PV658	35–37	301	295cm	
PV659	35–36	170	295cm	
TR670	1930–34	88	310cm	
TR67				DB–EB/55–65
TRS/TR671	1930–31	61	310cm	
TRL/TR672	1930–31	139	310cm	
TR673	1931–34	233	310cm	
TR674	1932–34	138	310cm	
TR675	1934	2	310cm	
TR676	1934–35	29	310cm	
TR677	1934	2	325cm	
TR678	1934–35	39	325cm	
TR679	1934	114	325cm	
TR70				EC/75
TR701	1935–37	214	310cm	
TR702	1935–37	11	325cm	
TR703	1935–37	181	325cm	
TR704	1935–37	530	325cm	
PV36			295cm	EC/75
PV36	1935–38	500		
PV36 ch.		1		
PV51–52	1936–38		288cm	EC/75–86
PV51		1.754		
PV51ch.		205		
PV52		1.046		
PV53–55.	1938–45		288cm	EC/84–86
PV53		1.204		
PV55		286		
PV54–56	1938–45		288cm	EC/84–86
PV54		814		
PV56		1.321		
PV57		275		
PV80	1938–46		325cm	EC/84–86
PV800 ch.		37		
PV801/801F		550		
PV802/802F		1.081		
PV810 ch.		180		
PV82	1947–48			ED/90
PV821		200	325cm	
PV822		300	325cm	
PV823		150	325cm	
PV824		150	355cm	
PV60–s.	1946–50		285cm	ED/90
PV60		3.006		
PV61 ch.		500		
PV444			260cm	
A	1944–50	12.504		B4B/40
B	1950–51	7.500		B4B/44
C	1951–52	8.000		B4B/44
D	1952–53	9.000		B4B/44
E	1953–54	31.950		B4B/44
H	1954–55	29.046		B4B/44
K	1955–57	33.918		B4B/51
L	1957–58	64.087		B16/60–85
PV445			260cm	
ch.				
A	1953–54	500		B4B/44
B	1954–56	1.099		B4B/44
D	1956–58	1.926		B4B/44
G	1958–60	57		B4B/44–51
L	1958–60	54		B16/60
11	1958–60	169		B16/60
11M	1958–60	225		B16/60
Pick–Up			260cm	
DH	1953–56	6.389		B4B/44
GL	1956–57	1.766		B4B/44
LL	1957	821		B16/60
06	1957–58	3.380		B16/60
06M	1958–60	38		B16/60
PV83	1950–58			ED/90
831/832		4.135	325cm	
PV831				
PV832				
PV832S				
PV835		2.081		
PV833			325cm	
PV834			355cm	
PV445 Duett			260cm	
Sedan				
PH	1955–56	1.183		B4B/44
GP	1956–57	1.813		B4B/44
LP	1957	946		B16/60
07	1957–58	5.130		B16/60
07M	1958–60	54		B16/60
Van				
DS	1953–56	1.333		44
GS	1956–57	136		44
LS	1957	527		B16/60
05	1957–58	1.840		B16/60
05M	1958–60	23		B16/60
P1900	1956–57	67	240cm	B14A/70
Amazon/P120			260cm	
A	1956–58	5.184		B16/60
B	1958–60	49.214		B16/60
D	1960–61	29.900		B16/60–85
E	1961–62	28.500		B18/75–90
F	1962–63	27.200		B18/75–90
G	1963–64	26.400		B18/75–90
K	1964–65	27.400		B18/75–90
L	1965–66	31.250		B18/75–95
M	1966–67	9.160		B18/75–95
PV544/P110			260cm	
A	1958–60	99.495		B16/60–76
B	1960–61	34.600		B16/60–76
C	1961–62	37.900		B18/75–90
D	1962–63	27.100		B18/75–90
E	1963–64	24.200		B18/75–90
F	1964–65	17.300		B18/75–90
G	1965	3.400		B18/75–95

Vehicles Véhicule Fahrzeuge Voertuigen Fordon	Years Année Jahre Jaren Årtal	Number Quantité Anzahl Nummer Antal	Wheelbase Empattement Radstand Wielbasis Hjulbas	Engine type/power (hp) Moteur/puissance (cv) Motortyp/Leistung (ps) Motortype/vermogen (pk) Motortyp/effekt (hk)
P1800			245cm	
A	1961–63	6.000		B18/100
B	1963	2.000		B18/100
D	1963–64	4.500		B18/108
E	1964–65	4.000		B18/108
F	1965–66	4.500		B18/115
M	1966–67	4.500		B18/115
P	1967–68	2.800		B18/115
S	1968–69	1.693		B20/118
E T	1969–70	2.799		B20/130
E U	1970–71	4.750		B20/120–135
E W	1971–72	1.865		B20/120–135
P210			260cm	
A	1960–61	11.744		B16/60
B	1961–62	8.299		B16/60
C	1962–63	6.174		B18/75
D	1963–64	7.674		B18/75
E	1964–65	7.899		B18/75
F	1965–66	7.149		B18/75
M	1966–67	7.600		B18/75
P	1967–69	4.420		B18/75
P130			260cm	
A	1961–62	10.500		B18/75
B	1962–63	29.500		B18/75
D	1963–64	44.600		B18/75–90
E	1964–65	59.800		B18/75–90
F	1965–66	72.550		B18/75–90
M	1966–67	62.950		B18/85–115
P	1967–68	32.600		B18/85–115
S	1968–69	27.500		B20/90–118
T	1969–70	19.918		B20/90–118
P220			260cm	
A	1962	1.400		B18/75
B	1962–63	6.875		B18/75
D	1963–64	9.675		B18/75
E	1964–65	11.450		B18/75
F	1965–66	15.200		B18/75–95
M	1966–67	17.200		B18/85–100
P	1967–68	8.500		B18/85–100
S	1968–69	2.897		B20/90
144			260–262cm	
M	1966–67	37.100		B18/85–115
P	1967–68	57.700		B18/85–115
S	1968–69	48.900		B20/90–118
T	1969–70	55.400		B20/90–118
U	1970–71	68.010		B20/90–105
W	1971–72	77.030		B20/90–110
Y	1972–73	87.900		B20/90–135
A	1973–74	91.768		B20/90–135
142			260–262cm	
M	1967	1.500		B18/115
P	1967–68	5.140		B18/85–115
S	1968–69	59.500		B20/90–118
T	1969–70	66.560		B20/90–118
U	1970–71	71.910		B20/90–130
W	1971–72	73.470		B20/90–135
Y	1972–73	70.550		B20/90–135
A	1973–74	64.356		B20/90–135
145			260–262cm	
P	1967–68	9.200		B18/85–115
S	1968–69	21.700		B20/90–118
T	1969–70	30.700		B20/90–118
U	1970–71	41.780		B20/90–105
W	1971–72	50.340		B20/90–110
Y	1972–73	56.320		B20/90–135
A	1973–74	58.277		B20/90–135

Vehicles Véhicule Fahrzeuge Voertuigen Fordon	Years Année Jahre Jaren Årtal	Number Quantité Anzahl Nummer Antal	Wheelbase Empattement Radstand Wielbasis Hjulbas	Engine type/power (hp) Moteur/puissance (cv) Motortyp/Leistung (ps) Motortype/vermogen (pk) Motortyp/effekt (hk)
164			270–272cm	
S	1968–69	14.100		B30/145
T	1969–70	20.200		B30/145
U	1970–71	20.390		B30/145
W	1971–72	21.660		B30/145–175
Y	1972–73	28.500		B30/145–175
A	1973–74	29.617		B30/145–175
B	1974–75	20.601		B30/175
1800ES			245cm	
W	1971–72	3.070		B20/120–135
Y	1972–73	5.007		B20/120–135
242/240			264cm	
B	1974-75	53.804		B20–B21/82–97
E	1975-76	45.144		B20–B21/82–100
H	1976-77	23.125		B19–B21/90–100
L	1977-78	19.230		B19–B21/90–123
M	1978-79	23.445		B19–B21/90–123
	1979–80	22.145		B19–B21–B23/90–140
	1980–81	17.809		B19–B21/97–133
	1981–82	17.049		B19–B21/97–133
	1982–83	12.893		B19–B21/97–133
	1983–84	7.887		B19–B21/97–133
244/240			264cm	
B	1974–75	82.976		B20–B21/82–123
E	1975–76	90.736		B20–B21/82–123
H	1976–77	100.055		B19–B21/90–123
L	1977–78	89.685		B19–B21/90–123
M	1978–79	117.855		B19–B21/90–123
	1979–80	106.012		B19-21-23-27–D20-24/68–141
	1980–81	94.111		B19-21-23-28–D20-24/68–155
	1981–82	126.696		B17-19-21-23-28–D24/82–155
	1982–83	125.639		B17-19-21-23-28–D24/82–155
	1983–84	133.104		B17-19-21-23-28–D24/82–155
	1984–85	73.235		B17-200-21-230-28–D24/82–155
	1985–86	69.511		B200–B230–D24/82–131
	1986–87	63.045		B200–B230–D24/82–131
	1987–88	55.318		B200–B230–D24/82–131
	1988–89	52.509		B200–B230–D24/82–131
	1989–90	42.846		B200–B230–D24/82–125
	1990–91	27.464		B200–B230–D24/82–125
	1991–92	20.790		B200–B230–D24/82–125
	1992–93	11.812		B200–B230–D24/82–125
264/260			264–265cm	
B	1974–75	9.674		B27/140
E	1975–76	25.987		B27/125–140
H	1976–77	12.045		B27/125–140
L	1977–78	15.590		B27/125–140
M	1978–79	20.950		B27/125–148
	1979–80	24.058		B27–B28/129–148
	1980–81	17.696		B28/155
	1981–82	6.390		B28/155
245/240			264cm	
B	1974–75	54.709		B20–B21/82–123
E	1975–76	60.640		B20–B21/82–123
H	1976–77	48.485		B19–B21/90–123
L	1977–78	47.490		B20–B21/90–123
M	1978–79	53.430		B19–B21/90–123
	1979–80	51.742		B19–21–23–D20-24–B27/68–141
	1980–81	50.352		B19–21–23–D20–D24–B28/68–155
	1981–82	66.194		B17-19-21–B23–D24–B28/82–155
	1982–83	71.295		B17-19-21–B23–D24–B28/82–155
	1983–84	85.729		B17-19-21–B23–D24–B28/82–155
	1984–85	68.188		B17-200-21–230–D24–B28/82–155
	1985–86	58.231		B200–B230–D24/82–131
	1986–87	47.860		B200–B230–D24/82–131
	1987–88	42.047		B200–B230–D24/82–131
	1988–89	36.980		B200–B230–D24/82–131
	1989–90	36.969		B200–B230–D24/82–125
	1990–91	27.046		B200–B230–D24/82–125
	1991–92	28.427		B200–B230–D24/82–125
	1992–93	23.337		B200–B230–D24/82–125

Vehicles / Véhicule / Fahrzeuge / Voertuigen / Fordon	Years / Année / Jahre / Jaren / Årtal	Number / Quantité / Anzahl / Nummer / Antal	Wheelbase / Empattement / Radstand / Wielbasis / Hjulbas	Engine type/power (hp) / Moteur/puissance (cv) / Motortyp/Leistung (ps) / Motortype/vermogen (pk) / Motortyp/effekt (hk)
262			264cm	
E	1975–76	3.099		B27/125
H	1976–77	230		B27/125
262C			264–265cm	
	1977–78	1.670		B27/140
M	1978–79	2.120		B27/141–148
	1979–80	1.920		B27–B28/129–148
	1980–81	912		B28/155
265			264–265cm	
E	1975–76	8.108		B27/125
H	1976–77	2.905		B27/125
L	1977–78	4.815		B27/125–140
M	1978–79	6.040		B27/125–148
	1979–80	6.481		B27–B28/129–148
	1980–81	2.315		B28/155
	1981–82	1.918		B28/155
	1982–83	1.018		B28/156
	1983–84	857		B28/156
	1984–85	704		B28/156
744			277cm	
	1984	14.359		B23/131
	1984–85	103.617		B200–B230–D24/82–177
	1985–86	90.088		B200–B230–D24/82–182
	1986–87	100.499		B200–B230–D24/82–182
	1987–88	102.604		B200–B230–B234–D24/82–182
	1988–89	101.500		B200–204–230–234–D24/82–200
	1989–90	100.576		B200–204–230–234–D24/82–200
	1990–91	31.531		B200–204–B230–D24/82–200
	1991–92	5.669		B200–204–B230–D24/82–200
764			277cm	
	1982	3.000		B28/156
	1982–83	29.917		B23–B28–D24/109–173
	1983–84	33.616		B23–B28–D24/109–173
	1984–85	28.181		B230–B28–D24/109–177
	1985–86	16.887		B230–B28–D24/109–182
	1986–87	20.342		B230–B280–D24/109–182
	1987–88	20.668		B230–B280–D24/109–182
	1988–89	18.310		B230–B280–D24/109–182
	1989–90	12.943		B230–B280–D24/109–170
745			277cm	
	1985	7.015		B230–D24/82–162
	1985–86	54.983		B200–B230–D24/82–182
	1986–87	53.915		B200–B230–D24/82–182
	1987–88	60.353		B200–B230–B234–D24/82–182
	1988–89	64.741		B200–204–230–234–D24/82–200
	1989–90	71.462		B200-204-230-234-D24/82-200
	1990–91	26.128		B200–204–230–234–D24/82–200
	1991–92	20.355		B200-204-230-234-D24/82-200
765			277cm	
	1985	993		B230–B28/116–162
	1985–86	7.443		B230–B28–D24/109–182
	1986–87	7.698		B230–B280–D24/109–182
	1987–88	6.953		B230–B280–D24/109–182
	1988–89	7.571		B230–B280–D24/109–182
	1989–90	6.787		B230–B280–D24/109–170
780			277cm	
	1985–86	683		B28–D24/129–170
	1986–87	2.035		B280–D24/129–170
	1987–88	2.334		B280–D24/129–170
	1988–89	2.166		B23–B280–D24/129–175
	1989–90	1.300		B204–B230–B280–D24/129–200
944			277cm	
	1990–91	52.508		B200–B204–B234–D24/82–170
	1991–92	50.323		B200–B204–B230–B234–D24/82–170
	1992–93	41.571		B200–B230–D24/82–170
	1993–94	43.218		B200–B230/111–165
964			277cm	
	1990–91	14.547		B200-B234-B280-B6304/165-204
	1991–92	11.956		B200–B234–B6304–D24/165–204
	1992–93	9.178		B200–B230–B6304/165–204
	1993–94	12.112		B200–B230–B6304–D24/116–204
945			277cm	
	1990–91	27.794		B200–B204–B234–D24/82–170
	1991–92	29.936		B200–B204–B234–D24/82–170
	1992–93	34.618		B200–B230–D24/82–170
	1993–94	37.877		B200–B230/111–165
965			277cm	
	1990–91	4.401		B234–B280–B6304/165–204
	1991–92	5.189		B200–B234–B6304–D24/165–204
	1992–93	4.420		B200–B234–B6304–D24/165–204
	1993–94	3.375		B200–B234–B6304–D24/165–204
854			266cm	
	1991–92	28.922		B5204–B5254/140–170
	1992–93	69.341		B5204–5252–5254/140–170
	1993–94	73.241		B5204–B5234–B5252–B5254/140–240
855			266cm	
	1992–93	11.605		B5204–5252–5254/140–170
	1993–94	65.073		B5204–5234–5252–5254/140–240

Vehicles / Véhicule / Fahrzeuge / Voertuigen / Fordon	Years / Année / Jahre / Jaren / Årtal	Number / Quantité / Anzahl / Nummer / Antal	Wheelbase / Empattement / Radstand / Wielbasis / Hjulbas	Engine type/power (hp) / Moteur/puissance (cv) / Motortyp/Leistung (ps) / Motortype/vermogen (pk) / Motortyp/effekt (hk)

"Volvo" cars built in Holland:

Vehicles	Years	Number	Wheelbase	Engine type/power
66 Saloon			225cm	
	1975–76	19.591		B11–B13/47–57
	1976–77	15.735		B11–B13/47–57
	1977–78	13.200		B11–B13/47–57
	1978–79	14.656		B11–B13/47–57
	1979–80	14.455		B11–B13/47–57
66 Estate car			225cm	
	1975–76	15.151		B11–B13/47–57
	1976–77	8.849		B11–B13/47–57
	1977–78	4.500		B11–B13/47–57
343/340			240cm	
343	1976	5.206		B14/70
343	1976–77	29.902		B14/70
343	1977–78	37.700		B14/70
343	1978–79	67.969		B14/70
343	1979–80	49.940		B14/70
343	1980–81	29.108		B14–B19/70–92
343	1981–82	47.066		B14–B19/70–92
340	1982–83	50.778		B14–B19/64–70
340	1983–84	31.658		B14/70
340	1984–85	29.400		B14–"D16"/55–70
340	1985–86	29.849		B14–B18–"D16"/55–79
340	1986–87	27.230		B14–B18–"D16"/55–79
340	1987–88	17.628		B14–B18–"D16"/55–79
340	1988–89	15.870		B14–B18–"D16"/55–79
340	1989–90	3.130		B14–B18–"D16"/55–79
360 (3–d)				
360	1983–84	7.743		B19/92–115
360	1984–85	9.073		B200/92–115
360	1985–86	5.994		B200/101–112
360	1986–87	5.836		B200/101–112
360	1987–88	3.129		B200/101–112
360	1988–89	1.760		B200/101–112
345/340				
	1979–80	28.665		B14/70
	1980–81	30.779	1.090kg	B14–B19/70–92
	1981–82	47.449		B14–B19/70–92
	1982–83	48.337		B14–B19/
	1983–84	26.617		B14/70
	1984–85	24.796		B14–"D16"/55–70
	1985–86	31.153		B14–B18–"D16"/55–79
	1986–87	36.698		B14–B18–"D16"/55–79
	1987–88	33.871		B14–B18–"D16"/55–79
	1988–89	29.024		B14–B18–"D16"/55–79
	1989–90	17.960		B14–B18–"D16"/55–79
	1990–91	2.595		B14–B18–"D16"/55–79
360 (5–d)			240cm	
	1983–84	13.781		B19/92–115
	1984–85	14.249		B200/92–115
	1985–86	15.153		B200/101–112
	1986–87	15.296		B200/101–112
	1987–88	11.322		B200/101–112
	1988–89	6.480		B200/101–112
340 (4–d)			240cm	
	1983–84	11.107		B14/72
	1984–85	12.719		B14–"D16"/55–70
	1985–86	19.469		B14–B18–"D16"/55–79
	1986–87	18.639		B14–B18–"D16"/55–79
	1987–88	11.314		B14–B18–"D16"/55–79
	1988–89	6.716		B14–B18–"D16"/55–79
360 (4–d)			240cm	
	1983–84	18.253		B19/92–115
	1984–85	15.608		B200/92–115
	1985–86	10.459		B200/101–112
	1986–87	11.502		B200/101–112
	1987–88	6.910		B200/101–112
	1988–89	3.475		B200/101–112
480			250cm	
	1985–86	851		B18/109
	1986–87	11.243		B18/109
	1987–88	15.944		B18/102–120
	1988–89	12.295		B18/102–120
	1989–90	9.968		B18/102–120
	1990–91	7.297		B18/102–120
	1991–92	7.439		B18/102–120
	1992–93	4.908		B18–B20/102–120
	1993–94	1.606		B18–B20/110–120
440			250cm	
	1988	19.689		B18/79–120
	1988–89	56.451		B18/79–120
	1989–90	45.605		B18/79–120
	1990–51	49.073		B18/79–120
	1991–92	52.965		B16–B18/82–120
	1992–93	44.859		B16–B18–B20/82–120
	1993–94	28.799		B16–B18–B20/82–120
460			250cm	
	1989–90	42.726		B18/87–120
	1990–91	25.484		B18/87–120
	1991–92	33.615		B16–B18/82–120
	1992–93	35.404		B16–B18–B20/82–120
	1993–94	24.272		B16–B18–B20/82–120

Vehicles / Véhicule / Fahrzeuge / Voertuigen / Fordon	Years / Année / Jahre / Jaren / Årtal	Number / Quantité / Anzahl / Nummer / Antal	Wheelbase / Empattement / Radstand / Wielbasis / Hjulbas	Engine type/power (hp) / Moteur/puissance (cv) / Motortyp/Leistung (ps) / Motortype/vermogen (pk) / Motortyp/effekt (hk)

Trucks designed in Sweden:

Vehicles	Years	Number	Wheelbase	Engine type/power (hp)
LV1	1928–29	497		DA/28
A				
"LV40"			330cm	
"LV41"			370cm	
B				
"LV42"			330cm	
"LV43"			370cm	
LV2	1928–30	498		DA/28
LV44			330cm	
LV45			370cm	
LV3				
LV60–61	1929–32	1.665		DB–EB/55–65
LV60			332,4cm	
LV61			370cm	
LV62–63	1929–30	761		DB/55
LV62			332,4cm	
LV63			370cm	
LV4	1930–32	544		DB–EB/55–65
LV64			332,4cm	
LV65			370cm	
LV66–67	1931–36	700		DC–HA–FC–FCH/75–90
LV66			380cm	
LV67			410cm	
LV68–70.	1931–36	1.670		DC–HA–FC–FCH/75–90
LV68			340cm	
LV69			380cm	
LV70			410cm	
LV70B	(1933–36)		460cm	DC–HA/75
LV71–72	1932–35	3.275		EB/65
LV71			340cm	
LV72			410cm	
LV73–74	1932–35	1.417		EB/65
LV73			340cm	
LV74			410cm	
LV75	1933–35	308	410cm	EB/65
LV76–78	1934–38	1.250	340cm	EB–EC/65–75
LV76				
LV77				
LV78				
LV79	1936–40	1.000	380cm	EC/75
L8				
LV81–82	1936–39	1.700		EC/75
LV81			340cm	
LV82			410cm	
LV83–86	1935–40	6.850		EC/75
LV83			340cm	
LV84			410cm	
LV85			470cm	
LV86			380cm	
L9	1935–39	2.950		DC–DCH–FC–FCH/75–90
LV93			340cm	
LV94			410cm	
LV95			470cm	
L18/L19	1937–43	900		DC–HA–FC–FCH–FDH/75–90
LV180			340cm	
LV181			380cm	
LV182			410cm	
LV183			470cm	
LV190			340cm	
LV191			380cm	
LV192			410cm	
LV193			470cm	
L29	37–51	2.383		FA–FAH–FB–FBG–FBH–VDA/95–140
LV290			340cm	
LV291			380cm	
LV292			410cm	
LV293			470cm	

Vehicles	Years	Number	Wheelbase	Engine type/power (hp)
L10				ECG–EC/50–86
LV101	1938–45	837	310cm	
LV102	1939–41	495	350cm	
LV103	1943–46	500	315cm	
L11	1940–46	3.000		ECG–EC/50–86
LV110			340cm	
LV111			380cm	
LV112			410cm	
LV105	1947–48	497	350cm	ED/90
L20	1948–50	1.003		ED/90
L201			350cm	
L202			390cm	
L12				
LV120–123	1940–49	7.200		EC/75–86
LV120			340cm	
LV121T			380cm	
LV122			410cm	
LV123			470cm	
LV125–128	1939–49	10.200		FC–FCG–FCH–FDH/–90
LV125			340cm	
LV126T			380cm	
LV127			410cm	
LV128			470cm	
LV128B			470cm	
L22	1949–54	4.700		ED/90
L221			340cm	
L223			410cm	
L224			470cm	
L13	1939–48	3.739		FC–FCG–FCH–FDH/–90
LV130			340cm	
LV131			380cm	
LV132			410cm	
LV133			470cm	
LV136			380cm	
LV137			410cm	
LV138			470cm	
LV1300	1948–50	1.005		FC/90
LV1301			340cm	
LV1302			380cm	
LV1303			410cm	
LV1304			470cm	
LV1305			530cm	
L23	1951–54	3.700		A6/105
L231			340cm	
L233			410cm	
L234			470cm	
L14	1944–51	2.100		FE/105
LV140			340cm	
LV141			380cm	
LV142			410cm	
LV143			470cm	
LV145			340cm	
LV146			380cm	
LV147			410cm	
LV148			470cm	
L15	1946–49	2.850		VDA/95
LV151			340cm	
LV152			380cm	
LV153			410cm	
LV154			470cm	
L24	1949–53	8.026		VDA/100
L246			340cm	
L248			410cm	
L249			470cm	
L29C–L29V	1946–51			
LV291C2			380cm	VDB/130
LV291V3			380cm	VDF/150
LV292C2			410cm	VDB/130
LV292V2			410cm	VDB/130
LV293C2LF			470cm	VDB/130

Vehicles / Véhicule / Fahrzeuge / Voertuigen / Fordon	Years / Année / Jahre / Jaren / Årtal	Number / Quantité / Anzahl / Nummer / Antal	Wheelbase / Empattement / Radstand / Wielbasis / Hjulbas	Engine type/power (hp) / Moteur/puissance (cv) / Motortyp/Leistung (ps) / Motortype/vermogen (pk) / Motortyp/effekt (hk)
L34	50–56	4.900		ED/90
L341			350cm	
L342			390cm	
L39 Titan	1951–59	7.108		VDF–D96–TD96/150–195
4x2				
L397/L3954			380cm	
L398/L3956			440cm	
L399K			470cm	
L399L/L3958			510cm	
6x2				
L398LF/L39526			440+124cm	
L399LF			470+124cm	
L399LF/L39528			510+124cm	
6x4				
L397FDB/L39534			380+123cm	
L398FDB/L39536			440+123cm	
L399FDB/L39538			510+123cm	
L49 Titan	1959–65	12.429		D96–TD96/150–230
4x2				
L49504			380cm	
L49506			440cm	
L49507			480cm	
L49508			520cm	
L49509				
L49526			440+124cm	
L49528			520+124cm	
L49534			380+127cm	
L49537			480+127cm	
L38 Viking		18.458		
L385	1953–54			VDC/100
4x2				
L386			340cm	
L388/L388LF			410cm	
L389/L389LF			470cm	
L385A	1954–62			D67/115
4x2				
L386A/L38503			340cm	
388A K/38505/TL388/38545			410cm	
L388A L/38506			440cm	
L389A/L38507			470cm	
L38509				
6x2				
L388A/L38525			410+120cm	
L389A/L38527			470+120cm	
L48 Viking	1959–65	21.780		
L48504			380cm	
L48506/L48526/L48546			440cm	
L48507			480cm	
L48508/L48528			520cm	
L36 Friske	1955–57	1.099		ED/90
L360				
L363			410cm	
L364			470cm	
L365	1955–56	90		D47/95
L37				
L370 Brage	1954–63	4.975		A6/105–115
L373/L37005			410cm	
L374/L37007			470cm	
L375 Starke	1954–62	13.400		D47/95
L378/L37505			410cm	
L379/L37507			470cm	
L46 Starke	1961–65	6.995		D47/95
L46505			410cm	
L46506			440cm	
L46506			470cm	
L47 Raske	1961–65	3.002		D47/95–120
L47505			410cm	
L47506			440cm	
L47507			470cm	
L382/L3851	1954–62	370		A6–D67/115–125
L386/L38513			340cm	
L387/L38514			380cm	
L388K/L38515			410cm	
L388L/L38516			440cm	
L389/L38517			470cm	
L42 Snabbe				
L4201/F82B	1956–65	5.206		B36AV/120
L34011/L421/L42011			260cm	
L34012/L422/L42012			300cm	
L34013/L423/L42013			340cm	
L4251/F82	1964–72	4.537		D36A–D39A/65–80
L42512			300cm	
L42513			340cm	
L43 Trygge				
L4301	1957–65	6.530		B36AV/120
L432/L43012			300cm	
L433/L43013			340cm	
L434/L43014			380cm	
L4351/F83	1963–72	6.432		D36A–D39A/65–80
L43512			300cm	
L43513			340cm	
L43514			380cm	
Raske TIPTOP	1962–65	3.498		
L47513			340cm	
L47514			380cm	
L47515			420cm	
Viking TIPTOP	1964–65	1.078		
L48513			340cm	
L48514			380cm	
L48515			420cm	
L48517			490cm	
Titan TIPTOP	1964–65			TD96/230
L4951		953		
L49513			340cm	
L49517			490cm	
L4956		476		
L49563			340+132cm	
L49566			460+132cm	
N84	1965–72	7.822		D50/107–117
N86	1965–73	12.785		D–TD70/185–207
N88	1965–73	20.142		D–TD100/166–260
F84	1968–74	4.128		D50–TD50/107–165
F85	1965–76	12.387		D50–TD50/107–147
F85S	1976–78	1.429		TD60/180
F86	1965–79	40.796		D70–TD70/144–210
F88/G88	1965–77	40.215		D100–TD100/165–290
F88	1965–77			
G88	1970–78			
F89/G89/CH230		21.005		TD120A/330
F89	1970–77			
G89	1970–78			
CH230	1977–79			
F82S	1972–75	856		D39B/80
F83S	1972–75	1.567		D39B/80
N7	1973–86	12.258		TD70/207–212
N10	1973–90			TD100–101–102/250–318
N12	1973–91			TD120–121–122/329–395
F4	1975–86	9.262		D39–Volvo TD40/80–126
F406				
F407				
F408				
F6	1975–85	36.477		
F609				D60/120
F610				TD60/147
F611				D–TD60/120–147
F612				TD60/147
F613				TD60/180
F614				TD60/180

Vehicles / Véhicule / Fahrzeuge / Voertuigen / Fordon	Years / Année / Jahre / Jaren / Årtal	Number / Quantité / Anzahl / Nummer / Antal	Wheelbase / Empattement / Radstand / Wielbasis / Hjulbas	Engine type/power (hp) / Moteur/puissance (cv) / Motortyp/Leistung (ps) / Motortype/vermogen (pk) / Motortyp/effekt (hk)
F10 (a)	1977–83			TD100/250–300
F12 (a)	1977–83			TD120/330–385
F10 (b)	1983–87			TD101–102/275–318
F12 (b)	1983–87			TD121–122/329–395
F10 (c)	1987–			TD101–102–103/275–320
F12 (c)	1987–			TD121–122–123/329–405
F6S	1978–85	8.386		TD60/180
F7	1978–86	36.002		TD70/212–245
CH230	1980–86	779		TD120–121/326–329
FL6				
FL6L	1985–			TD61–63/152–210
FL608				
FL610				
FL611				
FL612				
FL6M	1985–			TD61–63/180–230
FL612				
FL614				
FL615				
FL6H	1985–91			TD61/180–207
FL616				
FL617				
FL6E	1991–			TD61–63/207–230
FL618				
FL619				
FE6	1986–90			
FE613				TD61/174
FE614				TD61/205
FE615				TD61/205
FL7	1985–			TD71–73–D7/230–285
FL10	1985–			TD101–102–103–D10/285–360
FL12	1995–			D12A/380–420
FL4	1986–88	1.923		TD41/122
FS10	1986–92			TD101–102/299–318
FE7	1986–90			TD71/230–260
FE715				
FE716				
F16	1987–94			TD162–163/465–500
NL10	1989–			TD101–102–103/275–318
NL12	1989–			TD121–122–123/329–405
FS7	1991–			TD73/230-260
FS717				
FS719				
FH12	1993–			D12/340–420
FH16	1993–			D16/470–520

"Volvo" trucks designed in North America:

Vehicles / Véhicule / Fahrzeuge / Voertuigen / Fordon	Years / Année / Jahre / Jaren / Årtal	Engine type/power (hp) / Moteur/puissance (cv) / Motortyp/Leistung (ps) / Motortype/vermogen (pk) / Motortyp/effekt (hk)
FE	1990–	Volvo VED7–Caterpillar 3116/185–260
NE	1991–95	Volvo TD73–TD123–D12/230–370
Conventional	1995–	Volvo VED12–Caterpillar 3176-3406– Cummins M11-N14–Detroit S60/280–525
Integral Sleeper	1995–	Volvo VED12/Caterpillar 3176-3406– Cummins M11-N14–Detroit S60/280–525
IS ES	1995–	Volvo VED12–Caterpillar 3176-3406– Cummins M11-N14–Detroit S60/280–525
WG	1995	Volvo VED7-VED12–Caterpillar 3306-3176– Cummins L10-M11-N14– Detroit S60/230–370
Autohauler	1995–	Cummins M11–Detroit S60/280–370
Xpeditor	1995–	Volvo VED12–Caterpillar 3306– Cummins L10-M11/280–350hk
High Cabover	1995–	Cummins N14–Detroit S60/330–525
Autocar	1995–	Volvo VED12–Caterpillar 3306-3406– Cummins L10-M11-N14– Detroit S60/260–525

Vehicles / Véhicule / Fahrzeuge / Voertuigen / Fordon	Years / Année / Jahre / Jaren / Årtal	Number / Quantité / Anzahl / Nummer / Antal	Wheelbase / Empattement / Radstand / Wielbasis / Hjulbas	Engine type/power (hp) / Moteur/puissance (cv) / Motortyp/Leistung (ps) / Motortype/vermogen (pk) / Motortyp/effekt (hk)
Buses:				
B1–B4	1934–37		470cm	DC–HA–FC–FCH/75–90
B1		132		
B4		11		
B2–B3	1934–36			DC–HA–FC–FCH/75–90
B2		25		
B3		16		
B10–12	1936–43			DC–HA–FC–FCH–FDH/75–90
B10			420cm	
B12			470cm	
B11–14	1936–42			DC–HA–FC–FCH–FDH/75–90
B11			470cm	
B14			520cm	
B20–22	1937–42			FC–FCH–FDH/90
B20		251	470cm	
B23		78	520cm	
B22–24.	1937–42			FC–FCH–FDH/90
B22		267	520cm	
B24		52	580cm	
B40–41	1937–46			FA–FAH–FB–FBH–FBG/–135
B40		75	530cm	
B41		40	600cm	
B50–s.	1938–40		530cm	FBH/135
B50		22		
B52		15		
B51	1944–52	3.841		FE–VDA–VDC/95–105
B511			420cm	
B512			470cm	
B513			520cm	
B514			470cm	
B53	1946–51	400		VDB/130
B531			550cm	
B532			600cm	
B533			570cm	
B62	1949–51			VDB–VDF/130–150
B626			470cm	
B627			520cm	
B64	1950–51	5		VDF/150
646			600cm	
B65	1951–64	2.573		D96AL/150
656/65504			500cm	
657/65506			550cm	
658/65508			600cm	
B61	1951–65	6.056		VDC–D67/100–125
B616/61503			470cm	
B617/61505			520cm	
B618/61506			550cm	
B619/61597			590cm	
B614–s.		285		VDC–D67/100–125
614	1951		470cm	
614F/61515	1954–59		520cm	
616F/61513	1954–59		470cm	
B63	1952–65	3.577		D96/150–162
637/63506			550cm	TD96AS/185
638/63508			600cm	
B72	1952–62			D96/150–162
B727/72505			520cm	
B72506			550cm	
B70	1958–64	650		D47/90
B70501			410cm	
B70503			470cm	
B71	1962–65	1.978		D67/125
B71514			500cm	TD67/150
B71516			550cm	
B71518			600cm	
B75	1963–65	652		D96AL/150
B75506			550cm	
B75508			600cm	
B54	1966–71	500		D50A–TD50A/105–135
B54–47			470cm	
B54–52			520cm	
B57	1966–83			D70–TD70
B57–50			500cm	
B57–55			550cm	
B57–60			600cm	
B57–65				
B58	1966–80	17.184		D100–TD100
4x2				
B58–55			550cm	
B58–56			564cm	
B58–60			600cm	
B58–61			610cm	
B58–65				
Articulated bus				
"Hägglund"			525+650cm	
"Volvo"			550+650cm	
BB57	1970–83			
BB57–50			500cm	
BB57–55			550cm	
BB57–60			600cm	
BB57–65			650cm	
B59	71–78	2.180		THD100/250
B59–55			550cm	
B59–56			564cm	
B59–59			590cm	
B55	74–	1.021		Volvo TD70/186
B6				
B609	1976–	161		D60A/120
B609–38.5			385cm	
B609–44.5			445cm	
B609/50.5			505cm	
B6F	1976–82	316		TD60/180
B6F–38.5			385cm	
B6F–44.5			445cm	
B6F–50.5			505cm	
B10R	1978–92			THD100
B10R–55			550cm	THD102
B10R–56			563,9cm	
B10R–59			590cm	
B58E				
B6FA	1979–			TD60B/180
B6FA–44.0			440cm	
B6FA–50.6			506cm	
B6FA Mark II				TD60B/180
B6FA–44.0			440cm	
B6FA–50.6			506cm	
B10M	1979–			THD100–101
4x2				
B10M–55			550cm	
B10M–56			563,9cm	
B10M–60			600cm	
B10M–61			609,6cm	
B10M–65				
6x2	1984–			
B10M–50			500cm	
B10M–53			530cm	
B10M–70			700cm	
B10MD	1982–			
4x2			495,3cm	
6x2			563,9cm	
Articulated	1979–			
w/steerable third axle			550cm	
w/rigid third axle			550cm	
B10M Bimode	1988–			THD101KB/285 + BBC44BO2052/152kW
B9M	1982–			THD101/242
B9M–46			460cm	
B9M–55			550cm	
B9M–60			600cm	
B10C	1989		636cm	THD101KC/310

Vehicles / Véhicule / Fahrzeuge / Voertuigen / Fordon	Years / Année / Jahre / Jaren / Årtal	Number / Quantité / Anzahl / Nummer / Antal	Wheelbase / Empattement / Radstand / Wielbasis / Hjulbas	Engine type/power (hp) / Moteur/puissance (cv) / Motortyp/Leistung (ps) / Motortype/vermogen (pk) / Motortyp/effekt (hk)
B7F	1983–87			TD70H/213
B7F–50			500cm	
B7F–55			550cm	
B7F–60			600cm	
B7F–65			650cm	
B7FA	1983–87			TD70H/213
B7FA–50			500cm	
B7FA–55			550cm	
B7FA–60			600cm	
C10M	1984–85	79		THD101/276–310
C10M–63			633cm	
C10M–70			700cm	
B7	1987–		50–61dm	TD71G/211
B7–50			500cm	
B7–55			550cm	
B7–61			610cm	
Leyland				
Lynx	1988–92			Cummins L10/210
55				–Gardner 6HXCT/205–234
56,3				–Volvo THD102KF/245
Tiger	1988–91			
Olympian	1988–93		490,0–563,9cm	Cummins LT10/180–250
4x2				–Gardner 6LXB/180
9.6m			495,3cm	
10.3m			563,9cm	
11.1m			490cm	
Swift	1988–91			Cummins 6BT/115–130
3,65m			365cm	
4,4m			440cm	
B10M MkIII	1988–			THD101–THD102
4x2				
B10M–55			550cm	
B10M–60			600cm	
B10M–65			650cm	
6x2				
B10M–50			500cm	
B10M–70			700cm	
Articulated, w/steerable third axle			550+720cm	
			550+740cm	
Articulated, w/rigid third axle			550cm	
Steyr				
Citybus			330cm	
SC6F72	1990–		330cm	DB OM616/72
SC6F85				DB OM601/85
SC6F115				Volvo B230/115
Bus chassis				
4x2				
SS11			581cm	DB OM447h/11.967cc/240
STS11				
SR11				
SL11			581cm	OM447hA/11.967cc/280
SFL12				
SL12				
6x2				
SG18			525+660,2cm	DB OM447hA/11.967cc/280
B12	1991–		600–610cm	TD122–123–D12/356–420
B6	1991–		410–450cm	TD63E/180
B6–41				
B6–45				
B10B	1992–		550–600cm	THD102–103
B10B LE	1993–		360–600cm	THD103/245–286
B10MMk IV	1993–			
Volvo Olympian	1993–			
Drögmöller				
EuroPullman				
E 325			610cm	D–B OM441LA–OM402LA/340–381
EuroComet				
E330 H/11,3			540cm	D–B OM402LA/381
E 330 H			610cm	D–B OM402LA/381
SuperComet				
E 430			530+cm	D–B OM402LA/381
E 430 U			530+cm	D–B OM402LA/381
B12–500			594,5cm	Volvo TD123/356–405
B10L				
4x2	1994–		300–600cm	THD104/245–286
Articulated	1995–			THD104/245–286

Special and military vehicles:

Vehicles / Véhicule / Fahrzeuge / Voertuigen / Fordon	Years / Année / Jahre / Jaren / Årtal	Number / Quantité / Anzahl / Nummer / Antal	Wheelbase / Empattement / Radstand / Wielbasis / Hjulbas	Engine type/power (hp) / Moteur/puissance (cv) / Motortyp/Leistung (ps) / Motortype/vermogen (pk) / Motortyp/effekt (hk)
TVB	1940–41	148	280cm	FBT/128
TVC	1942–43	168	335cm	FBT/140
HBT				FCT/90
TPV	1944–46	210		EC/86
TP21	1953–58	720		ED/90
TL1				
TL11	1953–54	100		A6/105
TL12	1956–57	165		A6/115
TL22	1954–59	857		A6/105–115
TL31	1956–62	920		D96AS–TD96AS/150–185
L2304	1959–61	91		B16/60
L3304	1963–64			B18/65
L3314 Laplander	1961–70	7.737		B18–B20/65–82
L3314PU				
L3314HT				
L3315	1966–69	1.116		B18–B20/65–82
C202	1977–81	3.222		B20/82
BV200–s.	1963–			B18–B20
BV202				
BV203				
C3	1974–84	8.718		B30/117
C303				
C304				
C306				

Agricultural tractors:

Vehicles / Véhicule / Fahrzeuge / Voertuigen / Fordon	Years / Année / Jahre / Jaren / Årtal	Number / Quantité / Anzahl / Nummer / Antal	Wheelbase / Empattement / Radstand / Wielbasis / Hjulbas	Engine type/power (hp) / Moteur/puissance (cv) / Motortyp/Leistung (ps) / Motortype/vermogen (pk) / Motortyp/effekt (hk)
T4			180cm	
T41	1943–46	500		A4G/40
T42	1944–50	400		A4F/48
T43	1946–50	1.600		A4H/48
T2				
T21	1946–48	1.800	170cm	C4F/22
T22	1947–52	9.469	170cm	C4F/22.5
T23	1947–52	556	170cm	C4B/28.5
T24	1952–57	9.825	177cm	CF22/27.5
T25	1952–55	6.445	177cm	CB22/31
BM24/25	54–59	962	177cm	CF22–CB22/27,5–31
BM10	1947–52	6.400	165cm	/23
BM20–21				
GBMV-1/BM20	1944–50	4.000	180cm	WA5T2/41
BM21	1951–52	1.013	180cm	/43
T3				
T31	1949–57	6.919	184–196cm	D4F/35–36
T32	1950–57	788	196cm	D4B/45
T33	1950–56	2.483	201cm	D4F/36.5
T34	1952–56	284	201cm	D4B/42
BM 31–34	1954–57	44		D4F–D4B/35–45
BM35/T35–s.				1053T/42,5
BM35	1952–59	4.206	196cm	
BM36	1952–59	6.040	201cm	
T35	1953–58	825	196cm	
T36	1953–59	1.632	201cm	
BM Teddy	1953–55		177cm	
BM200		1.140		Austin/32
BM210		1.260		Austin/29
T5			217,5cm	1054/57
T55	1953–59	1.256		
BM55	1953–59	1.745		
BMS55	1954–59	161		
T230/Viktor			185cm	1052/30
T230	1956–61	4.976		
BM Viktor	1955–61	10.929		
T1				
BM15	1956	275		B14C/27
T15	1956	975		B14C/27
BM425/T425	1957–62	11.193		B16C/32
Boxer				
T350 Boxer	1959–67	26.815	230,5cm	1113TR/56
T350PKD	1964–67	400		
T350 I	1963–67	1.224		
T470 Bison-s.				1114TR/73–75
T470	59–66	3.695	217,5cm	
T471	1962–63	50	240cm	
T470 I	1962–66	474	220cm	
473	1964	90		
Buster				
T320 Bensin	1962–63	650	195cm	B18C/37
T320 Diesel	1961–64	15.720	195,3cm	Perkins/37
T400	1964–69	22.589	210cm	Perkins/42,5
T400 PKD	1965–66	547		
T400 I	1965–69	823		
Lisa T873		1		Volvo TD50/147
Parca 714	1965–70		242,5cm	Scania D8/156
Boxer			230,5cm	1113/69
T600	1967–70	12.200		
T600 PKD	1967–70	1.500		
T600 I	1967–70	594		
Bison				
T800	1966–79	4.466	269cm	D50/99,9
T800 I	1966–68	149		D50/99,9
T810	1969–79	3.550	269cm	TD50/128,2
T814	1969–79	1.647	284cm	TD50/128,2

Vehicles / Véhicule / Fahrzeuge / Voertuigen / Fordon	Years / Année / Jahre / Jaren / Årtal	Number / Quantité / Anzahl / Nummer / Antal	Wheelbase / Empattement / Radstand / Wielbasis / Hjulbas	Engine type/power (hp) / Moteur/puissance (cv) / Motortyp/Leistung (ps) / Motortype/vermogen (pk) / Motortyp/effekt (hk)
T26				
T2600	1981–83	1.477	275cm	D60B/117
T2650	1979–83	523	275cm	TD60B/140
T2654	1979–83	1.255	285cm	TD60B/140
T500–s.			217cm	D39/61
T500	1975–78	6.376		
T500 I	1976–78	286		
T22				
T2200	1978–81	1.819	223cm	D39/56
T2204	1979–81	320	217cm	D39/56
T2250	1978–81	1.960	228cm	D39/68
T2250 I	1978–81	90		D39/68
T2254	1979–81	865	217cm	D39/68
T675				1113
T430–s.			210–218,5cm	D25/42.5
T430	1969–78	23.764		
T430 I	1970–78	1.125		
T650–700			244cm	
T650	1970–82	26.120		D42/73
T650PKD	1971–76	2.080		
T650 I	1970–82	1.502		
T700	1976–82	4.291		
T700 I	1976–82	205		
Mini	1970–			
700				/7
820				/8
1000				/10
1200				/12
1202				/12
1412				/14
1520				/15
Volvo BM Valmet				
505	1982–			311DS/65
605	1982–			311DS/72
705	1982–			411DS/83
805	1982–			411DS/95
905	1984–			611D/105
305	1985–			309DS/53
405	1985–			309DS/61
2005	1985–87	455		TD60B/140
2105	1985–87	545		TD60K/163

Wheel loaders:

Vehicles / Véhicule / Fahrzeuge / Voertuigen / Fordon	Years / Année / Jahre / Jaren / Årtal	Number / Quantité / Anzahl / Nummer / Antal	Wheelbase / Empattement / Radstand / Wielbasis / Hjulbas	Engine type/power (hp) / Moteur/puissance (cv) / Motortyp/Leistung (ps) / Motortype/vermogen (pk) / Motortyp/effekt (hk)
H10				
H10–35	1954–61			1053/43
H10/55	1954–61			1054/57
H10/55				
H10/55S				
LM21	1959–70			1113/63
LM218				
LM218Td				
LM22				1114/83
LM222	1962			
LM225	1962–66			
LM422	1967–			D913/47
LM62				
LM620	1965–70			1113ALH/69
LM621	1970–73		235cm	D42/80
LM621	1973–78			D42/80
LM622	1978–82			D42/80
LM64				
LM640	1965–70			1113ALH/69
LM641	1970–73		235cm	D42/80
LM641	1973–78			D42/80
LM642	1978–82			D42/80
LM84				
LM840	1966–72			D50A/110
LM841	1972–78		243cm	D50B/112
654	1963–69			D50A/113
854	1962–69			D70A/157
1254	1967–72		258cm	D100/200
1640	1970–72		347cm	Scania D11R41/215
845	1970–73		270cm	D50B/112
846	1972–79			D50B–D60A/115–125
1240	1972–79			D70B/160
1641	1972–80			TD100A/240
4200	1978–80			Perkins D39L/64
4200B				/90
4300	1977–82			TD42/107
4300B				/118
4400			286cm	TD60B/143
4500	1979–83		300cm	TD70H/186
4600				TD100/252
4600B				TD100/264
L30	1987–		272,5cm	Perkins 4.236/69
L50	1986–		270cm	D45B/82
L70	1986–		284cm	TD45B/110
L90	1986–		300cm	TD61G/145
L120	1986–		320cm	TD71G/190
L160	1986–		355cm	TD102GB/252
L50B	1993–		275cm	Perkins TD40GA/92
L70B	1994–		284cm	
L90B	1992–		300cm	TD61GB/148
L120B	1992–		320cm	TD71G/190
L150	1991–		355cm	TD102GC/231
L180	1992–		355cm	TD122GH/275
L50C	1995–		275cm	TD40KAE/97
L70C	1995–		284cm	TD61GD–63KDE/118–122
L90C	1995–		300cm	TD63KBE/153
L120C	1995–		320cm	TD73KDE/201
L150C	1995–		355cm	102KCE/234
L180C	1995–		355cm	122KHE/269
L330C	1995–		406cm	TD164KAE/498
Zettelmeyer				
ZL302			150cm	Deutz F4M 1008/28
ZL401			180cm	Deutz F2L511/38
ZL402			185cm	Deutz F3L1011/37
ZL502			200cm	KF4L1011/48
ZL602			200cm	KBF4L1011T/58
ZL702			200cm	Deutz BF4L1011/66
ZL802			225cm	Deutz BF4M1012E/76
ZL1002i				Deutz BF4M 1013E/90

Vehicles / Véhicule / Fahrzeuge / Voertuigen / Fordon	Years / Année / Jahre / Jaren / Årtal	Number / Quantité / Anzahl / Nummer / Antal	Wheelbase / Empattement / Radstand / Wielbasis / Hjulbas	Engine type/power (hp) / Moteur/puissance (cv) / Motortyp/Leistung (ps) / Motortype/vermogen (pk) / Motortyp/effekt (hk)

Tractor dumpers:

Vehicles	Years	Number	Wheelbase	Engine type/power (hp)
Boxer Dumper				
DD1015				
630DS	1965–66			1113A/65
Bison Dumper				1114/73–75
473–DD1520				
473–DD1524				

Articulated dumpers:

Vehicles	Years	Number	Wheelbase	Engine type/power (hp)
631	1966–67			1113A
631B	1967–69			1113A/67
860–s.				
860	1968–69			D50A/110
860A	1969–70			D50A/112
860T	1970–73		405cm	TD50B/150
860TL	1973–75		405cm	TD50B/150
860S	1976–79			TD60A/170
861			405cm	TD60B/170
Terrainchassis				
860TC				
869TC				
861TC				TD60B/170
TC40			405cm	
TC59			591cm	
5350–s.				TD70G/213
5350	1979–82		420cm	
5350B				
5350TC				
A20	1986–		432,2cm	TD71G/201
6x4				
6x6				
A25–s.				
A25	1986–			TD71K/244
4x4			465cm	
6x4			417,5cm	
6x6			417,5cm	
A25B				TD71K/244
4x4			465cm	
6x6			416,5cm	
A25C	1993–			TD73KCE/251
4x4				
6x6			416,5cm	
A30	1991–		417,3cm	TD102KF/280
A35	1986–		448cm	TD121GA–122GA/326–330
A40	1995–			TD122KFE/398

Rigid dump trucks:

Vehicles	Years	Number	Wheelbase	Engine type/power (hp)
Volvo BM				
425B				
425C				
442B			340cm	Scania DS1402/401
442C				
540			365cm	Scania DSI14–CumminsKT1150C450–Detroit 12V71TT/438–456
555			430cm	Detroit 16V71N/617
565			430cm	Detroit 16V71TV/674
Euclid				
R32			365cm	TD122KAE/375
R35			373cm	Cummins KT19C
R40	1995–			Cummins QTA19C/525
R60			429cm	Cummins KTTA19C–VTA28C/664–668
R65	1994–			Cummins VTA28C/760
R85B	1990–		462cm	
R90	1995–			Cummins KT38C/925
R130			531cm	CumminsKTTA38C–Detroit12V-149TIB/1.200
R150			531cm	CumminsKTTA38C–Detroit12V-149TIB/1.200

Vehicles	Years	Number	Wheelbase	Engine type/power (hp)
R170			564cm	Cummins KTA40C–Detroit 16V-149TIB/1.650
R190			564cm	Cummins 200E–Detroit 16V-149TIB/2.000
R220	1995–		564cm	Dieselelectric

Road graders:

Vehicles	Years	Number	Wheelbase	Engine type/power (hp)
55	1954–55			VDC/65
85/100	1955–61			D67/87
100	1961–62			D67/110
115	1962–65			D67/110
116	1965–71			D70A/135
118	1971–72			D70B/135
310	1968–71			D70A/157
312	1971–77			D70B/160
3200				
3300				
3400				
3500	1977–82			TD70/185
3700				TD70/199
510	1972–75			TD100/265

Excavators:

Vehicles	Years	Number	Wheelbase	Engine type/power (hp)
BM Volvo/Volvo BM				
GM410	1966–70			D913/47
GM600–s.				
GM611	1964–65			1113/60
GM612	1965–69			1113/60
GM614	1969–72			1113/66
GM616	1974–76			D42/80
GM616B	1976–81			D42/80
GM646	1977–81			TD42/86
6300	1984–92			TD45B/114
EL70	1992–95			TD45B/114
EL70C	1995–			Deutz TD48GAE/119
Åkerman				
Wheeled				
H3MB	1986–		255cm	TD31ACE/67
H5M	1991–		250cm	Iveco 8041 Si25/107
H7MC	1985–		250cm	TD61ACE/145
H10MB	1985–		278cm	TD61ACE/166
EW130	1993–		250cm	VMETD40GB/103
EW150	1993–		250cm	VMETD40KC/113
EW200	1993–		250cm	TD61GE/145
EW230	1993–		278cm	TD61ACE/166
EW230B	1994–			TD61GE/166
Tracked				
H3B	1986–			TD31ACE/67
H5	1991–			Iveco 8041Si25/107
H7C	1985–			TD61ACE/145
H10B	1985–			TD61ACE/166
H14B	1984–			TD71ACE/209
H16D	1984–			TD100G/262
H25D	1990–			TD121L/386
EC130	1993–			VMETD40GB/103
EC150	1993–			VMETD40KC/113
EC200	1993–			TD61GE/145
EC230	1993–			TD61ACE/166
EC230B	1994–			TD61GE/166
EC300	1992–			TD71ACE/209
EC420	1993–			TD101GE/262
EC450	1995–			TD122KKE/309
EC620ME	1993–			TD121KG/386
EC650	1995–			TD122KIE/386

Vehicles / Véhicule / Fahrzeuge / Voertuigen / Fordon	Years / Année / Jahre / Jaren / Årtal	Number / Quantité / Anzahl / Nummer / Antal	Wheelbase / Empattement / Radstand / Wielbasis / Hjulbas	Engine type/power (hp) / Moteur/puissance (cv) / Motortyp/Leistung (ps) / Motortype/vermogen (pk) / Motortyp/effekt (hk)
Mobile cranes:				
690	1968–70			1113A/66
691	1970–71			1113A/66
692	1971–74			D42/80
693	1974–80			D42/80
Forestry machines:				
BMB-230 Bamse Lisa		732	172cm	1052/30
SM870			292,5cm	D50/118
SM871			485cm	D50/118
Stor–Nalle	1964–	558		1113/65
SM360				
SM660				
SM661				
SM662 Niklas				1113/65
SM667 Timmer–Kalle			485cm	1113/65
Lill–Nalle	1966–	585	317cm	D913/47
SM460				
SM461				
SM668/868		1.794		
SM668	1968–69			1113
SM868	1969–74		402,5cm	D50/105
SM462	1970–74	356	460cm	D25/47

Bibliography

It's impossible to make a complete list of books which makes mention of Volvo or those companies which have been part of or have co-operated with Volvo.

Listed below are several books which either deal with Volvo's history, products, and joint partners, or are written by or about people who have held leading positions within the Volvo Group.

Wherever possible, an author, title, and publisher is given for each book, and also an indication of when the book was published. The ISBN number is given, which makes it possible to order the book in question from a book store or a library. If the book has been published in several special editions or in different languages, these editions are listed.

Many of the books disappeared from the shelves in book stores a long time ago, but can often be traced though libraries or at second-hand book shops.

In some cases, publications of an informative character which have been published by Volvo or by other Volvo Group companies are mentioned.

Amari, Giancarlo: Volvo. Editions EPA, Paris, France. 1981. ISBN 2-85120-157-3

Blom, Svante & Andersson, Lars (Editors): Torslandaverkens första 20 år. 1984. Published by Volvo Personvagnar AB.

Blom, Tore: Lokomobiler från Munktells Mek Verkstads AB. Rubens Maskinhistoriska Samlingar, Götene, Sverige. 1982. ISBN 91-7260-614-2.

van der Brugghen, Joan: Van da Vinci tot van Doorne. 1500-2000. Published by van Doorne's Transmissie b v Tilburg. 1988.

van der Brugghen, Joan: Dertig jaren Nederlandse personenwagens. 1958-1988. Published by Volvo Car b v Helmond. 1988

Car and Driver on Volvo 1956-1986. Brookland Books, Cobham, England. 1986. ISBN 1 869 826 051.

Clarke, R M (Editor): Volvo PV444 & PV544 1945-1965. Brookland Road Test Books, Cobham, England. ISBN 1-85520-172-0.

Clarke, R M (Editor): Volvo Amazon–120. Gold Portfolio 1956-1970. Brookland Books, Cobham, England ISBN 1-85520-130-5.

Clarke, R M: Selling Volvo 1956-1986.

Davis, Pedr & Davis, Tony: Volvo Down Under. A Swedish Success Story. Marque Publishing Company Pty Ltd, Blakehurst, Australien. ISBN 0-947079-14-9.

Ellegård, Kajsa: Människa – Produktion. Tidsbilder av ett produktionssystem. Cultural-geographic institution, University of Gothenburg, Sweden. 1983. ISBN 91-86472-02-X.

Ericsson, Gunnar I: Tjänstemannakåren vid Aktiebolaget Volvo 1939. 1982. ISBN 91-85636-01-0.

Ericsson Gunnar I: AB Volvos grundare och företagets verkställande direktörer. Biographical information. 2nd edition. 1993. ISBN 91-85636-02-9.

Ekman, Bo (editor):
• Arbete och värdighet. A book dedicated to Pehr G. Gyllenhammar. Swedish edition. Streiffert & Co Publishing Company HB, Stockholm, Sweden. 1985. ISBN 91-7886-000-8.
• Dignity at work. A book dedicated to Pehr G Gyllenhammar. English edition. 1985. ISBN 91-7886-001-6.

• En bok om Volvo. Swedish edition. Produced by Volvo Plc. 1985.
• A Book about Volvo. English edition. Produced by Volvo Plc. 1985.
• Ein Buch über Volvo. German edition. Produced by Volvo Plc. 1985

Forty Years of Selling Volvo. A portfolio of North American advertising. Brookland Books, Cobham, England. ISBN 1-85520-318-9.

40 years. The Story of Volvo's First Forty Years in America. Produced by Volvo Cars of North America, Inc. 1995.

Fransson, Gunnar: Från Köpings Mekaniska Verkstads Aktiebolag till Volvo Komponenter AB Transmissionsdivisionen. 125 years of factory history 1856-1981. Produced by Volvo Components Plc. Transmissiondivision, Köping & Lindesberg, Sweden. 1982.

Gunnarsson, Barbro & Yngve: Karmansbo och järnet. Produced by Karmansbo Herrgård & Volvo Plc. 1987.

Günther, Dieter & Wolf, Walter: Das grosse Buckel-Volvo Buch. F Ch Heel-Verlag, Bonn, Germany. 1986. ISBN 3-922858-30-9.

Günther Dieter & Wolf, Walter: Das grosse Buckel-Volvo Buch. F Ch Heel-Verlag, Bonn, Germany. 1989. ISBN 3-89365-138-1.

Günther, Dieter & Wolf, Walter:
• Volvo – Die P120-modelle. Autovision Verlag Günther, Wolf & Co. German edition. ISBN 3-9802766-1-9.
• Volvo P120. Autovision Verlag Günther, Wolf & Co. English edition. ISBN 3-9802766-6-X.

Gyllenhammar, Pehr Gustaf: Jag tror på Sverige, Askild & Kärnekull Förlag AB. 1973. ISBN 91-7008-337-1.

Gyllenhammar, Pehr Gustaf: People at work. Addison-Wesley Publishing Company, USA. 1977. ISBN 0-201-02499-3.

Gyllenhammar, Pehr Gustaf (in collaboration with Palmgren, Anders & Petersson, Christer): Även med känsla. Bonniers Fakta Bokförlag AB, Stockholm, Sweden. 1992. ISBN 91-34-51206-3.

Haventon, Peter: Volvo PV444. Den svenska folkbilen. Bienen & Haventon AB, Höör, Sweden. 1994. ISBN 91-971861-1-2.

Hedell, Olof: Från Munktells till Valmet – En 75-årig traktorepok. Media Nova, Stockholm, Sweden. ISBN 91-7143-021-0.

Hubert, Karel (editor): Lademans Bil-Lexicon: Volvo. Swedish edition. Orbis Publishing Limited. 1984. ISBN 91-88174-58-1.

Hälleby, Bertil: Så föddes en svensk bilindustri. Akademiförlaget. 1990. ISBN 91-24-16378-3.

Jack, Doug: The Leyland Bus. 1977.

Jack, Doug: Leyland Bus Mk II. Revised edition. The Transport Publishing Company, Glossop, England. 1984. ISBN 0-86317-110-9.

Jensen, Jens: Vi bilbyggare.

Johansson, Carlerik: Vilda härliga Volvo Cup! Carlerik Johansson Information AB, Bergvik, Sverige. 1981.

Johansson, Christer & Rydholm, Claes
• Utmaningen. Volvo 850GLT. Produced by CommuniQué, Göteborg, Sweden. 1991.
• The Challenge. Volvo 850GLT. English edition. Produced by CommuniQué, Göteborg, Sweden. 1991.

Jonasson, Weimar: Volvo Verkstadsklubb 1927-1952.

Kennet, Pat:
• Volvo Lastbilar då och nu (edited by Lars Ericsson). Swedish edition. Frank Stenvalls förlag, Malmö, Sweden. 1981. ISBN 91-7266-052-X.
• Volvo Trucks. English edition.
• Les Camions du Monde: Volvo, French edition (edited by Thierry de Saulieu). EPA, Paris, France. 1982 ISBN 2-85120-152-2.
• German edition. Vogt Schild Druck und Verlag, Solothurn, Switzerland. ISBN 3-85962-069-X.

Kronan på verket 1735-1985. Published by Volvo Personvagnar AB, Olofströmsverken.

Lindh, Björn-Erik (editor): Autohistorica. Special edition of Automobilhistoriska Klubbens magazine for Volvos 50th anniversary 1977. ISSN 0345-1003.

Lindh, Björn-Erik:
• Volvo Personvagnarna – från 20-tal till 80-tal. Swedish edition. Förlagshuset Norden, Malmö, Sweden. 1984. ISBN 91-86442-06-6.
• Volvo. The Cars – from the 20s to the 80s. English edition. Förlagshuset Norden, Malmö, Sweden. 1984. ISBN 91-86442-08-2.
• Volvo 60 ans d'historie automobile. French edition. Éditions Xavier Richer, Paris, France. 1984. ISBN 2-901151-15-9.
• Volvo. Personenwagens van de jaren 20 tot de jaren 80. Dutch edition. Förlagshuset Norden AB, Malmö, Sweden. 1984.

Lindh, Björn-Erik:
• Volvo. Personvagnarna – från 20-tal till 80-tal. Revised Swedish edition. 1985. ISBN 91-86442-12-0.
• Volvo. The cars – From the 20s to the 80s. Revised English edition. 1986. ISBN 91-86442-14-7.
• Volvo. Von den 20ern in die 80ern Jahre. German

edition. Motorbuch Verlag, Stuttgart, Germany. 1987. ISBN 3-613-01215-4.
• Volvo–henkilöautot 1920-luvulta 1980-luvulle. Finnish edition. Förlagshuset Norden AB, Malmö, Sweden & Oy AB Pluskustannus, Finland. ISBN 951-99794-3-3.
• Volvo. Le automobili dagli anni Venti agli anni Ottanta. Italian edition. Förlagshuset Norden AB, Malmö, Sweden. 1985.

Lindh, Björn-Erik:
• Volvo Personenwagens van de jaren 20 tot de jaren 90. Revised Dutch edition. Förlagshuset Norden AB, Malmö, Sweden. 1988. ISBN 91-86442-15-5.
• Volvo – Personvagnarna – från 20-tal till 90-tal. Revised Swedish edition. 1988. ISBN 91-86442-16-3.
• Volvo. The cars – From the 20s to the 90s. Revised English edition.1988. ISBN 91-86442-17-1.
• Volvo. Von den 20ern in die 90ern Jahre. German revised edition.1988. ISBN 91-86442-19-8.
• Japanese edition. 1990. ISBN 3-907150-01-5.

Lindholm, Rolf & Norstedt, Jan-Peder:
• Volvo-rapporten, Arbetsmiljö i utveckling. Published by Svenska Arbetsgivareföreningen, Stockholm, Sweden. 1975. ISBN 91-7152-070-8.
• The Volvo Report. English edition. 91-7152-072-4.

Ljungqvist, Fredrik: Från hantverk till motorer. Volvos historia i Skövde. 1993. ISBN 91-630-2174-9.

Maasing, Iva:
• Hur jag får ut mest av min PV444. Bokförlaget Forum AB, Stockholm, Sverige.
• Hur jag får ut mest av min PV444. Second, extended edition. Bokförlaget Forum AB, Stockholm, Sweden. 1956.
• Hur jag får ut mest av min PV544. Third, extended edition. Bokförlaget Forum AB, Stockholm, Sweden. 1959.

Matras, John: Illustrated Volvo Buyers guide. Motorbooks International, Osceola, USA. 1993. ISBN 0-87938-713-0.

McNeil, Gerry & McConachie, Bob: Odyssey 77: The great gold tooth pick caper. The Toronto Sun Publishing Corporation Limited, Toronto, Canada. ISBN 0-919233-00-8.

Sahlström, Bengt: Articles in two special editions of Motorhistoriskt Magasin. Published ahead of Volvos 50th anniversary. 1977.

Nicol, Gladys: Volvo. William Luscombe Publisher Limited, London, England. 1975. ISBN 0-86002-138-6.

Niskanen, Hannu:
• Piikkilangankiristäjästä Power Plus. Published by Valmet AB Traktorfabriken. Jyväskylä, Finland. 1989. ISBN 951-95880-8-6.
• Barbed wire tightener to Power Plus. English edition. 1990. ISBN 951-95880-9-4.
• Från taggtrådsspännare till Power Plus. Valmet-traktorns färgstarka fyrtio år. Swedish edition. 1989.ISBN 951-95881-0-8.
• Fra Pigtrådstramning til Power Plus. Danish edition. 1990. ISBN 951-95881-1-6.

Olsson, Christer:
• Volvo–Lastbilarna under sextio år. Swedish edition. Förlagshuset Norden, Malmö, Sweden 1987. ISBN 91-86442-50-3.
• Sixty years of truckmaking. English edition. 1987. ISBN 91-86442-56-2.
• Volvo Sessenta anos fabricando caminhões. Portuguese edition. 1987.
• Volvo. Zestig jaar vrachtwagens. Dutch edition. 1987. ISBN 91-86442-58-9.
• Volvo Kuusikymmentä vuotta kuormaautoja. Finnish edition. 1987. ISBN 91-86442-60-0.
• Les Camions Volvo. Soixante ans à historie. French edition. 1987. ISBN 91-86442-62-7.
• Volvo Lastbilerene igennem tres år. Danish edition. 1987. ISBN 91-86442-64-3.
• Volvo. Sechzig Jahre Lkw-Bau. German edition. 1988. ISBN 91-86442-68-6.
• Volvo sesenta años fabricando camiones. Spanish edition. 1988. ISBN 91-86442-72-4.
• Japanese edition. Verlagshaus Norden AG, St Gallen, Switzerland. 1990. ISBN 3-907150-02-3.

Olsson, Christer:
• Volvo–Lastbilarna igår och idag. Revised edition. Förlagshuset Norden, Malmö, Sweden. 1990. ISBN 91-86442-76-7.
• German revised edition. Verlagshaus Norden AG, St Gallen, Switzerland & Motorbuch Verlag, Stuttgart, Germany. 1990. ISBN 3-907150-07-4.

Olsson, Christer:Landsvägens Riddare. Verlagshaus Norden AG, St Gallen, Switzerland. 1990. ISBN 3-907150-05-8.

Olsson, Christer:
• Project FH. Swedish/English edition. Verlagshaus Norden AG, St GAllen, Switzerland. 1993. ISBN 3-907150-15-5.
• Dutch/French edition. 1993. ISBN 3-907150-16-3.
• Danish/English edition. 1993. ISBN 3-907150-17-1.
• German/French edition. 1995. ISBN 3-907150-19-8.

Olsson, Christer:
• Volvo Göteborg Sverige. Verlagshaus Norden AG. Swedish edition. 1995. ISBN 3-907150-57-0.
• Volvo Gothenburg Sweden. English edition. 1995. ISBN 3-907150-58-9.
• Volvo Göteborg Schweden. German edition. 1995. ISBN 3-907150-59-7
• Volvo Gothenbourg Suède. French edition. 1995. ISBN 3-907150-60-0.
• Volvo Göteborg Zweden. Dutch edition. 1995. ISBN 3-907150-61-9.

Osberg, Mats: Milstolpar. En bok om Volvo i Skövde. 1995. ISBN 91-630-3165-5.

Road & Track on Volvo 1957-1974.

Road & Track on Volvo 1974-1985. Brookland Books, Cobham, England. 1985. ISBN 0 948207 31 0.

Road & Track on Volvo 1977-1994. Brookland Books, Cobham, England, 1994. ISBN 1-85520-254-9.

Robson, Graham: The Story of Volvo cars. Patrick Stevens, Cambridge, England. 1983. ISBN 0-85059-591-X.

Von Rosen, Lars: Landsverk i Landskrona. Produced by Landsverksgruppen & VME Industries. 1992.

Rydenfelt, Sven: Från tornspiror till grävmaskiner. Åkermans i Eslöv 1890-1990. Ett företags öden och äventyr under 100 år. Published by Åkermans Verkstad AB. 1990. ISBN 91-7970-995-8.

Schröder, Halwart: Volvo PV 444/544. 1800 S/E/ES. Amazon 121/122/123GT. 1945-73. Schrader Verlag, Suderburg, Germany. ISBN 3-922617-90-5.

Sessions, Ron & Motta, William A (editor/art director): Guide to the All-New Volvo 850GLT. Published by Road & Track, USA. 1992.

Strugala, Karel: Volvo nákladí automobily. Prague, Czech Republic. 1994.

Sundqvist, Sven-Ivan: Exit PG. T Fisher & Co. 1994. ISBN 91-7054-726-2.

Torslandaverkens invigning. Book published by Volvo Plc. 1964.

Vertes, Josef: Konstruktörerna som skapade 1960-talets säkerhets bilar. 1991. ISBN 91-630-0780-0.

Volvo 440. Published by Volvo Car b v. 1988.

Volvo 480.
• Swedish edition. 1986. Published by Volvo Car b v.
• English edition. 1986.
• Dutch edition. 1986.

Volvo 1927-1995. Latest annual edition. Is available in Swedish, English, French, German. Produced by Volvo Personvagnar, Göteborg, Sweden.

Whyte, Andrew: Volvo 1800 and family 1944-73. PV444/544, P120, P1900/1800-series. Osprey Publishing Limited, London, England. 1984. ISBN 0-85045-555-3.

Wik, Erik: Volvo BM Arvikaverken 1895-1985. Published by Volvo BM. 1985.

Östberg, Martin: En smedjas förvandling – ÖSA's historia. Produced by FMG ÖSA AB, Alfta, Sweden. 1990.